a taste of china

KEN HOM

a taste of china

THE DEFINITIVE GUIDE TO REGIONAL COOKING

PAVILION

First published in Great Britain in 1996 by
PAVILION BOOKS
This revised edition published in 2005

An imprint of **Chrysalis** Books Group plc

The Chrysalis Building
Bramley Road
London W10 6SP
www.chrysalisbooks.co.uk

Text © 1990 by Taurom Incorporated

ISBN 1 86205 707 9

A CIP catalogue record for this book is available from the British Library.

2 4 6 8 10 9 7 5 3 1

Cover design: Mark Latter
Cover photography: Jean Cazals
Cover Styling: Sue Rowlands and Jane Suthering
Typeset by: SX Composing, Essex, UK
Printed by: Grafica Veneta S.p.A. Italy

This book can be ordered direct from the publisher. Please contact the
Marketing Department, but try your bookshop first.

CONTENTS

foreword   7

1 a personal odyssey   9

2 the tastes and flavours of China   26

3 influences from within and without   64

4 the imperial legacy   84

5 the glorious cuisine of Guangzhou (Canton)   98

6 family traditions   116

7 city and country fare   139

8 restaurant cooking   167

9 snacks and street foods   185

10 food for the body and soul: the medicinal and the vegetarian   207

11 reflections   226

index   233

DEDICATION

This book is dedicated with love and affection to Martha Casselman who has made this project, as well as many others, possible and to the people of China

author's note

The spelling of Chinese words and place names follows the pinyin system of converting Chinese characters to the Roman alphabet. This system has been officially adopted by the People's Republic of China since 1979 and it closely resembles actual Mandarin pronunciation. I have used this system when referring to certain recipe names and specific food items as well as certain regions within China. For instance, I have used Sichuan, instead of Szechuan. However, I felt it necessary to make exceptions for the spellings of certain very well known dishes, such as Peking duck, dim sum, and for a few ingredients which are better known by their Cantonese names. In the case of better known places, the pinyin spelling is followed by the perhaps more familiar name, for example, Kaiping (Hoiping) and Guangzhou (Canton).

foreword

This book has touched and moved me in many ways. The people of China welcomed me with warmth and genuine cordiality They shared their homes, guided me to their favourite restaurants, told me about markets, referred me to other, valuable contacts; some even shared precious crops from their small private fields. As I travelled to almost every region of China, to well-known cities as well as remote farm villages, I was able to grasp a sense of history, the culture, and the lives of the people. After my experiences during visits over the past two years, I eagerly anticipate future trips to this huge and complex nation.

This is not the definitive book of the foods of China; no such volume can be written. What I have written reflects my experiences in and tasting the foods of China as they are today. Sometimes I ate meals in restaurants and homes and sometimes, when I was very lucky, I got to share in making them.

I was unimpressed with the official menus, ingredients, and food preparation in many of the state-owned restaurants; I would not recommend most of the usual tourist fare; nor was I ever offered the elaborately decorated, often tasteless dishes which seem to exist only in coffee-table books produced in China for its overseas markets.

What *did* impress me were simple foods served in good, private restaurants, in homes, and in the street stalls of China's cities and villages. Much of what I ate was a metaphor for the spirit of China: lusty, savoury, and earthy, almost plain in presentation, deceptively simple in taste. The recipes I gathered there reflect this range of sensations. Tested in my own kitchen, they are, for the most part, easy to duplicate outside of China. My friend and photographer, Leong Ka Tai, did not try to translate our day-to-day experienced but, rather, the atmosphere of the China I was discovering.

Before I left California for my first long stay in China, I hoped to find real food, unself-consciously and naturally prepared, and I did. *This* is the real taste of China, which I invite you to share with me.

Ken Hom, October 1989

8

a personal odyssey

CHAPTER 1
A PERSONAL ODYSSEY

As a child I left home and now have just returned
My accent unchanged but my sideburns gray
The village children know me not, but laughing they ask:
Where do you come from, stranger?
He Zhizhang, Tang Dynasty, a.d. 618–905

In spite of the saying that you can't go home again, you can. The question is, what or where is home? To a Chinese-American, or any "overseas Chinese," emotional ambiguities are built into any answer. The Chinese experience outside of China has created what has been called "sojourner mentality": No matter what economic success emigrant Chinese achieve, the pull of the homeland remains powerful. All too often, a combination of racial prejudice and deeply rooted cultural family ties – including ancestor reverence – have caused or forced these emigrants into the thousands of "Chinatowns" that exist today throughout the world. There they dream of returning one day to the homeland.

This was my own experience. Ever since I was a small child growing up in Chicago, my mother maintained that we must return one day to *gu xiang* (or, in the Cantonese dialect, *heung ha*), "the village of our ancestors." And as Westernized as I was, I could not deny the emotional attraction of this call. Where one's ancestors lived and died, where the small family shrines are kept; where the family's roots were nourished – these are no slight matter. My mother insisted that before she grew too old to travel, a return to the family's *gu xiang* was a necessity; and the opening of China made this possible. She also insisted that as Westernized as I fancied myself, it was my filial duty to accompany her. As the time was ripe for my own personal odyssey, I offered no resistance to her demand.

The links on her side of the family had been broken by the wars and political turbulence that have been China's lot in the twentieth century. Despite the turmoil, however, my mother had managed to maintain contact with our family's one surviving connection to the ancestral village, a cousin on my father's side. It was to his home that we directed our steps, setting off, by way of Hong Kong and Macao, to the village of Kaiping (Hoiping) in the Foshan region of Guangdong province.

On our journey from America, and at my urging, Mother reviewed the family history. She had always been told that our ancestors were originally from Gansu, somewhere in northern China. I have also heard from other relatives that we have family in Beijing (Peking) with whom we have lost contact. This could be true because near our ancestral village there is a temple where the sexton, Mr. Guan Huoling, told me that many people in the area indeed trace their roots to the north. In the temple there is a likeness of one Guan Jingqi who, it is believed, migrated with his extended family from the north of China over nine hundred years ago. The temple was built with money sent "home" by overseas Chinese to revere him as the founding father of the area's families.

Whatever the mythic origins of the family, my mother was born on April 24, 1924, in Kaiping (Hoiping). Her father at first glance appears to have been a classic example of the imperial scholar-bureaucrat. He was the first from his area to graduate from a university, his studies made possible by the generosity of his paternal grandfather, who had already emigrated to San Francisco, establishing there what turned into a thriving import-export business. After graduating from Beijing University he was appointed to a position, first in Beijing (Peking), then in Shanghai, in the salt monopoly, which in those days was a powerful government department.

Here we see a blending of old China with modernizing China. Traditionally, merchant-business people had little prestige and no authority in China. Society was dominated by the Imperial bureaucracy and the landed gentry. Official ideology and the status system positioned and kept merchants at the bottom of the social scale. Gentry and bureaucrats never emigrated. Only needy peasants and workers undertook the long and arduous journey to the "Golden Mountains" supposedly awaiting them in Singapore, America, Australia, or wherever. In the nineteenth century, wars, natural disasters, overpopulation, and a stagnant economy drove millions of them out, mostly to Singapore and other parts of southeast Asia. By far the larger percentage of this first wave of Chinese emigrants returned home whenever their finances allowed them to do so.

The name of the general area from which my family comes is Sze Yup, which in Cantonese means "the four districts." Its rocky soil could produce only enough food to feed its population for four months of the year. Much of this agricultural production was devoted to cash crops – fruit, indigo, sugarcane, tobacco – for the benefit of the gentry who owned the land. Rice, the staple of southern China, was always expensive, and in bad years unobtainable. To survive, people turned to other trades, traveling to and from the port cities of Macao, Guangzhou (Canton), and Hong Kong as peddlers, artisans, shopkeepers, or simple "coolies."

The Cantonese had long enjoyed relations with the non-Chinese world. Indeed, for a long time the only open port allowed to trade with foreigners was Guangzhou, with majestic Yankee Clippers making Guangzhou a regular port of call. Exaggerated tales of the wealth to be had in America percolated through the ports to the hinterland and its poor population. For the Cantonese, the West was a challenge but not unknown.

My family's home province, Guangdong (Canton province), alone accounted for almost all of the thousands of Chinese immigrants to America. Sixty percent of them came from one district of the area, Taishan (Toisan), next to my family's district. My great-grandfather was one of those ambitious peasants turned merchant adventurer who accepted the challenge. Although he experienced racial discrimination and prejudice, he nevertheless was able to build a profitable enterprise in America. It was the pull of opportunity abroad as well as the push of adversity at home that led to so many overseas Chinese, but his was an extraordinary success.

The money he sent to his family remaining in China enabled them to buy land and join the elite, as it were, to afford education, and even to send my maternal grandfather to the University.

In the China of the last Emperor, however, change was underway, with modern ideas and practices being introduced. My enlightened grandfather, for example, rejected the still prevalent custom of bound feet and seclusion for his two daughters and educated them instead. They lived with their mother, a marvellously talented cook my mother tells me, in Guangzhou (Canton), while he worked in Beijing (Peking) and Shanghai. My mother continued her education in Guangzhou until Hong Kong and the adjacent area fell to the Japanese invaders in 1941. At this point the family returned to the ancestral village, joining my grandfather who, as an official of the Chinese government, had something to fear from the Japanese conquerors. From Kaiping (Hoiping) the family retreated even farther to Shaoguan where they stayed in hiding until the end of the war, returning by stages to Guangzhou in 1948.

It was there also in 1948 that my mother and my father met. He was already an "overseas Chinese" and in his early thirties. Having just finished his American military service in Europe, he was on a visit from America. His family's history was only slightly different from my mother's. Again, it is a tale of poverty at home and opportunities abroad. My father's grandfather set out to seek a better life, or at least some money, for himself and his family. At first he tried Singapore, but one of the peculiarities of the overseas Chinese is their extreme clannishness based upon geographic origin and distinctive dialects as well as family ties. The Singapore region was dominated by Chinese from the Hokkien area and a Cantonese-speaking Chinese was at an extreme disadvantage. Thus, great-grandfather set out for America where he did well enough to be able to send home money for the family to expand its land holding into a sizeable one. Moreover, he brought his son (my grandfather) and his son's family to America, leaving one grandson (my uncle) to supervise the family property and maintain the family roots. My one known relative in China is my cousin, the son of that uncle left in charge of the family estate.

After what by Chinese standards was a whirlwind courtship, my parents were married, on June 30, 1948. Soon thereafter, the American consulate in Guangzhou (Canton) gave my mother the right to emigrate. That is how I came to be born the next year in Tucson, Arizona, and not in a village in Guangdong. After suffering through war with its privation and disruption and all the social turmoil of postwar China, my mother was happy to start a new life in America. But she was not to realise her own American dream. Eight months after I was born, my father died in December, 1949.

Mother found herself in a precarious situation. A stranger in a strange land, unable to speak the language, she was forced to eke out a living for herself and her son from unskilled, low-paid factory work. Even after she joined the extended family of my mother's cousins in Chicago, her lot was one of hard work. I have always understood why my mother so often harked back to her earlier life in China.

Such were the thoughts in my mind as we left Hong Kong on the final leg of our journey. Laden with gifts for my cousin's family, we went first by the high-speed hydrofoil boat to Macao. There we crossed the border and rented a car and driver to take us to Kaiping (Hoiping), about a four-hour drive. The area has a population of some 600,000 people. It has a subtropical climate, reminiscent of Hong Kong, moderately warm in the winter, very hot in the summer, and humid the year round. The Tan Jiang River and its tributaries provide abundant water and many beautiful river scenes. The countryside is lush and green, capable of producing three crops of rice per year. On the day we arrived, a warm, misty rain fell, shrouding everything in a blue-gray haze that made our journey rather dreamlike.

13

my mother's story

As we approached the village, my mother excitedly pointed out the medieval-looking fortress towers, called *paulou*, that dot the terrain and overlook the rice fields. These, she explained, were watch towers and a place of refuge against attacks by pirates or bandits or neighbouring clans. Our driver located the family house and my mother and I walked through the gates of the field into the courtyard where we were met by our assembled relatives, joyously, shyly, haltingly, formally and spontaneously all at once. This was a sweet homecoming. We were led into an ample stone house, with grayish stone floors and dark brick walls, cool and yet glowing with warm hospitality. Photographs of the American members of the family, sent by my mother and other relatives over the years, were on display. To announce our arrival to the village at large, my cousin and his son set off strings of firecrackers. It was a tearful and very happy reunion. I remember thinking how natural it all seemed. Because I speak our Cantonese village dialect, I felt quite at home in the language, with the people, and with my mother in that house. It really was as if I had been there before.

The highlight of our first day was a banquet prepared in our honour. As with all special events in China, sharing of food is an integral part of the celebration. That day I witnessed what my mother's culinary behaviour had always exemplified: meals are a cultural matter, symbolic as well as nutritional, a metaphor and a vehicle for social and familial interaction. The meal began with the ritual washing of the rice.

The best rice, grown right in the family fields, had been set aside for this occasion. Rinsed several times, the rice was carefully drained on a bamboo flat basket. A water pump, linked to the well directly below the house, brought fresh water to the kitchen. My cousin went to a small pond near the house to net some grass carp for the meal – only the freshest fish would do!

And what a banquet it was! There were eleven courses, all cooked separately in two large woks. Most of the food was home grown, and all of the relatives – twenty members of the extended family – had helped in the preparation. Because it was melon season and because my mother had told them it was a favourite of mine, we enjoyed bitter melon stir-fried with lean pork. Chinese water spinach, freshly plucked from the garden, was cooked with fermented bean curd. Lean pork stir-fried with soybean sprouts was another dish. (The authentic recipe called for pig's intestine but, unsure of my cultural adaptability, they had substituted lean pork.) At midpoint in the meal a delicious stew of dried oysters and bean curd sticks was a delight. We also enjoyed some of the best long beans I have ever had, served with silk squash and crispy cloud ear fungus, a superb dish. Throughout the meal, our beverage was a clear rabbit broth, laced with spices and the medicinal herbs – there is no sharp distinction made in Chinese cuisine between the culinary and medicinal. Another bean curd dish, this time red-cooked bean curd, was followed by red-cooked carp, the fish that just minutes before had been swimming in the nearby pond. With the special rice we also had a braised goose dish and platters of roast pig and roast duck that had been purchased, already prepared, especially for the feast, since roasting is rarely done in Chinese homes. The presence of so much meat and poultry demonstrated that this was indeed a special occasion, one that allowed for indulgence and demanded extraordinary fare. It certainly impressed me and if anything I overindulged myself during that long, delightful afternoon.

Before this memorable banquet, I joined my cousin in performing another important ritual. Since I was returning home and because we are the oldest males of the family, we poured wine into cups and offered it to our ancestors, bowing three times toward the family shrine as a sign of respect. Food was set aside as an offering to the spirits of the departed. Whatever food the spirits do not eat is then consumed by the family.

Ancestor worship lies at the root of religion in China, and until very recently underpinned traditional family life in China for thousands of years. The rituals of ancestor worship are connected to funeral rites, the selection and tending of graves or shrines and regular sacrificial offerings. Food and incense are typical offerings. Smoke carries up messages to the ancestors. My cousin's family perform such rituals. These require bowing before graves and conveying the prayerful request that the ancestors intervene on one's behalf in this world.

In agricultural societies where so much depends upon the unpredictable vagaries of nature, these appeals to lost fathers are

a family homecoming

understandable. It is believed that bodies of the dead, who are buried in the family field plots, or their ashes – my family's practice – mingle with and favourably affect the agricultural gods or spirits of the soil. Thus, the living are bound together with the dead in a common enterprise. The dead may intervene for the living; the living respect and make offerings to the dead. The ancestor reverence rituals are important in easing the lot of the dead as they progress through the various stages of afterlife. Such a system ensures respect for the family structure. That it solidifies the dominant position of the males, the fathers, is only one aspect of the matter. It also serves to maintain the family in good times and bad. Mortuary sacrifices involve securing the family's future as well as the condition of the ancestors. In participating in this ritual, I realised an important aspect of my cultural heritage, re-creating a vital link with my parents' past, though at the same time I knew I could never make it entirely my own.

After two days exploring the area, as my mother and I took our leave of the family for Hong Kong, many thoughts crowded in on me. To have a family still thriving in the ancestral village, to have blood relatives who were so similar to me and yet so different, to see my mother's joy and serenity at having watched me bowing to our ancestors, to have shared a magnificent family feast exemplifying the best in Chinese cuisine, all of these things flooded my mind and filled me with warm emotions. As we sailed along the beautiful Tan Jiang River, I imagined that this was the route taken by many of my own ancestors as they left China seeking better opportunities, bearing with them their culture, their cuisine, their history, as well as their hopes and fears. How sad it must have been for them to leave their ancestral home; how much must they have longed to return. For me, the experiences of my own personal journey had been deeply enriching. A piece of my heart is forever in Kaiping.

jiuwang chao dan
stir-fried eggs with yellow chives

Stir-fried eggs are a popular food in the countryside: chickens are plentiful and eggs are abundant. During the stay with my relatives we enjoyed many such egg dishes. My cousin's wife gave me this recipe, which is typical of the dishes she ordinarily cooks. Urban dwellers, even in China, rarely get to enjoy these yellow chives, but country dwellers grow their own. A paler version of Chinese green chives, while growing they are sheltered from the sun, blocking the formation of chlorophyll. The chives are delicate and tender, with an earthy taste; they must be cooked immediately after they are picked. You may substitute Chinese green chives or spring onions if necessary, but Western chives have a completely different taste.

4 eggs, beaten
2 teaspoons sesame oil
1 teaspoon salt
225 g/8 oz Chinese yellow or green chives
4 whole spring onions
1½ tablespoons peanut oil

In a medium-sized bowl, combine the eggs with the sesame oil and ½ teaspoon of the salt. Set aside. Cut the chives and spring onions on a slight diagonal into 7.5-cm/3-in pieces.

Heat a wok or large frying pan until it is hot. Add the oil, remaining salt, the chives, and spring onions and stir-fry until the chives and spring onions are wilted, about 2 minutes. Then add the eggs and continue to cook until the eggs have just set. Quickly place on a platter and serve at once.

Serves 3 as part of a Chinese meal, or 1 as a single dish.

hongshao doufu
red-cooked bean curd family style

Bean curd is ideal for braising as it readily absorbs flavours and colours. Chinese bean curd seems to me to be the best in the world, smooth and satiny in texture and invariably perfectly prepared.

Here is a particularly tasty and easy-to-prepare recipe which I first sampled with my Kaiping (Hoiping) relatives. It was surrounded by many other dishes, but I was immediately impressed by its striking qualities. One of the ingredients, hoisin sauce, added colour and a slightly sweet flavour to the bean curd. The dish reheats nicely.

450 g/1 lb firm bean curd
8 whole spring onions
125 ml/4 fl oz peanut oil
1½ tablespoons peanut oil
2 tablespoons coarsely chopped garlic
2 tablespoons rice wine
2 tablespoons hoisin sauce
1 tablespoon light soy sauce
1 tablespoon dark soy sauce
1 teaspoon sugar
225 ml/8 fl oz chicken stock
1 tablespoon sesame oil

Cut the bean curd cake into 2.5 × 7.5 × 2.5-cm/l × 3 × 1-in pieces. Lay them on kitchen paper and drain for 10 minutes.

At a slight diagonal, cut the spring onions into 7.5-cm/3-in pieces.

Heat a wok or frying pan until hot. Add the 125 ml/4 fl oz of peanut oil, and when it is hot, fry the bean curd on both sides until it is golden brown. Drain the bean curd well on kitchen paper.

Drain and discard the oil. Wipe the wok or frying pan clean, reheat, and add 1½ tablespoons of peanut oil. Then add the spring onions and garlic and stir-fry for 30 seconds. Put in the rest of the ingredients except the sesame oil. Bring the mixture to the boil, return the fried

a personal odyssey

bean curd pieces, and cook over high heat for 10 minutes or until the bean curd has absorbed most of the sauce. Add the sesame oil, and give the mixture a final turn. Serve at once.

Serves 4 as part of a Chinese meal, or 2 as a single dish.

jiuhuang rousi chao mifen
rice noodles with yellow chives and pork

After my second visit to our family home, my mother and I left for Hong Kong by ship. Since it wasn't to leave until late afternoon, we thought it advisable to eat something before boarding. The restaurant at the dock appeared no better or worse than the usual such establishment; that is, the food promised to be dreadful. Much to our surprise, we were served this delightful rice noodle dish. Light and flavourful, it was just the thing to carry us through the long overnight trip to Hong Kong. It is perfect for lunch or a light supper. Easy to make, it can be prepared in advance as it reheats very nicely.

350 g/12 oz dried thin rice noodles
225 g/8 oz lean pork
1 teaspoon rice wine or dry sherry
1 teaspoon light soy sauce
3½ teaspoons sesame oil
½ teaspoon cornflour
225 g/8 oz Chinese yellow or green chives or spring onions
4 tablespoons peanut oil
2 peeled garlic cloves, lightly crushed
2 tablespoons oyster sauce
1 tablespoon rice wine or dry sherry
1 tablespoon light soy sauce
1 tablespoon dark soy sauce
5 tablespoons chicken stock or water
1 teaspoon salt
1 teaspoon sugar

Soak the dried rice noodles in warm water for 20 minutes. Drain thoroughly.

Cut the pork into thin slices, then stack the slices and finely shred them. In a small bowl, combine the pork with the rice wine or sherry, soy sauce, ½ teaspoon of the sesame oil, and the cornflour.

Cut the chives or spring onions into 7.5 cm/3-in segments.

Heat the wok or frying pan until hot. Add half the oil and the garlic cloves. When the garlic has slightly browned, about 15 seconds, add the pork and stir-fry for 2 minutes. Remove the pork and garlic with a slotted spoon.

Reheat the wok and add the remaining oil. When it is very hot, add the rice noodles, and chives and stir-fry for 30 seconds. Then add the oyster sauce, rice wine or sherry, soy sauces, chicken stock or water, salt, and sugar. Continue to stir-fry over medium heat for 5 minutes. Return the pork to the wok or pan and mix well, continuously stir-frying for another minute. Give the mixture several good stirs, add the remaining sesame oil, turn onto a platter, and serve.

Serves 4 as part of a Chinese meal, or 2 as a single dish.

hongshao wanyu
red-cooked grass carp with tangerine peel

The carp enjoys a favoured place among aquatic foods in Chinese cuisine. As long ago as the Zhou Dynasty in the tenth century b.c. carp was "domesticated," that is, reared in ponds and bred selectively. Today, every farmer tries to maintain a fish pond where the carp thrives in circumstances that would weaken and kill other fish. Small wonder that the carp is a symbol of vigour, endurance, and strength. It is also a sign of respect, so he used.

"Red cooking" means braising with a strong, reddish sauce. The technique is usually applied to meat but it works well with any fresh, firm white fish.

15 g/½ oz dried tangerine or citrus peel

1.1–1.4 kg/2½–3 lb firm, white-fleshed fish such as carp, rock fish, cod, halibut, haddock, scrod or red snapper, or sole, cleaned and left whole

2 teaspoons salt

4 tablespoons cornflour

450 ml/16 fl oz peanut oil

2 tablespoons finely chopped garlic

3 tablespoons finely chopped peeled fresh ginger root

4 tablespoons finely chopped spring onions

3 tablespoons rice wine or dry sherry

1 tablespoon whole bean sauce (yellow bean sauce)

2 tablespoons dark soy sauce

1 tablespoon sugar

6 tablespoons chicken stock or water

Soak the tangerine or citrus peel for 20 minutes in warm water or until it is soft. Rinse under running water, squeeze out any excess liquid, finely chop, and set aside.

Make three or four slashes on each side of the fish to help it cook faster and allow the flavours to penetrate. Rub the fish on both sides with the salt. Sprinkle the cornflour evenly on each side of the fish.

Heat a wok or deep frying pan until hot. Add the oil, and when it is hot, deep-fry the fish on each side for 5 to 8 minutes until it is brown and crispy. Remove the fish and drain on kitchen paper.

Pour off most of the oil, leaving 2 tablespoons, and reheat the wok or pan. Add the chopped tangerine peel, garlic, ginger, and spring onions and stir-fry for 30 seconds. Put in the rest of the ingredients. Return the fish to the pan, spooning the ingredients over the top of the fish. Cover and cook over low heat for 8 minutes. When the fish is cooked, carefully remove it to a serving platter, and serve at once.

Serves 4 as part of a Chinese meal, or 2 as a single dish.

doujiao zai chao sigua yuner
long beans stir-fried with silk squash and cloud ears

One of the best vegetarian dishes I have eaten anywhere was prepared in the kitchen of my own family in Kaiping (Hoiping). It's a brilliant combination of authentically Cantonese tastes and textures. The long beans were fresh from the fields, crisp and extremely sweet, the silk squash had a soft, spongy texture and earthy flavour which was a nice contrast to its coarse skin. The cloud ears had a soft but elastic texture and subtle flavour. Quickly stir-fried with the other ingredients they made this a unique dish, good as a vegetarian main course or in combination with a meat dish.

25 g/1 oz cloud ear fungus
225 g/8 oz Chinese long beans or green beans
450 g/1 lb silk squash or courgettes
2 tablespoons peanut oil
2 tablespoons finely chopped shallots
2 tablespoons coarsely chopped garlic
2 teaspoons finely chopped peeled fresh ginger root
2 tablespoons oyster sauce
2 tablespoons rice wine or dry sherry
2 tablespoons light soy sauce
2 teaspoons salt
1 teaspoon sugar
125 ml/4 fl oz chicken stock

Soak the cloud ear fungus in warm water for at least 15 minutes. Rinse them several times in cold running water to remove any sand. Drain thoroughly and set aside.

If you are using Chinese long beans, trim the ends and cut them into 7.5-cm/3-in segments. If you are using green beans, trim the ends and cut them in half.

Peel off the tough outer skin of the silk squash, or top and tail the courgettes. Cut the vegetable at a slight diagonal into 5-cm/2-in pieces.

Heat a wok or large frying pan until hot and add the oil. Put in the shallots, garlic, ginger, cloud ears, and beans. Stir-fry for 1 minute, then add the silk squash or courgettes, oyster sauce, rice wine or sherry, soy sauce, salt, sugar, and chicken stock. Cook over high heat, uncovered, until the vegetables are tender, about 5 minutes. Serve at once.

Serves 4 as part of a Chinese meal, or 2 as a single dish.

chao douya
stir-fried soybean sprouts with pork

Soybean sprouts are a nutritious and economical food, used in China as an "instant vegetable." Similar to mung bean sprouts but longer and with a large yellow bean seed attached, soybean sprouts add crunchiness and a nut-like flavour to recipes. They are available in Chinese markets, though the more widely available mung bean sprouts, which can be found in most supermarkets. are an acceptable substitute.

The soybean has been cultivated in China for over three thousand years, so I am never surprised to encounter it in any of its myriad forms. I enjoyed this version in a meal my cousin prepared for us in Kaiping (Hoiping). It's a simple stir-fry of marinated pork bits, the whole enhanced by shrimp paste, making a delicious and satisfying meal. Shrimp paste, by the way, is a quite typical south Chinese condiment; its strong odour is rendered more pleasant by cooking.

225 g/8 oz lean pork
1 teaspoon rice wine or dry sherry
1 teaspoon light soy sauce
½ teaspoon sesame oil
½ teaspoon cornflour
700 g/1½ lb soybean sprouts or mung bean sprouts
2 tablespoons peanut oil
2 slices peeled fresh ginger root, crushed
1 tablespoon peanut oil
1 teaspoon shrimp paste
2 teaspoons light soy sauce

a personal odyssey – recipes

Chop the pork into small coarse bits. In a small bowl, combine it with the rice wine or sherry, soy sauce, sesame oil, and cornflour.

Wash the sprouts in cold running water, picking out any wilted pieces or darkened sprouts. Drain well.

Heat a wok or large frying pan until hot. Add 2 tablespoons of oil and the ginger pieces. When the ginger has browned, remove it with a slotted spoon. Put in the pork and stir-fry for 2 minutes. Remove the pork with a slotted spoon.

Reheat the wok or pan and add the remaining oil. When it is very hot, add the shrimp paste and stir-fry it for 10 seconds. Then add the sprouts and soy sauce. Continue to stir-fry for 4 minutes. Return the pork to the wok and mix very well with the sauce, continuously stir-frying for another minute. Give the mixture several good stirs, turn onto a platter and serve.

Serves 4 as part of a Chinese meal, or 2 as a single dish.

zheng ji
steamed chicken

On my first visit to my ancestral home, as part of the ritual of paying homage to our ancestors, I had to prostrate myself before the household shrines. As I did so, my cousin was dispatching a sacrificial chicken in the yard which was then quickly plucked and cleaned, rubbed with salt and steamed. The two of us offered it up to our common ancestors, bowing three times before the shrines. The chicken was then quickly cut into small portions and served to all the family with its ginger-spring onion sauce that brought out the full flavour. The liquid from the steamed chicken was poured over the rice for an additional treat. Even without ancestor reverence this dish is delicious.

One chicken, about 1.6 kg/3 lb
1 tablespoon sea salt
DIPPING SAUCE
Pinch of sugar
½ teaspoon salt

2 teaspoons light soy sauce
2 tablespoons finely chopped peeled fresh ginger root
5 tablespoons finely chopped spring onions
2 tablespoons peanut oil
1 teaspoon sesame oil

Rinse the chicken under cold running water and blot completely dry with kitchen paper. Rub the salt inside the cavity and on the skin of the chicken. Place the chicken, breast side down, on a heatproof platter, and set aside for 15 minutes.

Set up a steamer or put a rack into a wok or deep pan. Fill the steamer with about 5 cm/2 in of hot water. Bring the water to a simmer. Put the plate with the chicken into the steamer or onto the rack. Cover the steamer tightly and gently steam over medium heat for 1 hour. Replenish the water in the steamer from time to time. Remove the platter with the cooked chicken and pour off all the liquid.

In a small bowl, combine the sugar, salt, soy sauce, ginger, and spring onions well. In a small pan, heat the peanut and sesame oils until they smoke. Pour the hot oils over the ginger mixture. Chop the chicken into serving portions and serve immediately with the sauce.

Serves 8 as part of a Chinese meal, or 4 as a single dish.

a personal odyssey – recipes

CHAPTER 2
THE TASTES and FLAVOURS of CHINA

With good food, there is a different look and fragrance: sometimes pure as
autumn clouds, or beautiful like amber; a smell divine. There is no need to
apply the tongue or teeth to detect its exquisiteness
Menu of Su Yuan, Yuan Mei, 1715–1798

China is a huge country with vast geographical and climatic variation. Its history is measured in thousands of years, and for centuries its people have numbered in the hundreds of millions. Until the last century, it was a nation that had been more or less unified politically, bureaucratically, and linguistically (in its written language) for two millennia. During this time the people experienced many periods of social and political innovation and experimentation, times of flexibility and social mobility, of new ideas and open trade. They are undergoing such a period today. In such times, novelty is allowed or even encouraged. This is apparent in China's cuisine more than in other aspects of her culture as the Chinese join foreign influences to their venerable traditions and beliefs. In this way they assimilate them and make them their own.

China's foods have thus developed in a context of permanence and change, of ancient traditions and exciting innovations. While natural catastrophes – floods, earthquakes, droughts – have regularly surged across and altered the land, the Chinese nonetheless know the "good earth." From the sub-tropical south through the central mountains to the temperate north, the land, the fisheries, the rivers, and the oceans have always been exploited to their fullest.

The country is heavily populated, but there is relatively little fertile land, so the Chinese learned early on to use everything edible as food. They also employed the most ingenious techniques to produce it, believing that "human resolution can overcome heaven's destiny." No civilisation has ever done more with its food resources than China and her efforts continue. With 22 percent of the world's population and only 7 percent of the world's arable land, China sustains over one billion people.

Over the centuries, the Chinese have developed a unique style or approach, a philosophy concerning food. Most apparent is an accent on the freshness of ingredients and the balance of tastes. The Chinese use spices and flavourings in moderation. Ginger, spring onions, garlic, soy sauce, chilli bean sauce, and other seasonings are clearly but never obtrusively present. Thus, the Chinese differentiate themselves from their southeastern Asian neighbours – who, they allege, bury the flavours of food – and from their Japanese and central Asian neighbours – whose food, they say, is bland and tasteless. Freshness, balance, purity, clarity, and texture: these are the qualities that bespeak good cooking.

Everywhere I went in China, to markets, restaurants, and private homes, I encountered variety, pungency, and an atmosphere redolent with aromas and flavours. In the stores and food stalls in almost every region, for example, dozens of varieties of chilli bean pastes and sauces were available. In the condiment shops of Guangzhou, shoppers would bring their own bottles and have them filled with their favourite spicy mixture. The number of different condiments was

the tastes and flavours of china

impossible to count. I could have watched for hours.

Thanks to the recent liberalisation of the Chinese economy, ingredients are now readily available that were scarce or entirely lacking a few years ago. One of the unfortunate results of the Cultural Revolution was that it forcibly created a unified food economy and eliminated private gardens. Now, for the first time in many years, the Chinese are able to grow, buy, and prepare diverse foods. Fresh vegetables, spices, flavourings, and other traditional ingredients are becoming increasingly available. Private restaurants and food stalls are once again thriving. Cooking schools are reviving and teaching a new generation that had almost lost the arts and techniques of Chinese cuisine. There is still much to be regained, but I was heartened by the progress already made.

Throughout my travels in China, I was constantly impressed by the wide variety of food and ingredients. Despite regional variations, I felt a sense of unity which came from the shared techniques and flavours which are unique to China. This is due to more than the emphatic use of ginger, spring onions, and garlic, the trinity of Chinese seasonings; nor is the unity reducible to applications of soy sauce.

I saw people shop two and three times a day, not only because of a lack of refrigeration or inadequate storage space, but also from a compulsion to get the freshest foods possible. If this means returning to the shops a few times daily, so be it. In China, the freshest ingredients are the best, and the Chinese marry these with the most appropriate seasonings, spices, and sauces. One would think there is a limit to the number of dishes resulting from this simple yet masterful combination, but my very recent visits confirmed that there will always be surprises.

Almost all the ingredients called for in this book can now be obtained in ordinary supermarkets, as well as in Chinese or Asian grocers. I have listed acceptable substitutes if the original is unavailable. You will find advice on what to look for when shopping for these exotic ingredients, how to use them, and how to store them.

A word on monosodium glutamate, also known as MSG, Ve Tsin, Accent, or seasoning or taste powder. A flavour-enhancer and tenderiser, it was developed by Japanese scientists over half a century ago. About 250,000 tons of it are produced each year. Scientists still are not sure how this chemical works, but it does seem to bring out the natural salt flavour of foods and can help revive or enliven the taste of bland food and old vegetables. Some people suffer discomfort, the so-called "Chinese restaurant syndrome," if they eat food containing MSG but there is no danger. Unfortunately, with the advent of state-owned restaurants and limited distribution of some ingredients, it is widely used throughout China. The very best chefs, cooks, and restaurants, however, avoid MSG and rely instead, as they should, on the freshest and finest ingredients that need no enhancing. I agree with them wholeheartedly.

The food markets of China are full of exotic vegetables – wild rice shoots, fresh straw mushrooms, fresh bamboo shoots, smoked garlic, pea shoots, yellow cucumbers – whose range is impossible to find in the West. The good news, however, is that *most* ingredients, seasonings and vegetables *are* available and becoming increasingly so with expanding trade and the spread of an international style of cuisine. Today, with a little effort, you can duplicate many of the culinary wonders of China quite easily. All the recipes included in this book were tested with easily obtained ingredients.

INGREDIENTS

BAMBOO SHOOTS (*Dendrocalamus; Phyllostachys*)
Bamboo shoots are the young edible shoots of certain kinds of bamboo (part of the grass family). There are as many different types of bamboo shoots as there are kinds of bamboo – and at least ten of the hundred or so are marketed. They generally fall into two broad categories: spring shoots and winter shoots, the winter being smaller and more tender than the spring ones, which tend to be quite large. Expensive, fresh bamboo shoots are found only seasonally in markets in China; however, canned ones are available in the West and are more reasonably priced. Canned bamboo shoots tend to be pale yellow with a crunchy texture and, in some cases, a slightly sweet flavour. They come peeled and either whole or thickly sliced. Rinse them thoroughly and blanch them for two minutes in boiling water before

use. Transfer any remaining shoots to a jar, cover them with fresh water, and refrigerate them. If the water is changed daily they will keep two or three days. Slice blanched bamboo shoots before proceeding with the recipe.

Fresh bamboo shoots are prepared by first stripping off all their leaves and then trimming the hard base. Only the tender center core is edible, which is cut and blanched for at least five minutes to remove its bitterness. The shoots are then ready to be stir-fried or cooked.

BEAN CURD – Doufu (*Leguminosae glycine max*)

Bean curd is also known by its Chinese name, doufu, or by its Japanese name, tofu. It has played an important part in Chinese cookery for over a thousand years because it is highly nutritious, rich in protein, and goes well with other foods. Bean curd has a distinctive smooth texture but a bland taste. It is made from yellow soybeans which are soaked, ground, mixed with water and then cooked briefly before being solidified. It is usually sold in two forms: as firm, small blocks or in a soft, custard-like variety, but it is also available in several dried forms and in a fermented version. The soft bean curd (sometimes called silken tofu) is used for soups and other dishes, while the solid type is used for stir-frying, braising, and deep-frying. Solid bean curd blocks are white in colour and are packed in water in plastic containers. Once opened, they can be kept in their containers in the refrigerator for up to five days, provided the water is changed daily. To use solid bean curd, carefully cut the amount required into cubes or shreds using a sharp knife, then cook it gently. Too much stirring can cause it to disintegrate, though this does not affect its nutritional value.

Fermented Bean Curd (Red, Chilli, and Regular)

This is a cheese-like form of bean curd preserved in rice or in wine, in brine with rice, or in chillies, and sold in glass jars at Asian speciality markets. It is very popular in China where it is eaten by itself with rice or used in cooking or as a condiment. It is used as a flavouring agent, especially with vegetables. A little adds zest to any vegetable dish. Once it begins to cook, it produces a fragrant odour that enriches the vegetables. It comes in several forms: the red fermented bean curd has been cured in a brine with red rice, rice wine, and sometimes with crushed dried chilli peppers, and the regular one has been made with wine. Once the jar has been opened, fermented bean curd will keep indefinitely if resealed and refrigerated. You can only find this at Asian speciality markets. There is no substitute for this unique ingredient.

Pressed Seasoned Bean Curd
When water is extracted from fresh bean curd cakes by pressing them with a weight, the bean curd becomes firm and compact. Simmered in water with soy sauce, star anise, and sugar, the pressed bean curd acquires a smooth, resilient texture that is quite unusual. Cut into small pieces, it can be stir-fried with meat or vegetables; when cut into larger pieces it can be simmered. In China, pressed seasoned bean curd is a popular ingredient. Buy it at Asian speciality markets, or substitute fresh firm bean curd.

Bean Sprouts (*Leguminosae phaseolus aureus; glycine max*)
Now widely available, these are the sprouts of the green mung bean, although some Chinese markets also stock yellow soybean sprouts which are much larger. Bean sprouts should always be very fresh and crunchy. They will keep for several days loosely wrapped in kitchen paper and inside a plastic bag stored in the vegetable crisper of a refrigerator. It is paradoxical that bean sprouts, now so common in the West, have become a luxury in China where keeping the bean sprouts fresh is difficult because they are so perishable and refrigeration is so expensive. However, this refreshing food has enjoyed a revival in the more highly priced restaurants.

Bird's Nest
A truly exotic food, and one of the most sought-after delicacies of China. Historically, it was most abundant in southern China, and is now sought after in affluent Hong Kong and Taiwan. This is literally bird's nest made of regurgitated spittle of a certain type of swift from the East Asian tropics: Thailand, Vietnam, Java, and the Philippines. Their nests are found in large mountainside caverns where workers climb on long bamboo scaffolding to retrieve them. Bird's nest is said

bean curd – bird's nest

to be good for one's complexion and is prescribed for convalescing patients. There are shops in Hong Kong and Taiwan specialising in bird's nest, which comes in all grades. The best ones are the "white nests" and "pink or blood nests," which are actually complete cups. The nests are expensive and are usually sold precleaned, that is, feathers and other bits are hand-plucked from the nests. It is sold dried and must be soaked before using, as instructed in recipes calling for it. The result, like shark's fin, is a bland, soft, crunchy jelly that relies for flavour on whatever sauce or broth it is served with. It is an acquired taste.

BITTER MELON (*Momordica charantia*)
This unusual vegetable is also an acquired taste that has as many detractors as it has fans. While I found it quite abundant throughout my travels in China, especially during the warm summer months, I discovered that even the Chinese must learn to love it. Bitter melon has a bumpy dark to pale green skin, and has a slightly bitter quinine flavour that has a cooling effect in one's mouth. I ate it stir-fried with chillies, and braised with fermented bean curd. In some parts of China it is often dried and used as medicine. The greener the melon, the more bitter its taste, and many cooks look for the milder yellow-green varieties. To use, cut in half, seed, and discard interior membrane. Then, to lessen its bitter taste, either blanch or salt it, according to instructions in your recipe. Store in the bottom of your refrigerator in a loose plastic or paper bag. It should keep there for three to five days, depending on the condition in which it was bought.

BLACK BEANS
These small black soybeans, also known as salted black beans or fermented black beans, are preserved by being fermented with salt and spices. They have a distinctive, slightly salty taste and a pleasantly rich smell, and are used as a seasoning, often in conjunction with garlic or fresh ginger. Together, they are among the most popular flavours of southern China, and their aroma stimulated my appetite as I walked through the busy, narrow streets of Guangzhou (Canton). Inexpensive, shoppers usually purchase only as much of them as they

need for a day or so. They are easy to find in the West and I see them often in supermarkets. You can can find them in cans marked "Black Bean Sauce," but I prefer those packed in plastic bags. In China, the black beans are usually used whole or coarsely chopped for a more pungent flavour. Although some recipes say to rinse them before using, I notice that most chefs in China do not bother with this. The beans will keep indefinitely if stored in the refrigerator or in a cool place.

CAUL FAT
Actually the lower stomach lining of a pig or cow, this lacy membrane melts during cooking and keeps meats and fillings moist and delicious. It is highly perishable so buy it in small quantities and use quickly. For longer storage, wrap the caul fat carefully and freeze. To defrost, rinse in cold water. I find that soaking layers of caul fat in cold water helps to separate them without tearing its fragile webs. You can order caul fat from your local butcher.

CHILLIES, FRESH (*Capsicum frutescens*)
Fresh chillies – the seed pods of the capsicum plant – are used extensively and are popular in Chinese cuisine. However, the type of chilli most often found is not as pungent or spicy as the ones found in many parts of southeast Asia and parts of the United States. Although relatively new to Chinese cuisine, as it comes from the Americas, the chilli has spread rapidly throughout Asia. Although they are not a standard ingredient in southern Chinese cooking, I found them widely used throughout the western and northern parts of the country. In China, fresh chillies are small to medium size, and generally red, but they also come in shades of green. Smaller varieties can be found, but the larger, longer ones are the ones most available. Their taste is mildly spicy and pungent and they are also popular for their colour especially in garnishes. Ordinarily chopped or sliced, and used in many dishes and sauces, one of my great discoveries was to taste mild chillies stir-fried whole.

Throughout this book, I have used the mildest variety I can find. I have cut down the amounts to compensate for the slightly hotter ones found in the West. Look for fresh chillies that are bright, with no brown patches or black spots. Use red chillies wherever possible, as they are generally milder than green ones.

To prepare fresh chillies, first rinse them in cold water. Then, using a small, sharp knife, slit them lengthways. Remove and discard the seeds. Rinse the chillies well under cold running water, then prepare them according to the instructions in the recipe. Wash your hands, knife and chopping board before preparing other foods, and be careful not to touch your eyes until you have washed your hands thoroughly with soap and water.

CHILLIES, DRIED RED

A beautiful sight in food shops, at the front of restaurants and in the homes of Sichuan are the long strings of dried red chillies. Used less frequently in other areas of China, dried chillies are essential to many Sichuan-inspired dishes. They are used in either whole or ground form. Some are small and thin, 12–25mm/½–1 in long. They are used to season oil for stir-fried dishes, or split and chopped and used in sauces and for braising. They are normally left whole, cut in half lengthways, or finely ground with the seeds left in. Dried chilies will keep more or less indefinitely stored in a tightly covered jar in a cool, dry place.

CHILLI OIL/CHILLI DIPPING SAUCE

Chilli oil is sometimes used as a dipping condiment as well as a seasoning in China, where it is generally milder than the commercially made chilli oil from Sichuan Province, and certainly never as hot as the oil from Southeast Asia. Of course, as chillies vary, so do the oils vary in strength and flavour. You can purchase chilli oil from Chinese markets. The Thai and Malaysian versions are especially hot; the Taiwanese and Chinese versions are more subtle. Such commercial products are quite acceptable, but I include this recipe because the homemade version is the best. Remember that chilli oil is too dramatic to be used as the sole cooking oil; it is best used as part of a dipping sauce or as a condiment, or combined with milder oils. I include the spices (pepper and black beans) as additional flavours because then I can also use it as a dipping sauce.

Once made, chilli oil will keep for months if it is stored in a tightly sealed glass jar and kept in a cool, dark place.

175 ml/6 fl oz peanut oil
2 tablespoons chopped dried red chillies
1 tablespoon whole unroasted Sichuan peppercorns
2 tablespoons whole black beans

Heat a wok over a high heat and add the oil and the rest of the ingredients. Continue to cook over a low heat for about 10 minutes. Allow the mixture to cool undisturbed and then pour it into a jar. Let the mixture sit for 2 days, and then strain the oil. It will keep indefinitely.

CHILLI BEAN SAUCE (see *Sauces and Pastes*, page 50)

CHILLI POWDER
Chilli powder is made from dried red chillies. It is pungent and aromatic, ranging from hot to very hot, so is thus widely used in many spicy dishes. In Sichuan, it is often combined with ground roasted Sichuan peppercorns.

CHINESE BROCCOLI (*Brassica alboglara*)
Chinese broccoli is not like European-type broccoli. It is very crunchy and slightly bitter and more resembles Swiss chard in flavour. It is quite delicious with an earthy, "green" taste. It has deep olive green leaves and sometimes white flowers. It is usually available only at Chinese markets but is well worth the search. If you can find it, look for stems which are firm and leaves which look fresh and green. It is prepared in exactly the same way as broccoli and should be stored in a plastic bag in the vegetable crisper of the refrigerator where it will keep for several days. Where Chinese broccoli is not available, substitute ordinary broccoli.

CHINESE CHIVES (*Allium tuberosum*)
Chinese chives, widely used in China, are related to common chives

chillies – chinese chives

and are of the garlic family. Their taste is stronger and more garlic-like than our chives and their flowers can be used as well as the blades. They have an earthy, onion taste and are delicious by themselves or cooked with other foods. Chinese chives can be found in Chinese markets but they are very easy to grow in home herb gardens. Look for wide flat blades and sprays of white, star-shaped flowers. They can be substituted for regular chives but adjust the quantity to allow for their stronger flavour. Rinse and dry the chives, store them in slightly damp kitchen paper inside a plastic bag in the refrigerator and use as soon as possible. Chinese yellow chives are Chinese chives which have been grown in the dark and are pale and have a more subtle flavour than the green Chinese chives. In China they are used extensively, especially in restaurants, but are hard to find in the West. Select the freshest leaves possible. Trim any decaying parts. Wash and dry thoroughly and store between sheets of kitchen paper in the lower part of your refrigerator for only one or two days, as they are highly perishable. They have a rich, earthy taste and flavour – yet are delicate and fragile at the same time.

CHINESE FLOWERING CABBAGE (*Brassicacae chinensis var. parachinensis*)

Chinese flowering cabbage is part of the large mustard green cabbage family and is found frequently in dishes in China, especially in the south, where it is usually known by the more familiar Cantonese name, *choi sum*. Chinese flowering cabbage has green leaves and may have small yellow flowers which are eaten along with the leaves and stems. In China this is one of the most common and popular leafy vegetables and is delicious stir-fried.

CHINESE LEAVES (*Brassicacae pekinensis*)

Chinese leaves, also popularly known as Peking cabbage and Napa cabbage, are common throughout China. This cabbage comes fresh in various sizes from long, compact and bullet-shaped to fat and squat-looking. All types are tightly packed with firm, pale green (or in some cases slightly yellow), crinkled leaves. This versatile vegetable is used in China for soups or it is stir-fried with meats, absorbing flavours easily because of its sponge-like quality. Used raw or lightly cooked, the cabbage is a sweet, crunchy vegetable with a mild but distinctive taste that chefs like to match with foods with richer flavours. Store it as you would ordinary cabbage.

CHINESE LONG BEANS (*Vigna sesquipedalis*)

These beans are popular in China and can be found in great abundance in the markets there. They are also known as yard-long beans and can grow to 90 cm/3 ft in length. Not related to short, Western green beans, long beans originated in Asia. There are two varieties: the pale green ones and the dark green, thinner ones. Buy those that are fresh and bright green, with no dark marks. You will usually find long beans sold in looped bunches, and there is no need to string them before cooking. In China, they are stir-fried with meats or with fermented bean curd. They have a crunchy taste and texture like runner beans but cook faster. Store the fresh beans in a plastic bag in the refrigerator and use within four days.

CHINESE MUSHROOMS, DRIED

There are many grades of these wonderful mushrooms said to have been cultivated for more than a thousand years in southern China. Black or brown in colour, they add a particular flavour and aroma to Chinese dishes. The best, and most popular in China, are very large ones with a lighter colour and a highly cracked surface; these are usually the most expensive. Chinese markets specialising in dried food carry all grades heaped in mounds, with the most expensive mushrooms elaborately boxed, sometimes in plastic. Fresh mushrooms (popularly known by their Japanese name, Shiitake) are not an adequate substitute and the Chinese almost never use them fresh, preferring the dried version's distinct, robust, smoky flavours, and the way they absorb sauces, taking on a succulent texture. They are used as seasonings, finely chopped and combined with meats, fish, and shellfish. Keep them stored in an air-tight jar in a cool, dry place.

To use Chinese dried mushrooms

Soak the mushrooms in a bowl of warm water for about 20 minutes or until they are soft and pliable. Squeeze out the excess water and cut off and discard the woody stems. Only the caps are used.

Strain the soaking water through a fine sieve to remove any sand or residue from the dried mushrooms and save it to use in soups and in water for cooking rice.

Chinese Tree Fungus

These tiny, black, dried leaves are also known as cloud ears; when soaked, they puff up to look like little clouds. Soak the dried fungus in hot water for 20 to 30 minutes until soft. Rinse well, cutting away any hard portions. Fungi are valued for their crunchy texture and slightly smoky flavour. You can find them at Chinese markets, usually wrapped in plastic or cellophane bags. They keep indefinitely in a jar stored in a cool, dry place.

Chinese Wood Ear Fungus

These fungi are the larger variety of the Chinese tree fungi described above. Prepare, soak, and trim them in the same manner. Once soaked, they will swell up to four or five times their size. Rinse well and cut away any hard portions. Sold in Chinese markets they keep indefinitely when stored in a cool, dry place.

CHINESE WHITE CABBAGE – Pak Choi (*Brassicacae chinensis*)

Chinese white cabbage, popularly known as pak choi or bok choy, has been grown in China for centuries. Although there are many varieties, the most common and best known is the one with a long smooth stem, milky-white and large, crinkly, dark green leaves. The size of the plant indicates how tender it is. The smaller the better, especially, in the summer when the hot weather toughens the stalks. Pak choi has a light, fresh, slightly mustardy taste and requires little cooking. In China, pak choi is used in soup or is stir-fried. Now widely available in supermarkets, look for firm crisp stalks and unblemished leaves. Store pak choi in the vegetable crisper of your refrigerator.

CHINESE WHITE RADISH (*Raphanus sativus*)

Chinese white radish is also known as Chinese icicle radish, as mooli, or by its Japanese name, daikon. It is long and white and rather like a carrot in shape but usually much larger. A winter radish, it can withstand long cooking without disintegrating and thus absorbs the flavours of the food it is cooked with, yet retains its distinctive radish taste and texture. In China, these root vegetables are usually found in home dishes, treated the way Western cooks use potatoes or carrots. They are never used without being peeled. Look for firm, heavy, solid, and unblemished ones. They should be slightly translucent inside, solid and not fibrous. You can find them in some supermarkets and most Chinese or Asian markets. Store in a plastic bag in the vegetable crisper of your refrigerator where they will keep for over a week.

CINNAMON STICKS OR BARK
Cinnamon sticks are curled, paper-thin pieces of the bark of the cinnamon tree, the Chinese version being rather thick. They are highly aromatic and more pungent than the common cinnamon sticks, but the latter are an adequate substitute. They add a robust taste to braised dishes and are an important ingredient of five-spice powder. Store cinnamon sticks or bark in a tightly sealed jar to preserve their aroma and flavour. Ground cinnamon is too strong and not a satisfactory substitute.

CITRUS PEEL (Dried Tangerine Peel, Dried Orange Peel)
In the markets of China you will often find freshly peeled greenish lemons with the fruit sold separately from the peel. Many people take the peels home and dry them to use in fish or meat dishes. The best citrus peels are those of Chinese tangerines, which have a rich, slightly sweet orange flavour. Dried citrus peel is sold in Asian or Chinese stores or can be easily made at home. Wash and rinse the fruit well. Cut each fruit into eight wedges. Use a sharp knife to cut off the fruit sections and then carefully separate the white pith from the peel. Dry the peel on a rack in a warm place until it is hard. Stored in an airtight jar, the dried peel will last for months. When you are ready to use the peel, rehydrate it in a bowl of warm water for 20 minutes or until it is soft.

CORIANDER – Chinese Parsley – Cilantro (*Coriandrum sativum*)

39

chinese tree fungus – citrus peel

Fresh coriander is one of the relatively few herbs used in Chinese cookery and is a standard in southern China. It looks like flat parsley but its pungent, musky, citrus-like character gives it an unmistakable flavour. Its feathery leaves are often used as a garnish, or it is chopped and then mixed into sauces and stuffings. When buying fresh coriander, look for deep green, fresh-looking leaves.

To store coriander, wash it in cold water, drain it thoroughly or spin dry in a salad spinner and put it in a clean plastic bag along with a couple of sheets of moist kitchen paper. I learned this technique from my cooking associate, Gordon Wing, and it works wonderfully. Stored like this in the vegetable crisper of your refrigerator, fresh coriander will keep for several days.

CORNFLOUR

In China and throughout Asia there are many flours and types of starch, such as water chestnut powder, taro starch, and arrowroot, which are used to bind and thicken sauces and to make batter. Cornflour is also now widely used in Chinese cooking, although traditional cooks prefer a bean flour because it thickens faster and holds longer. In China, sauces are light and barely coat the food, and food never "swims" in thick sauces. As part of a marinade, cornflour helps to coat food properly and to give dishes a velvety texture. It also protects food during deep-frying by helping to seal in the juices, producing a crisper coating than flour, and can be used as a binder for minced stuffings. Cornflour is invariably blended with cold water until it forms a smooth paste and added at the last moment to sauces. The mixture will look milky at first, but when the dish is properly prepared, the cornflour turns clear and shiny as it thickens the sauce.

DRIED SHRIMPS

Seafood of all forms – fresh or dried – is a favourite of Chinese people. Dried shrimps are used to perk up fried rice or mixed with meat dishes to give an added dimension. Tiny dried shrimps are sold in packages and may be found in Asian specialty markets. Look for the brands with the pinkest colour and avoid grayish ones. Dried shrimps will keep indefinitely sealed in a glass container and stored in a cool, dry place.

the tastes and flavours of china

When cooked, the dried shrimps add a delicate taste to sauces; cooking moderates the shrimps' strong odour.

AUBERGINES (*Solanum melongena*)
Another popular and inexpensive food found throughout China. These pleasing purple-skinned vegetables range in size from the larger plump ones, easy to find in all produce stores, to the small thin variety which the Chinese prefer for their more delicate flavour. Look for those with smooth unblemished skin. Chinese cooks normally do not peel aubergines, since the skin preserves texture, taste, and shape. Large aubergines should be cut according to the recipe, sprinkled with a little salt, and left to sit for 20 minutes. They should then be rinsed and any liquid blotted dry with kitchen towels. This process extracts bitter juices and excess moisture from the vegetable before it is cooked, giving a truer taste to a dish. The aubergine also absorbs less moisture after this process. This procedure is unnecessary if you are using Chinese aubergines.

EGG WHITE
Egg whites are often used in Chinese recipes as ingredients of batters and coatings, sealing in flavour and juices and making a light and protective coating for foods when plunged into warm oil, especially for velveting. One egg white from a large egg generally measures about 2 tablespoons. Egg whites freeze well in tablespoon-size cubes in an ice tray.

FIVE-SPICE POWDER
Less commonly known as five-flavoured powder or five-fragrance spice powder, this brownish powder is a mixture of star anise, Sichuan peppercorns, fennel, cloves, and cinnamon. A good blend is pungent, fragrant, spicy, and slightly sweet at the same time. The exotic element it gives a dish is worth any effort it takes to find it in the spice section of good supermarkets or Asian speciality markets.

FLOUR
Glutinous Rice Flour: This flour, made from glutinous rice, gives quite a chewy texture to the dough and is widely used in China for

making rich dim sum pastries. However, it is not an acceptable substitute in recipes that call for regular rice flour, but can be stored in the same way.

Rice Flour: This flour is made from raw rice and is used to make fresh rice noodles. Store it as you would wheat flour.

FUNGUS (see *Chinese Mushroom,* page 37)

GARLIC (*Alliaceae sativum*)

The pungent flavour of garlic is part of the fabric of China's cuisine, and it would be inconceivable to cook without this distinctive, highly aromatic smell and taste. It is used in numerous ways: whole, finely chopped, crushed, and pickled. In China I have even found it smoked. It is used to flavour oils as well as spicy sauces, and is often paired with other equally pungent ingredients such as spring onions, black beans, curry, shrimp paste, or fresh ginger. In China, cooks often add a smashed clove of garlic to the hot oil. The garlic becomes fragrant and is said to have "sweetened" the oil; it is then removed and discarded before other ingredients are added.

Select fresh garlic which is firm and heavy, preferably with cloves that are pinkish in colour. It should always be stored in a cool, dry place, but not in the refrigerator where it can easily become mildewed or begin sprouting.

GARLIC SHOOTS

Frequently you see garlic shoots in China's markets alongside spring onions and various forms of Chinese chives. These are young garlic shoots before they begin to form a bulb. Harvested early in the spring, they add a delicate perfume and mild, delicate flavours to food which are highly prized among China's discerning diners. They look a little bit like spring onions and their green tops may also be used as a garnish or flavouring.

GINGER ROOT (*Zingiber officinale*)

In traditional Chinese cooking fresh ginger root is as essential as the wok. It is said that ginger root from Canton is the most aromatic, but,

42

the tastes and flavours of china

like garlic, it is an indispensable ingredient of all Chinese cookery. Its pungent, spicy, and fresh taste adds a subtle but distinctive flavour to soups, meats, fish, sauces, and vegetables. These rhizomes are golden-beige in colour with a thin dry skin. They range from small, broken-off bits to large knobbly "hands." In China you can find peeled ginger root at the markets; older, ginger root is used for medicinal broths. Look for ginger root which is firm, solid, and clear-skinned.

Young stem ginger often makes a seasonal appearance in the markets of China, but is hard to find in the West. Knobbly-looking, moist and pink, the early spring growth, young stem ginger is usually eaten in various stir-fried dishes. So tender it does not need peeling, fresh young ginger can be eaten on its own as a vegetable. It is also commonly pickled in China. A popular way to eat pickled young ginger is with preserved "thousand-year-old" duck eggs as a snack. It is often served in restaurants or private homes as an hors d'oeuvre.

Ginger root wrapped in plastic will keep in the refrigerator for up to two weeks. Peeled ginger root covered in rice wine or dry sherry in a jar and refrigerated will last for several months. This has the added benefit of producing a flavoured wine.

Ginger Juice

Made from fresh ginger, the juice is used in marinades to give a subtle ginger taste without the pungency of the fresh chopped pieces. Here is a simple method of extracting the juice: cut fresh unpeeled ginger root into 25-mm/1-in chunks and drop them into a running food processor. When the ginger is finely chopped, squeeze out the juice by hand through a cotton or linen towel. Or, mash the ginger with a kitchen mallet or the side of a cleaver or knife until most of the fibers are exposed. Then simply squeeze out the juice by hand through a cotton or linen towel.

Leeks (*Allium porrum*)

This vegetable is grown and used primarily in northern China. It is treated as an onion and stir-fried with meats. The leeks found in China are large, cylindrical and resemble a giant spring onion with a white husk, like garlic. Leeks found in the West are a good substitute. Leeks have a mild, slightly sweet onion flavour. To use, cut off and discard the green tops and roots and halve the leek lengthways. Wash them well. Store them in a plastic bag in a vegetable crisper of your refrigerator.

LILY BUDS (*Lilium lancifolium*)
Also known as tiger lily buds, golden needles, or lily stems, dried lily buds are an ingredient in *muxi (mu shu)* dishes and hot and sour soups. They provide texture as well as an earthy taste to any dish. Soak the buds in hot water for about 30 minutes or until soft. Cut off the hard ends and shred or cut in half according to the recipe directions. You can find them in Chinese markets; they are quite inexpensive. Store them in a jar in a dry place.

MALTOSE SUGAR (see *also Sugar,* page 55)
This type of malt sugar is a liquid syrup that adds a wonderful richness to stews and sauces without a cloying sweetness. It may be stored at room temperature and is only found in Chinese markets. Honey may be used as a substitute.

NOODLES
In China, people eat noodles of all kinds, day and night, in restaurants and at food stalls. They provide a nutritious, quick, light snack and usually are of good quality. Several styles of Chinese noodle dishes have now made their way to the West, including the fresh thin egg noodles which are browned (cooked) on both sides and the popular thin rice noodles. Both kinds can be bought in Chinese markets fresh and dried. Below is a list of the major types of noodles.

Wheat Noodles and Egg Noodles
These are made from hard or soft wheat flour and water. If egg has been added the noodles are usually labelled as egg noodles. Many supermarkets and delicatessens also stock both the dried and fresh variety. Flat noodles are usually used in soups and round noodles are best for stir-frying or pan-frying. The fresh ones freeze nicely if they are well wrapped. Thaw them thoroughly before cooking.

To cook wheat and egg noodles

Noodles are very good cooked and served with main dishes instead of plain rice. I think dried wheat or fresh egg noodles are best for this.

225 g/8 oz fresh or dried Chinese egg or wheat noodles

If you are using fresh noodles, immerse them in a pot of boiling water and cook them for 3 to 5 minutes or until you like their texture. If you are using dried noodles, either cook them according to the instructions on the packet, or cook them in boiling water for 4 to 5 minutes. Drain and serve.

If you are cooking noodles ahead of time or before stir-frying them, toss the cooked and drained noodles in 2 teaspoons of sesame oil and put them into a bowl. Cover this with plastic wrap and refrigerate for up to 2 hours.

Rice Noodles

Rice noodles are popular in southern China, where they are widely known as Sha He noodles, the name deriving from a small village outside the city of Guangzhou (Canton). The fresh ones are called "fen noodles," and are prepared in a different manner (see Fen Noodles). The dried noodles are opaque white and come in a variety of shapes. One of the most common examples is rice stick noodles, which are flat and about the length of a chopstick. They can also vary in thickness. Use the type called for in the recipes. Rice noodles are very easy to use. Simply soak them in warm water for 20 minutes until they are soft. Drain them in a colander or a sieve and they are then ready to be used in soups or to be stir-fried.

Fen Rice Noodles (also known as Sha He Noodles)

The Chinese make large sheets of *fen*, which means rice noodles, from a basic mixture of rice flour, wheat *starch* (not flour), and water. This pasta is steamed in sheets and then, when cooked, is cut into noodles to be eaten immediately. A very popular street snack in southern China, the fresh noodles are most often served with a sauce.

Bean Thread (transparent) Noodles

These noodles, also called cellophane noodles, are made from ground

lily buds – bean thread

mung beans and not from a grain flour. Freshly made ones can sometimes be seen in China, fluttering in the breeze on lines like drying clothes. They are available dried, and are very fine and white. Easy to recognise, packed in their neat, plastic-wrapped bundles, they are stocked by most Chinese markets and some supermarkets. They are never served on their own, but are added to soups or braised dishes or are deep-fried and used as a garnish. They must be soaked in warm water for about 5 minutes before use. As they are rather long you might find it easier to cut them into shorter lengths after soaking. If you are frying them, they do not need soaking beforehand but do need to be separated. A good technique for separating the strands is to pull them apart while holding them in a large paper bag which stops them from flying all over the place.

OILS

Oil is the most commonly used cooking medium in China. While animal fats, usually lard and chicken fat, are used in some regions, particularly in northern parts of China, the oil of choice is peanut. It is also the most expensive.

Throughout this book I have indicated wherever oils can be reused. In cases where this is possible, simply cool the oil after use and filter it through cheesecloth, muslin, or a fine strainer into a jar. Cover it tightly and keep in a cool, dry place. If kept in the refrigerator it will become cloudy but it will clarify again when the oil returns to room temperature. For purity of flavours, I use oils only once. Never use them more than twice; constantly reused oils increase in saturated fat content. In the finest restaurants in China, fresh oil is *always* used.

Corn Oil

Corn oil is a healthful, mostly polyunsaturated oil that is good for cooking and also has a high burning point. I use corn oil in a pinch but find it rather heavy and am always aware of its distinctive smell and taste. It is used in China, but it is not as popular as vegetable or peanut oil.

Other Vegetable Oils

Some of the cheaper vegetable oils are available in China: these include rapeseed, cottonseed, soybean, safflower, and sunflower oils. They are light in colour and bland in taste and so can be used in cooking, although they tend to smoke rather quickly, making them less suitable for the high temperatures required for stir-frying and deep-frying. In China, they are used mainly by food stalls and the cheaper restaurants. They are quite edible but simply not as good nor as effective as peanut oil.

Peanut Oil

The Chinese prefer to cook with peanut oil because it has a pleasant, mild, and unobtrusive taste. It can be heated to a high temperature without burning and this makes it perfect for both stir-frying and deep-frying. The peanut oils found in China are cold pressed and have the fragrance of freshly roasted peanuts. Some Chinese supermarkets stock a number of Chinese brands, their names appearing in Chinese characters on the labels. These are well worth searching for, but if you cannot find them, use a good quality peanut oil from your local supermarket.

oils

Sesame Oil

This aromatic and strongly flavoured, thick, rich, golden brown or dark coloured oil is made from toasted and roasted sesame seeds, which have a distinctive, nutty flavour and aroma. It is widely used in China, although in limited amounts and not normally for cooking. Only in northern China do cooks sometimes combine it with other oils as a cooking oil. Added as a final seasoning, or used as a marinade, it subtly enriches a dish without overcoming its basic flavour.

OYSTERS, DRIED

Like much dried seafood found in China, these oysters are frequently used in finely minced form to enhance dishes. They come in a wide range of grades and sizes and add a new dimension to the taste of foods. Use dried oysters carefully because they can overwhelm a dish with their assertive flavours. Soak them until soft for at least one hour in a bowl of warm water, or even as long as overnight. If you wish, you may substitute smoked oysters that have been canned in oil. These may be more easily found in Western supermarkets.

PEANUTS

Raw peanuts are used to add flavour and a crunchy texture and are especially popular in China. They are stir-fried before being added to dishes. They can be found at health food shops, good supermarkets, and Chinese markets. The thin red skins need to be removed before you use the nuts. To do this, simply immerse them in a pot of boiling water for about 2 minutes. Drain them and let them cool, and the skins will come off easily.

RED-IN-SNOW CABBAGE

This hardy winter vegetable peeks through the snow with red or crimson colours, thus its name. The cabbage is pickled and can be bought in cans at Asian speciality markets. It adds a pungent, slightly sour taste to dishes when used as a flavouring, or it can be used as an interestingly textured vegetable ingredient in stir-fried dishes.

RICE

Long-Grain Rice

This is the most popular rice for cooking in China where there are many different varieties. Although the Chinese go through the ritual of washing it, rice purchased at supermarkets doesn't require this step.

Short-Grain Rice

Short-grain rice is most frequently found in northern China and is used for making rice porridge, a popular morning meal. I find it to be coarse and rough.

Glutinous Rice

Glutinous rice is also known as sweet rice or sticky rice. It is short, round and pearl-like, with a higher gluten content, and is used in China for stuffings, rice pudding, and in pastries. It is used for rice dishes, sometimes wrapped in lotus leaves, and served after Chinese banquets. It is also used for making Chinese rice wine and vinegar.

Most Chinese markets and some supermarkets stock it. Glutinous rice must be soaked for at least 2 hours (preferably overnight) before cooking. You may cook it in the same way as long-grain rice.

To wash rice

An optional step, if you wish to do as the Chinese do. Put the required amount of rice into a large bowl. Fill the bowl with cold water and swish the rice around with your hands. Carefully pour off the cloudy water, keeping the rice in the bowl. Repeat this process several times until the water is clear.

RICE WINE

An important component to the flavours of China. This wine is used extensively for cooking and drinking throughout all of China, but I believe the finest of its many varieties to be from Shaoxing in Zhejiang Province in eastern China. It is made from glutinous rice, yeast, and spring water. Chefs frequently use it not only for cooking but also in marinades and for sauces. Now readily available in the West from Chinese markets and some wine shops, it should be kept tightly corked at room temperature. Do not confuse this wine with *sake,* which is the Japanese version of rice wine and quite different. A good quality, dry pale sherry can be substituted but cannot fully match its rich, mellow taste. Other Western grape wines are not an adequate substitute.

SALT (Kosher, Rock, and Sea Salt)

Table salt is the finest grind of salt. Many chefs feel that kosher or sea salt has a richer flavour than ordinary table salt. Sea salt is frequently found in bins at the Chinese markets. Rock salt is most often known for its role in freezing ice cream, but the larger crystals make an excellent medium of heat conduction, and rock salt is often used in certain kinds of Chaozhou (a regional southern cooking style), especially with chicken or squab dishes.

SAUCES AND PASTES

Chinese cuisine involves a number of thick, tasty sauces or pastes. They are essential to the authentic taste of the food and most are easy to find in bottles or cans in Chinese markets and some supermarkets.

Canned sauces, once opened, should be transferred to screw-top jars and kept in the refrigerator where they will last indefinitely.

Chilli Sauce

Chilli sauce is a bright red, hot sauce which is made from chillies, vinegar, sugar, and salt. It is sometimes used for cooking, but it is most often used in China as a dipping sauce. There are various brands available in supermarkets and Chinese markets, and you should experiment until you find the one you like best. If you find it too strong, dilute it with hot water. Do not confuse this sauce with the chilli bean sauce which follows.

Chilli Bean Sauce

This is a thick, dark sauce or paste, hot and spicy, made from yellow soybeans, chillies, and other seasonings. Widely used in cooking in western China, there are as many types and varieties as there are people. Be sure to seal the jar tightly after use and store in the refrigerator. Do not confuse it with chilli sauce which is a hot, red, thinner sauce made without beans and used mainly as a dipping sauce.

Hoisin Sauce

Widely used in southern China, this is a thick, dark, brownish red sauce which is made from soybeans, vinegar, sugar, spices, and other flavourings. It is sweet and slightly spicy. In the West, it is often used as a sauce for Peking duck instead of the traditional sweet bean sauce. Hoisin sauce is available in cans and jars and may also be labelled barbecue sauce.

Oyster Sauce

A popular seasoning from the fishing villages in southern China, this important sauce is an essential ingredient of Cantonese (southern) cuisine. It is thick and brown and is made from a concentrate of oysters cooked in soy sauce, seasonings, and brine. Despite its name, oyster sauce does not taste fishy. It has a rich flavour and is used not only in cooking but as a condiment, diluted with a little oil, for vegetables, poultry, or meats – a very popular southern Chinese use. It is usually

the tastes and flavours of china

sold in bottles and can be bought in Chinese markets and some supermarkets. Search out the most expensive ones; their higher quality is worth the price.

Sesame Paste

This rich, thick, creamy brown paste is made from toasted sesame seeds, unlike Middle Eastern tahini whose seeds are ground raw. If the paste has separated in the jar, empty the contents into a blender or food processor and blend well. Chinese sesame paste is used in both hot and cold dishes, and is particularly popular in northern and western China. It is sold in jars at Chinese markets. If you need and can't get it for a recipe, use smooth peanut butter instead.

Shrimp Paste

Used in the south of China, this ingredient adds an exotic flavour and fragrance to dishes. Made from shrimps which are ground and fermented, it has an odour before cooking much stronger than its taste. It is like anchovy paste in texture. It can be found in Chinese markets, usually in glass jars. Refrigerated, it will keep indefinitely.

Sweet Bean Sauce

Used in northern China as accompaniment to Peking Duck. It is slightly saltier than Hoisin sauce.

Yellow Bean Sauce/Bean Sauce

This thick, spicy, aromatic sauce is made with yellow beans, flour, and salt, fermented together. Correctly blended, it is quite salty but provides a distinctive flavour to Chinese sauces and is a frequent addition in Chinese cookery.

There are two forms: whole beans in a thick sauce; and mashed or puréed beans (sold as crushed bean sauce). I prefer the whole bean variety because it is slightly less salty and has a better texture.

SESAME SEEDS

These are dried seeds of the sesame plant. Unhulled, the seeds range from grayish white to black in colour, but once the hull is removed, the sesame seeds are tiny, somewhat flattened, cream coloured, and pointed on one end. Sesame seeds are valued throughout Asia, as a flavouring agent and as a source of oil and paste. Keep them in a glass jar in a cool, dry place or keep them frozen. Either way, they will last for weeks.

To toast sesame seeds

Heat a frying pan over a burner until hot. Add the sesame seeds and stir occasionally. Watch them closely, and when they begin to lightly brown, about 3 to 5 minutes, stir them again and pour them onto a plate. When they are thoroughly cool, store them in a glass jar in a cool, dark place.

Alternatively, you could preheat the oven to 160°C/325°F/Gas Mark 3. Spread the sesame seeds on a baking sheet. Roast them in the oven for 10 to 15 minutes until they are nicely toasted and lightly browned. Allow them to cool and place in a glass jar until you are ready to use them.

SHALLOTS

Shallots are mild-flavoured members of the onion family. They are small, about the size of pickling onions, with copper-red skins. They have a distinctive onion taste without being as strong or overpowering as ordinary onions. Readily available, they make an excellent substitute for fresh Chinese shallots, which are difficult to find, even in Chinese markets. They are expensive, but their sweet flavour permeates food; a few go a long way. Keep them in a cool, dry place (not the refrigerator) and peel, slice, or chop them as you would an onion. In China, shallots are also sold pickled as a snack to go with preserved eggs.

SHARK'S FIN

Another exotic delicacy of China. Southern Chinese restaurants and expensive restaurants in other areas of China sometimes offer a long list of shark's fin dishes. Extremely expensive, this is a conspicuous symbol of extravagance. Shark's fin is found dried in many dry food shops in China. The fin means the dorsal "comb fin" or the two ventral fins of any of a variety of sharks; indeed, in China, fins are imported from all over the world. Preparation usually involves an elaborate process of soaking and boiling in several changes of water and stocks. However, thanks to modern technology, it is now possible to purchase prepared shark's fin in the freezer section of the Chinese market.

Like bird's nest, another highly sought after Chinese delicacy, it has little flavour but is prized for its clear, gelatinous strands and texture. It is usually served with a rich stock, as in Shark's Fin Soup, or stuffed in poultry or scrambled with eggs and crab.

SICHUAN PEPPERCORNS
Sichuan peppercorns are known through China as "flower peppers" because they look like flower buds opening. They are reddish-brown in colour with a strong, pungent odour which distinguishes them from the hotter black peppercorns. They are actually not a pepper at all, but are the dried berries of a shrub which is a member of the citrus family. Their smell reminds me of lavender, while their taste is sharp, numbing and mildly spicy. They can be ground in a conventional pepper mill but should be roasted (see below) before they are ground to bring out their full flavour. An expensive item, they are sold wrapped in cellophane or plastic bags in Chinese stores. They will keep indefinitely if stored in a well-sealed container.

To roast Sichuan peppercorns
Heat a wok or heavy frying pan to a medium heat. Add the peppercorns (up to 4 tablespoons at a time) and stir-fry them for about 5 minutes until they brown slightly and start to smoke. Remove the pan from the heat and let them cool. Grind the peppercorns in a peppermill, clean coffee grinder, or with a mortar and pestle. Seal tightly in a screw-top jar to store. Alternatively, keep the whole roasted peppercorns in a sealed container and grind as required.

SICHUAN PRESERVED VEGETABLE
There are many types of Chinese pickled vegetables. One of the most popular is Sichuan preserved vegetable, a specialty of Sichuan Province. This is the root of the mustard green, pickled in salt and hot chilies. It is sold in cans in Chinese grocery stores and gives a pleasantly

crunchy texture and spicy taste to dishes. Before using it, rinse in cold water and then slice or chop as required. Any unused vegetable should be transferred to a tightly covered jar and stored in the refrigerator where it will keep indefinitely.

SILK SQUASH – Chinese Okra (*Luffa acutangula*)

A popular vegetable frequently found in markets in China, this is a long, thin, cylindrical squash, tapering at one end with deep, narrow ridges. Choose firm, unblemished dark green ones. Peel away the ridges. If the vegetable is young, you can leave on some of the green; if older, it's best to peel away all the skin. The inside flesh turns soft, spongy and tender as it cooks, tasting like a cross between a cucumber and courgette. Absorbent, it readily picks up flavours of the sauce or food it is cooked with.

SNOW PEAS/MANGETOUTS

Smaller varieties of mangetouts are found in the markets of China; the larger ones are found in the West. But all of them are sweet and crispy. This familiar vegetable combines a tender, crunchy texture and a sweet, fresh flavour. In China, mangetouts are simply stir-fried, with a little oil and salt, and bits of garlic and ginger root. Often they are combined with meats. Look for pods that are firm with very small peas, which means they are tender and young. Mangetouts are readily available at supermarkets. They keep for at least a week in the vegetable crisper of the refrigerator.

SOY SAUCES

Soy sauce is an essential ingredient in China's cooking. It is made from a mixture of soybeans, flour, and water, which is then naturally fermented and aged for some months. The distilled liquid is soy sauce. There are two main types:

Light Soy Sauce

As the name implies, this is light in colour, but it is full of flavour and is the best one to use for cooking. It is known in Chinese markets as Superior Soy and is saltier than dark soy sauce.

Dark Soy Sauce

This sauce is aged for much longer than light soy sauce, hence its darker, almost black colour. It is slightly thicker and stronger than light soy sauce and is more suitable for stews. I prefer it to light soy as a dipping sauce. It is known in Chinese markets as Soy Superior Sauce, and, although used less often than light soy, it is important to have some at hand.

SPINACH

Spinach is popular in China. The Western varieties of spinach are quite different from those used in China, nevertheless they make satisfactory substitutes for the Chinese variety. Spinach is most commonly stir-fried, so frozen spinach is obviously unsuitable. Chinese water spinach (*Ipomoea aquatica*) is what's most frequently cooked in China and is available in Chinese markets in the West. It has hollow stems and delicate, green, pointed leaves, lighter in colour than common spinach and with a milder taste. It should be cooked when it is very fresh, preferably on the day on which it is bought.

STAR ANISE

Star anise is the hard, star-shaped seed-pod of the anise bush. (It is also known as Chinese anise or whole anise.) It is similar in flavour and fragrance to common anise seed but is more robust and liquorice-like. Star anise is an essential ingredient of five-spice powder and is widely used in braised dishes to impart a rich taste and fragrance. Sold by Chinese markets in plastic packs, it should be stored in a tightly covered jar in a cool, dry place.

SUGAR

Sugar has been used – sparingly – in the cooking of savoury dishes in China for a thousand years. Excessive sugar destroys the palate, but when properly employed, it helps balance the various flavours of sauces and other dishes. Chinese sugar comes in several forms: as rock or yellow lump sugar, as brown sugar slabs, and as maltose or malt sugar. I particularly like to use rock sugar which is richer and has a more subtle flavour than that of refined, granulated sugar. It also gives a good luster and glaze to braised dishes and sauces. Buy it in Chinese markets, where it is usually sold in packages. You may need to break the lumps into smaller pieces with a wooden mallet or rolling pin. If you cannot find it, you can use white sugar or raw sugar (the amber, chunky kind).

VINEGAR

Vinegars are widely used in China as dipping sauces as well as for cooking. Unlike Western vinegars, they are usually made from rice. There are many varieties, ranging in flavour from the spicy and slightly tart to the sweet and pungent:

White Rice Vinegar: White rice vinegar is clear and mild in flavour. It has a faint taste of glutinous rice and is used in preparing sweet and sour dishes.

Black Rice Vinegar: Black rice vinegar is very dark in colour with a rich but mild taste. It is used for braised dishes, noodles, and sauces.

Red Rice Vinegar: Red rice vinegar is sweet and spicy in taste and is usually used as a dipping sauce for seafood.

All these vinegars can be bought in Chinese markets. They are sold in bottles and will keep indefinitely. If you cannot get Chinese vinegars, I suggest you use cider vinegar instead. Malt vinegar and wine vinegars cannot be substituted because their taste is too strong.

WATER CHESTNUTS

Water chestnuts do not actually belong to the chestnut family or, indeed, any nut family at all, but are a sweet, white and crunchy root vegetable about the size of a walnut.

They are especially popular in the south, where they are sometimes grown between rice plants in paddies. (This is why the fresh ones are often muddy on the outside. They must be peeled before eating or cooking.) Sweet, crisp water chestnuts have been eaten in China for centuries, where they are eaten as a snack, having first been boiled in their skins, or peeled and simmered in rock sugar. They are also used in many cooked dishes.

Here, fresh water chestnuts can sometimes be obtained from Chinese markets or some supermarkets. When buying fresh ones, look for a firm, hard texture. The skin should be tight and taut, not wrinkled. If they are mushy, they are too old. Feel them all over for soft, rotten spots. If you peel them in advance, cover them with cold water to prevent them from turning brown and store them in the refrigerator. They will keep, unpeeled, in a paper bag in the refrigerator for up to two weeks.

Canned water chestnuts are sold in many supermarkets and Chinese markets. A pale version of the fresh ones, they have a good texture but little taste because both the crispness and the flavour are lost in the canning process. Rinse them well in cold water before you use them, and store any unused ones in a jar of cold water. They will keep for several weeks in the refrigerator if you change the water daily. Fresh jicama, a crisp tuber, is a suitable substitute for water chestnuts and preferable to the canned. Crunchy and juicy, with the texture of water chestnuts, it is available through most of the year, especially in Chinese and Hispanic markets.

WHEAT GLUTEN
This is made from washing out the starch from wheat dough until only the adhesive substance remains. Once it is made, it can be boiled or deep-fried, then cooked with other ingredients. It is a staple and mock meat for Chinese vegetarians. I had many tasty versions of this unusual food throughout China.

WHEAT STARCH
Wheat starch is a flour-like powder left after the protein is removed from the wheat flour. It is used as a wrapping for dumplings in China. Bought in Chinese markets, it will keep indefinitely tightly sealed and kept in a cool, dry place.

WONTON/HUNTUN SKINS
Wonton skins, sometimes called wonton wrappers, are made from egg and flour and can be bought fresh or frozen from Chinese markets. They are thin pastry-like wrappings, stretched like freshly made noodles, which can be stuffed with minced meat and fried, steamed, or used in soups. They are sold in little piles of 7.5-cm/3-in squares or sometimes a bit larger, wrapped in plastic. The number of squares or

vinegar – wonton

skins in a package varies from about 30 to 36, depending upon the supplier. Fresh wonton skins will keep for about five days if stored in cling film or a plastic bag in the refrigerator. If you are using frozen wonton skins, just peel off the number you require and thaw them thoroughly before you use them.

YUNNAN AND JINHUA HAM

China produces some of the best hams in the world. In China you will see preserved whole Yunnan and Jinhua (from Zhejiang province) hams hanging in food shops, but the ham is also available in cans. It is a popular staple, used as seasoning or in many Chinese dishes as an ingredient. Unfortunately, it is not obtainable in the West. I find Italian prosciutto and American Smithfield hams acceptable substitutes for the wonderfully rich, smoky-flavoured Chinese hams. Sold in Chinese markets in slices or large pieces, it will keep for months tightly wrapped in the refrigerator. If a small amount of mold appears on the skin, simply scrape it away or cut it off. Use the ham as a flavouring or seasoning.

EQUIPMENT

The true tastes and flavours of China can be achieved through the appropriate cooking techniques, and proper technique requires proper equipment. Therefore a discussion of traditional Chinese cooking equipment is in order. While not absolutely essential for cooking Chinese food, there are a few items which will make it very much easier. Most are inexpensive, and all are serviceable over quite a long period of time. Look for authentic implements from a Chinese or Asian market; you can now find good versions of all these implements in speciality gourmet stores and in many department stores that feature good cooking equipment.

WOK

The most useful piece of equipment is the wok. It allows you to stir-fry, quickly moving the food without it spilling all over the place. You will find the wok useful for all types of other cooking too, such as blanching bulky vegetables like spinach, or to cook a large quantity of food. Another advantage is that the shape of the wok allows heat to spread evenly over its surface, thus making for the rapid cooking which is fundamental to stir-frying. When used for deep-frying, the wok saves cooking oil because the base is smaller, requiring less oil, but still providing important depth.

Chinese kitchens are completely different from Western kitchens. For instance, most homes have woks which are set on top of braisers in which wood or charcoal is burned to produce the high heat so important for Chinese cooking. However, this does not mean that those living outside of China are unable to cook Chinese food authentically. During many years of teaching and demonstrations, I have found the most appropriate wok for a Western-type stove is the wok which has one long wooden handle, about 30–35 cm/12–14 in in length, and a slightly flattened bottom which allows it to rest securely on a Western stove top. Although these design changes seem to go against the purpose of the traditional rounded shape, which is to concentrate intense heat at the center, living outside a Chinese kitchen requires adjustment.

Choosing a wok
Choose a medium-sized wok, preferably about 30–35 cm/12–14 in in diameter, with deep sides and a slightly flattened bottom. Some woks on the market are too shallow or too flat on the bottom, making them no better than a large frying pan. Select one which has weight to it, and, if possible, choose one made of carbon steel rather than of the lighter stainless steel or aluminum. The latter types tend to scorch and do not withstand the high temperatures required for this type of cooking. I do not like nonstick woks; not only are they more expensive, but they cannot be seasoned like an ordinary wok which then adds flavour to the food. Electric woks are also unsatisfactory because they do not heat up to a sufficiently high temperature and tend to be too shallow. Remember, it is better to cook a small quantity of food in a medium-sized wok than to try to accommodate a large quantity in a small one.

Seasoning a wok

All woks (except nonstick ones) need to be seasoned. Many need to be scrubbed first as well to remove the machine oil which is applied to the surface by the manufacturer to protect it in transit. This is the *only* time you will ever scrub your wok – unless you let it rust. Before its first use, scrub your wok with kitchen cleanser and water to remove as much of the machine oil as possible. Dry the wok and place it over a low heat. Add 2 tablespoons of cooking oil and rub this over the inside of the wok using kitchen paper until the entire surface is lightly coated with oil. Heat the wok slowly for 10 to 15 minutes and then wipe it thoroughly with a pad of more clean kitchen paper. The paper should become blackened from the machine oil. Repeat this process until the kitchen paper wipes clean. Once seasoned, your wok will darken with use. This is a good sign.

Cleaning a wok

Do not scrub a seasoned wok. Just wash it in plain water without detergent. Dry it thoroughly, preferably by putting it over a low heat for a few minutes before putting it away. This should prevent the wok from rusting, but if it does rust, scrub it off with kitchen cleanser and repeat the seasoning process. If you wish to store it for a long while or if you live in a humid climate, rub the inside of the wok with 1 tablespoon of cooking oil for added protection before storing.

WOK ACCESSORIES

Wok stand

This is a metal ring or frame used to keep a traditionally shaped, round-bottomed wok steady on the burner, and is useful *only* if you are using this kind of wok. It is also necessary when using such a wok for steaming, deep-frying, or braising.

Wok lid

A wok lid is a dome-like cover which is used for steaming. Usually made from aluminum and inexpensive, it normally comes with the wok but it may be purchased separately from a Chinese or Asian

the tastes and flavours of china

market. Any large, domed pot lid which fits snugly over the top of the wok can be used instead.

Spatula

A long-handled metal spatula shaped rather like a small shovel which is ideal for scooping and tossing food in a wok. Any good long-handled spoon may be used instead.

Rack

If you use your wok or a large pot as a steamer, you will need a wooden or metal rack or trivet to stand above the water level and support the plate of food to be steamed. Some woks are sold with a round metal stand, but most Asian speciality markets, department stores, and hardware shops stock triangular wooden stands or round metal stands which can be used for this purpose. You can improvise a stand by using an empty, inverted can of suitable size.

BAMBOO BRUSH

This bundle of stiff, split bamboo is used for cleaning a wok without scrubbing off the seasoned surface. It is an attractive, inexpensive implement but not essential: a soft sponge will do just as well.

CLEAVERS

No self-respecting Chinese cook would be seen with a knife instead of a cleaver. These heavy choppers serve many purposes; used for all kinds of cutting ranging from very fine shredding to chopping up bones. A Chinese cook will usually have three types: a lightweight one with a narrow blade for cutting delicate foods including vegetables; a medium-weight one for general cutting, chopping, and crushing purposes; and a heavy one for heavy-duty chopping. Of course, you can prepare Chinese food using good quality, sharp knives, but if you decide to buy a cleaver you will be surprised at how easy it is to use. Choose a good quality stainless steel one and keep it well sharpened. A medium-sized, all purpose, stainless steel cleaver, now widely available, is the best kind to have.

CHOPPING BOARD

The Chinese traditionally use a soft wood block for chopping. Such a block is not only difficult to maintain, however, but also accumulates bacteria, so I prefer a hardwood block or a white acrylic board. These are strong, easy to clean, and last indefinitely. There is so much chopping and slicing to be done when preparing food for Asian-style cooking that it is essential to have a large, steady cutting board. (For health reasons never cut cooked meat on a board which you have also used for chopping raw meat or poultry. Keep a separate board for this purpose. And always properly clean your cutting boards after use. Vinegar or lemon juice works well but you may prefer to use a stronger solution.)

STEAMERS

Bamboo steamers are among the most ancient of Chinese cooking utensils. These attractive, basket-like bamboo steamers come in several sizes; the 25-cm/10-in size is the most suitable for home use. Bamboo steamers are filled with food and placed on top of a pot or over a wok of boiling water. One of the advantages of the design is that several steamers can be stacked on top of one another. Bamboo steamers can be bought at Asian speciality markets and at cookware and department stores. (Alternatively, any kind of wide, metal steamer can be used.) Before using a bamboo steamer for the first time, wash it and steam it empty for about 5 minutes.

SANDY OR CLAY POTS

These attractive lightweight clay pots are also known as sandy pots or sand pots because their unglazed exteriors have a sandy texture. Indeed, they are made from a mixture of clay and sand, and their interiors are glazed to help conduct heat and to hold in moisture. They come in a variety of shapes and sizes, equipped with tight-fitting matching lids which have a small steam vent. Sometimes they are encased in a wire frame. The pots are designed to be used on the stove top (since most people in China do not have ovens) and are used for cooking rice and for braised dishes and soups. The resulting dishes are aromatic and infused with intense flavours and tastes.

Never put an empty sand pot onto the heat, or put a hot sand pot onto a cold surface; in other words, avoid drastic temperature changes, or the pot is likely to crack. However, the pots can be used over high gas heat. If you are using a sand pot on a electric stove, be sure to use an asbestos pad to insulate the clay pot from direct contact with the intense heat of the electric coils. The pot should always have some liquid in it when cooking. Because of the hot steam released as soon as you raise the lid from the pot, always open it *away* from you.

Although any good enamelware casserole or cast-iron pot can be used as a substitute, clay pots are attractive and inexpensive; and you can serve direct from stove to table.

CHOPSTICKS

Chopsticks are not just used for eating but also for stirring, beating, and whipping in Chinese cooking. Special long chopsticks are available for these purposes, but it is not necessary to purchase them. Any long spoons, spatulas, or forks will suffice. Chopsticks can be bought at many department stores, Asian speciality markets, the ethnic food section of supermarkets, and from many Chinese restaurants. I prefer wooden chopsticks, but in China plastic is often used for hygienic purposes.

MISCELLANEOUS TOOLS

A substantial, fairly large-sized strainer is helpful for removing deep-fried food from oil in the wok. Many of the recipes in this book call for oil to be drained from the wok, so a good colander or sieve, set inside a stainless steel bowl, is useful. Several stainless steel bowls are indispensable for cooking in general.

CHAPTER 3
INFLUENCES from WITHIN and WITHOUT

Fine wine and cups of jade
I wish I could drink all day
But the call to mount is urgent
And will not brook delay.
Should I lie drunk in action
Pray do not sneer nor spurn;
Of those who went to battle
How many did return?

Wang Han, 1333–1378

A great cuisine selects, refines, and combines the best of many influences. While sampling foods in restaurants and homes throughout China, I was impressed by how many common elements and similarities there are between "Chinese" foods and the cuisines of other parts of the world. On the one hand, there are ingredients, dishes, and recipes that I believed had been introduced to China long ago but which are, in fact, of Chinese origin, such as rice. On the other hand, it turns out that there are "traditional" Chinese dishes that were adopted from foreign sources. Tomatoes, for example, are to be found everywhere in China and I assumed that they had *always* been a part of Chinese cuisine. In fact, tomatoes are a recent introduction having arrived from the Americas barely one hundred years ago. The same is true of such popular ingredients as corn, squash, and chilli peppers, all of which entered China comparatively recently.

Farther back in time, during the Tang Dynasty (A.D. 618–907), near Eastern foods such as spinach, lettuce, almonds, sugar beets, and figs were adopted. These borrowings are more than matched by China's contributions to other cuisines. Food in the rest of Asia, for example, bears a strong Chinese influence, especially the cuisines of Japan, Korea, and Vietnam, Malaysia, and Thailand.

All of this is to be expected. Chinese traders and émigrés arrived with their customary foods and cooking techniques. Those who later returned to China brought with them new foods and recipes; foreign traders entering China did the same. So, over the centuries there has been a weaving back and forth, sometimes very slowly, sometimes quite rapidly, of the fabric of Chinese cuisine. The theme is clearly Chinese, the essentials having already been established by the end of the Song Dynasty (A.D. 1279), but there are always variations on the theme. Indeed, much of the history of China and its neighbours, and the development of their respective cuisines, is reflected in the migrations of people to and from China and movements within it.

The country is bounded by barriers of ocean, desert, and mountains. Where natural barriers were inadequate, the "Great Wall," extending over 4,800 km/3,000 miles from the Bohai Sea to the Gobi Desert, was erected and effectively blocked invasions and alien influences. And thus China, by official decree, was sealed off from the outside world, from any "barbarians" and "foreign devils" who presumed they had anything to offer the Imperial civilisation. Or so it might seem.

In fact, China has been open to the outside world for two thousand years, if usually on her own terms.

Through the centuries, the oceans were as much gateway as barrier and the deserts and mountains were threaded with caravan trails, especially the Silk Route. Even the Great Wall had openings through which commerce flowed. For example, during the Tang Dynasty, traders from many areas and nations – Japan, Korea, Arabia, India, and Persia – thronged Chinese ports, delivering their goods and trading for the many rich products of China.

Later, between the twelfth and fifteenth centuries, China's merchant and naval fleets far exceeded in number and commercial importance those of any other Asian or European fleets. By the thirteenth century, Chinese merchants had established regular commercial links with India, their vessels being the largest on the seas even though the trade involved a long and hazardous voyage. Until the nineteenth century, Chinese junks were the backbone of Asian sea-borne commerce: only the advent of steam and Western imperialism forced the decline of Chinese merchant shipping. Today, however, China again ranks among the top ten fleets of the world in tonnage.

For millennia, heavy commercial, religious, and military traffic has passed to and from China. Even before China's first consolidation under centralised rule in the third century A.D., the Han Dynasty had opened the fabled Silk Route. Running from Lanzhou (Gansu province) to Yumen (near the western terminus of the Great Wall) and then across desert plateaus and mountains to Samarkand, this route and some parallel and subsidiary pathways until the thirteenth century provided China's main contact with central Asia and with India.

The original purpose of the route was military: to guard China's expanding western border and to maintain contact with potential allies against mountain nomads of the northwestern frontier. But over the protected route Buddhism and, rather quickly, commerce began to flow. Thus, Chinese silks and other products reached Roman cities and places as far away as Siberia. Even until the nineteenth century, most of China's commercial contact with other societies still came along this great route.

As for the north, even the Great Wall could not seal off China completely. Commercial traffic to and from Korea and Manchuria was allowed to pass through it. The nomad tribes that the Wall was designed to keep out traded their only real commodity, horses, for Chinese products at the markets set up on the "wrong" side of the

Wall. Military forces also penetrated the Wall. In 1279, for example, the Mongols under Kublai Khan swept into China and established a dynasty that lasted until 1368. This was a unique interlude, for Mongol chauvinism did not allow them to be tainted by any Chinese culture. The Mongols retained instead most of their own customs, including their culinary practices.

When the Chinese successfully rebelled against Mongol rule, the Mongols retired to their central Asian steppes, leaving behind not much more than the culinary imprint of their passion for yogurt, game, goat, mutton, and the mare's milk derivative, *koumiss*. In fact, while it is probably true that the Mongols did not by themselves introduce mare's milk, butterfat (from mare's or cow's milk), and mutton to China, experts generally believe these three foods separate Mongol from Chinese cuisine. From Beijing to Kunming, I experienced this non-Chinese influence in many places. In Kunming, for example, restaurants serving mutton and goat cheese – pan-fried in a wok – suggested to me how such foods might have been served in the time of Kublai Khan.

China has, in turn, influenced those cultures from whom she borrowed, and the impact of Chinese culture on the cuisines of her neighbours is both clear and substantial. This was largely the result of the migrations of "overseas Chinese," those entrepreneurs whose reputations as shrewd and efficient businessmen were already firmly established.

Although Japan, Korea, and Thailand have distinctive culinary systems the Chinese influence is undeniable. Possibly the most important gift of the Chinese traveller was rice. The basic food of the East, perhaps its most valuable and useful plant, rice was first cultivated in China some three thousand years before it spread elsewhere. From exposure to Chinese dishes and techniques, the Koreans learned to use such spices as garlic and chilli pepper with meat dishes, usually pork and beef. In northern China, I saw many food stalls in markets offering distinctively Korean-style foods, serving them with pickled vegetables characteristically flavoured with garlic and chilli peppers. Filipino cooking has also been deeply affected by China. It has been said that the Chinese left an indelible mark on Philippine cooking and that

Chinese gastronomy was the midwife of Philippine haute cuisine. In fact, no traditional Filipino meal is ever complete without one or more dishes of Chinese heritage.

Likewise, in terms of cooking and eating implements, both spoons and chopsticks, universal in Asia, are of Chinese origin. Similarly, the wok, that marvellously adaptable cooking tool found in many Asian kitchens, is of Chinese origin. Even in India, the great authority Madhur Jaffrey has written, "the ancient Chinese may have come here [Kerala, India] for black pepper but, in fair exchange, they left behind their woks, cleavers, plates, pickling jars and designs for roofs and river-craft." In these and many ways the influence of the great "Middle Kingdom" radiated out into the world.

The Great Wall and politics aside, the Chinese are neither nationalistic nor xenophobic when it comes to food or techniques. While their basic diet grew out of animal and vegetable foods that are plentiful and native to China, the people gradually adopted foreign foods, spices, herbs, techniques, and culinary ideas, when practical. As far back as the Han Dynasty (205 B.C.–A.D. 220), Chinese cooks adopted foreign methods to make the first wheat noodles and cakes.

The Tang Dynasty (A.D. 618–907) – the Golden Age of China – was one in which a taste for the exotic could be indulged. Thus, "the golden peaches of Samarkand" and many other foods entered China, including grapes, spinach, lettuce, figs, kohlrabi, sugar beets, leeks, and shallots. There are references to pine nuts, almonds, and pistachios as well, and it is no accident that the first known cookbook and the first nutrition textbook appeared then. Although known long before, it was during the Tang Dynasty that tea attained the popularity it has never lost. The growing influence of Buddhism and its emphasis on vegetarianism led to innovative uses of wheat products in the form of dumplings and fried dough strips, both of which one still sees everywhere in China – from street food stalls to restaurants and homes.

It was during the Song Dynasty (960–1279) that "Chinese cuisine" crystallised into its distinctive, enduring form. Over those three hundred years, her cooks, food writers, nutritionists, elite consumers, merchants, and food vendors deliberately created a style of cooking and eating. They established and applied a set of attitudes about food and its place in society to an abundant and varied supply of ingredients. By the end of the Song era, China had established a cuisine of great sophistication. Its high standards maintained tradition but nonetheless allowed for experimentation and innovation, demanding only that new dishes were appealing to the eye and the palate.

The next significant stage of integration of "foreign" foods came during the Ming Dynasty (1368–1644), when the earliest Western influences arrived from southern Europe. New World food such as peanuts, sweet potatoes, and corn were introduced by Portuguese and Spanish explorers as they made their way from the New World to India, China, and the Philippines in the early sixteenth century. Used at first only as "famine foods," only later did they become acceptable as sustaining secondary foods. However, by the end of the Ming period, a little over a hundred years later, even the Yao people who live in the remote mountains of southern China relied heavily on potatoes and sweet potatoes.

China's population, stable at about one hundred fifty million for centuries, almost quadrupled in the period from about 1700 to 1850. Corn, peanuts, sweet potatoes, and white potatoes, by then basic crops, provided the necessary extra calories to sustain an astonishing population increase. These "new" Western foods were consumed almost entirely by the poor, that is, the great majority of people. Enormous masses of people experienced a sustaining but limited diet; the elite, great in number but still a minority of the population, enjoyed gourmet fare made up of an astonishing variety of foods. It was this class that maintained what we today understand as Chinese cuisine. It is this cuisine, this taste of China, with its home-grown as well as its exotic influences, that I experienced in visits to my ancestral homeland.

yangrou xiangcai
stir-fried goat with fresh coriander

Southwest China is mountainous but blessed with a wonderfully moderate climate. It is one of the most interesting and exotic regions of China, being populated by more than twenty-four different ethnic groups. The province's large Muslim population means that beef and mutton as well as goat are readily available, though pork is as popular there among other groups as it is in the rest of the country.

I had a fabulous dining experience in a hotel restaurant in Kunming (Yunnan): "the goat multi-dish banquet". It usually averages forty dishes, but I was served one with fifty-four! One of the dishes that caught my fancy I must share with you. In it goat meat's strong assertive flavour is tamed by seasonings such as fresh coriander, resulting in a delicious, satisfying dish.

450 g/1 lb lean goat fillets, or lamb fillets, boneless
   loin or steaks
MARINADE
2 teaspoons dark soy sauce
2 teaspoons rice wine or dry sherry
1 teaspoon sesame oil
½ teaspoon salt
½ teaspoon freshly ground black pepper
2 teaspoons cornflour
125 g/4 oz fresh mild chillies
2 tablespoons peanut oil
Handful of fresh coriander, washed

Cut the meat into thin slices and combine it in a small bowl with the soy sauce, rice wine or sherry, sesame oil, salt, pepper, and cornflour. Let the meat marinate for 30 minutes.

Seed and cut the chillies into thin slices.

Heat a wok or large frying pan until hot. Add the oil and when it smokes add the meat, stir-frying for 2 minutes or until it is browned. Remove with a slotted spoon.

Add the chillies and stir-fry for 2 to 3 minutes. Put in the fresh coriander and stir-fry for another 2 minutes. Return the meat to the wok, give a couple of good stirs, and serve immediately.

Serves 4 as part of a Chinese meal, or 2 as a single dish.

gan bian niurou
crisp beef in chilli sauce

The Han Chinese eat very little beef, preferring pork, due to their history, method of farming, and philosophy. Muslim Chinese, on the other hand, don't eat pork and quite enjoy beef dishes. One of the tastiest such ones I sampled on a recent visit to southwest China was in a Muslim restaurant called Mosilinl Arge in a large hotel in Kunming. The beef was first coated in a light batter, fried twice for extra crispness, and then tossed in a clear chilli sauce that was at once sweet and spicy. Although I was rather full from an appetiser by the time this dish arrived, I could not resist it.

450 g/1 lb beef steak
MARINADE
1 tablespoon light soy sauce
2 teaspoons rice wine
1 teaspoon sesame oil
H teaspoon salt
tablespoons cornflour
1 tablespoon plain flour
450 ml/16 fl oz peanut oil
SAUCE
5 dried chillies, halved
1½ tablespoons peanut oil
3 tablespoons finely sliced garlic
1 teaspoon salt
3 tablespoons sugar
125 ml/4 fl oz water
1 teaspoon cornflour mixed with 1 teaspoon water

Place the meat in the freezer for about 20 minutes, or until it is firm to the touch. Cut it into slices against the grain, then finely shred the slices. Combine the meat with the marinade and mix very well.

Soak the dried chillies in warm water. When they are soft and pliable, cut them in half.

Heat a wok or frying pan until it is hot. Add the peanut oil and when it is very hot and almost smoking, add the beef and deep-fry in two batches. Remove with a slotted spoon and drain the meat in a colander.

Heat a small saucepan and when it is hot, add the 1½ tablespoons oil, garlic, and chillies and stir-fry for 20 seconds. Then add the rest of the sauce ingredients and simmer gently for 2 minutes. Keep the sauce warm until ready to serve.

Reheat the oil in the wok until it is very hot. Deep-fry the beef again until it is very crisp, about 1 minute. Remove the beef with a slotted spoon, drain on kitchen paper and place on a warm platter. Gently toss the beef with the sauce and serve immediately.

Serves 4 as part of a Chinese meal, or 2 as a single dish.

yumi zhou
rice porridge with sweetcorn

Rice since ancient times has been China's nutritious, congenially bland staple food. Sweetcorn, introduced in the early sixteenth century by Portuguese and Spanish explorers, is a relative newcomer to Chinese cuisine. Enthusiastically adopted by the people, it has become the third most important grain in the country after rice and wheat. Sweetcorn and rice cooked together make a nutritious and satisfying family-style dish. A versatile mixture, it provides a nourishing snack anytime and can also be used as a starter or main course. I sampled this version in Chengdu, Sichuan, at the Green Stone Bridge Free Market, the largest shopping area in the city.

influences from within and without

1.4 1/2½ pt water
2 teaspoons salt
175 g/6 oz short-grain rice
275 g/10 oz fresh corn kernels (about 2 ears), or frozen
    corn kernels
3 tablespoons finely chopped spring onions
1 tablespoon chilli bean sauce
GARNISH
2 teaspoons Sichuan peppercorns,
    roasted and crushed

Bring the water to the boil in a large pot, add the salt and then the rice.
Bring back to the boil, stir several times, cover loosely, and let the rice
simmer for 40 minutes at the lowest possible heat.

Add the corn and simmer for 20 more minutes. Stir in the spring
onions and chilli bean sauce. Before serving, sprinkle on the crushed
Sichuan peppercorns.

Serves 4 as part of a Chinese meal, or 2 as a single dish.

yumi chao lajiao
stir-fried sweetcorn with fresh chillies

*My appetite for sweetcorn, a food I love, was well assuaged in China, where
I enjoyed it in many forms throughout the various regions. This simple
version was prepared in a private restaurant in Kunming, Yunnan, one
among many not run by the state that have sprung up since the early 1980s.
The mild, fresh, whole chillies combine nicely with the subtle flavour, crunchy
texture, and sweetness of the corn. Try it as an easy accompaniment to any
meat dish.*

275 g/10 oz fresh corn kernels (about 2 ears), or frozen
    corn kernels
1½ tablespoons peanut oil
2 small mild red chillies, seeded and finely chopped

influences from within and without – recipes

1 teaspoon salt
¼ teaspoon fresh ground white pepper
1 teaspoon sugar
50 ml/2 fl oz chicken stock

If frozen, blanch the corn for 10 seconds in boiling water and drain.

Heat a wok or large frying pan until hot. Add the oil, chillies, fresh or blanched corn, and salt and stir-fry for 1 minute. Put in the pepper, sugar, and chicken stock and continue to cook for 3 minutes. Serve at once.

Serves 4 as part of a Chinese meal, or 2 as a single dish.

chao lajiao
stir-fried whole mild chillies

I enjoyed this wonderful dish on a train trip from Hangzhou to Suzhou, known as the Venice of China because of its canals. It was the first and only time I have ever eaten a dish composed entirely of whole cooked chillies. It worked well because the chillies were mild, fresh and in season, therefore cheap and delicious, especially accompanied by rice. Variously coloured, the chillies – from green to yellow, orange, and bright red – were a delight to the eye.

It is interesting to note that there are over two hundred varieties of chilies, ranging in taste from mild to devilishly hot. Chillies are more than spicy; they are quite nutritious as well, being rich in vitamins A and C and in iron, calcium, and traces of other minerals. They were introduced into Asia from the New World almost five hundred years ago and were immediately assimilated into Asian cuisines. In high mountain areas of the Sichuan region where cabbages and sweet potatoes do not thrive, chillies supplied much-needed vitamins.

350 g/12 oz fresh whole mild chillies, preferably of different
   colours
2 tablespoons peanut oil

influences from within and without

1 teaspoon salt
2 tablespoons chopped garlic
1 tablespoon light soy sauce
2 teaspoons sugar
125 ml/4 fl oz chicken stock

Wash the chillies and pat them dry. Leave them whole.

Heat a wok or large frying pan over high heat. When hot, add the oil, salt, and garlic. Put in the chillies and stir-fry for 1 minute. Then add the soy sauce and sugar, and pour in the chicken stock and continue to stir-fry until most of the liquid has evaporated. Pour the mixture onto a platter and serve at once.

Serves 4 as part of a Chinese meal, or 2 as a single dish.

yuxiang qiezi
fish-flavoured aubergines with pork

This dish does not taste "fishy," but it does use the spices and seasonings usually employed when preparing fish: hot, sour, salty, and sweet at the same time. It sounds (and tastes) very Sichuan and indeed it is. This delightful version is from the Shu Feng Yuan restaurant/collective in Chengdu, Sichuan. Unlike other versions I have eaten in Europe, North America, and Hong Kong, this one used whole aubergines. The smaller variously coloured varieties used in China are generally the tastiest.

700 g/1½ lb Chinese or regular aubergines
450 ml/16 fl oz peanut oil
450 g/1 lb minced pork
2 tablespoons finely chopped garlic
2 tablespoons finely chopped
   ginger root
3 tablespoons finely chopped
   spring onions
2 tablespoons dark soy sauce

3 tablespoons rice wine or dry sherry
3 tablespoons Chinese black rice vinegar
2 tablespoons sugar
1 tablespoon Sichuan peppercorns, roasted
  and crushed
2 teaspoons ground red chilli
125 ml/4 fl oz chicken stock

If using ordinary aubergines, cut into quarters lengthways. Heat a wok or large frying pan until hot. Add the oil, and when it is hot, deep-fry the aubergines whole. Remove them with a slotted spoon and drain them on kitchen paper. Arrange them on a serving platter.

Pour off most of the oil, leaving 3 tablespoons, and reheat the wok. Add the pork, garlic, ginger, and spring onions and stir-fry for 30 seconds. Put in the rest of the ingredients, except the stock. Continue to cook for 2 minutes over high heat, then add the stock and simmer for another 3 minutes.

Add the aubergines and simmer in the sauce for 3 minutes and serve at once.

Serves 4 as part of a Chinese meal, or 2 as a single dish.

chao nai
stir-fried milk

influences from within and without

I have sampled many versions of this dish in Hong Kong and in the province of Guangdong where it was served most memorably to me at the Qing Hui Yuan restaurant in Shunde. The "milk" is really a thick custard, which they stir-fried with prawns, barbecued Chinese pork, and pine nuts, a perfect combination of taste and textures. I was told by the residents of the town that cows are abundant in the area and that milk-based dishes have been part of the local cuisine for a long time. In a country with almost no dairy products, Cantonese milk dishes date from the Portuguese influence of over three hundred years ago. Exposed to the European tradition, the Cantonese created flavourful dishes that cook the milk first to make it more digestible.

450 ml/16 fl oz milk
1 teaspoon salt
½ teaspoon freshly ground white pepper
4 tablespoons cornflour
1 tablespoon peanut oil, for the tin
1½ tablespoons peanut oil
1 teaspoon salt
225 g/8 oz Chinese barbecue pork or mild ham,
  coarsely chopped
125 g/4 oz medium-sized uncooked prawns unpeeled (but
  without heads) or 350-375 g/ 12-13 oz peeled uncooked
  prawns, coarsely chopped
125 g/4 oz pine nuts

Combine the milk, salt, pepper, and cornflour in a medium-sized saucepan and mix until smooth. Then simmer the mixture over low heat for 8 minutes or until it has thickened to the consistency of soft scrambled eggs. Oil a baking tin, pour in the cooked milk mixture, and allow it to cool thoroughly. Cover with cling film and refrigerate. This can be done the day before.

Heat a wok or large frying pan until hot and add the oil and salt. Then add the barbecue pork or ham and prawns, and stir-fry the mixture for 1 minute. Add the milk mixture and pine nuts, and stir-fry for 3 minutes or until the entire dish is heated through. Serve at once.

Serves 4 as part of a Chinese meal, or 2 as a single dish.

hongshao yangrou
braised goat casserole

Although goat dishes may be found in many places, most Chinese find goat not to their taste. It is primarily eaten in the western regions of China, probably reflecting Muslim influence. Here is a recipe from the western province of Yunnan in which goat, or even lamb, is braised in a casserole

*with an array of spices and other seasonings. The casserole makes a hearty
meal in itself, but it can also serve as part of a larger meal. Since the dish
reheats well, you could make it well ahead of time to freeze.*

1.4 kg/3 lb boneless goat or lamb shoulder,
   rind removed
4 spring onions
4 slices peeled fresh ginger root
3 tablespoons fermented bean curd
4 tablespoons rice wine or
   dry sherry
3 tablespoons light soy sauce
2 tablespoons dark soy sauce
4 whole star anise
3 tablespoons sugar
1½ tablespoons whole Sichuan
   peppercorns, roasted
2 cinnamon bark pieces or
   cinnamon sticks
3 tablespoons hoisin sauce
2 teaspoons salt
1 teaspoon freshly ground black pepper
350 ml/12 fl oz chicken stock
900 ml–l 1/3½–4 pt of water, or more

influences from within and without

Cut the meat into 5-cm/2-in dice. Blanch the meat in a large pot of
boiling water for 5 minutes. Remove the meat and discard the water.

In a large pot or casserole, add the blanched meat and all the other
ingredients, adding more water as necessary so that all the meat is
covered with liquid. Bring the mixture to the boil over medium heat,
skim off any fat or foam that rises to the surface, and turn the heat
down as low as possible. Cover and braise for 2 hours or until the meat
is very tender.

Skim off any surface fat and serve at once.

Serves 6 as part of a Chinese meal, or 3 as a single dish.

yangru bing
toasted goat cheese

Cheese is a food rarely, if ever, associated with Chinese cuisine. Although there are no taboos associated with milk and dairy products, they are generally not eaten by the Chinese, for historical, climatic, and other reasons. For instance, by age six, the Chinese — and the majority of the world's people — cease producing the enzyme lactase required for digesting milk and unprocessed dairy products. Processed milk products such as evaporated and sweetened condensed milk and mild cheeses are only now being introduced into some regions of China, though whole milk, yogurt, and especially goat cheeses have been popular for decades among the Muslims and other minority groups in the province of Yunnan, in the southwest.

Friends introduced me to this regional specialty at the Kang Le Xiao Wu restaurant in Kunming. We ate the firm, mild cheese lightly toasted, as a very enjoyable appetiser to begin our meal.

225 g/8 oz firm, mild goat cheese or feta
Freshly ground black pepper

Cut the goat cheese into 6-mm/¼-in slices, then into 5 x 7.5 cm/ 2 x 3-in pieces.

Preheat the grill. Lay the goat cheese slices on a baking tray. Place it under the grill and cook until brown, about 5 minutes. Turn them over, brown the other side, sprinkle with the pepper and serve warm.

Serves 4 as part of a Chinese meal, or 2 as a single dish.

yan jian rou
stir-fried chilli pork

Sichuan food is hot, spicy, and sensual, and the chilli is one of the mainstays of that region's cuisine. Unlike in the West, restaurants there do not offer chillies in oil or a paste at the table to augment tastes. Instead they season a

influences from within and without – recipes

dish before it arrives. Fragrant, roasted Sichuan peppercorns combined with freshly crushed dried chillies ensure that diners have a tasty dish, though not all chillies used are hot. In this recipe mild chilies are combined with thinly sliced pork to create a pleasing, nutritious dish which is colourful, fragrant, and flavourful. I discovered it in the Shu Feng Yuan restaurant/collective in Chengdu, Sichuan.

450 g/1 lb lean pork
1 tablespoon light soy sauce
2 tablespoons rice wine or dry sherry
Pinch of salt
2 teaspoons sesame oil
225 g/8 oz fresh mild chillies
3 tablespoons peanut oil
3 tablespoons finely chopped garlic
1 teaspoon ground red chilli powder
1 teaspoon Sichuan peppercorns, roasted
   and crushed
3 tablespoons water
1 tablespoon light soy sauce
2 teaspoons sugar

influences from within and without

Cut the pork into 7.5-cm/3-in thin slices and combine with the soy sauce, 1 tablespoon rice wine, salt, and sesame oil.

Cut the chillies in half lengthways and seed them.

Heat a wok or large frying pan until hot. Add 1½ tablespoons of the peanut oil and the pork and stir-fry for 1 minute. Remove the pork with a slotted spoon.

Reheat the wok or frying pan. Add the remaining oil. When it is very hot, add the fresh chillies, garlic, chilli powder, and peppercorns and stir-fry for 30 seconds. Then add the water, 1 tablespoon rice wine or sherry, soy sauce, and sugar and cook for another 30 seconds. Return the meat to the mixture and heat through. Stir well, turn onto a platter, and serve.

Serves 4 as part of a Chinese meal, or 2 as a single dish.

jidan chao xihongshi
stir-fried eggs with tomatoes

Whoever travels to the remoter parts of China is guaranteed some surprises. I experienced one in Yunnan province when I visited the tiny village of Yi Liang Gou Jie, a place that even my friends who live in the province had never been to. A colourful place, it teems with activity and yet looks like something out of the sixteenth century. Everywhere our party went (photographer, his assistant, the driver, and me) crowds would surround us, peering at us as if we were some alien beings. This, of course, we were, with our Western garb, high-tech equipment, and strange language. Whenever we smiled, they would break out into congenial laughter.

After some hours of walking around the town, we were famished. We stumbled upon a rustic tea house/restaurant. Quite unpretentious, it had no sign or nameplate, but someone's goat was tethered in front. We ordered the speciality of the house, Yunnan duck, several seasonal vegetable dishes, and this delectable stir-fry of eggs and tomatoes. It was quite a repast for the middle of nowhere at the no-name cafe. The delicate flavour of the fresh eggs was nicely balanced by the sweet acidity of the ripe tomatoes.

6 eggs, beaten
2 teaspoons sesame oil
1 teaspoon salt
450 g/1 lb fresh ripe tomatoes
6 whole spring onions
1½ tablespoons peanut oil
½ teaspoon salt

In a medium-sized bowl, combine the eggs with the sesame oil and salt and reserve.

Cut the tomatoes into quarters and then into eighths.

With the side of a cleaver or knife, crush the spring onions, then finely shred them.

Heat a wok or large frying pan until hot. Add the oil, salt, and spring onions and stir-fry for 30 seconds. Then add the tomatoes and eggs

influences from within and without – recipes

and continue to cook stirring continually until the eggs are set, about 5 minutes. Quickly place on a platter and serve at once.

Serves 4 as part of a Chinese meal, or 2 as a single dish.

xiao long yan rou
lamb steamed with spice-flavoured cornmeal

This is one of the most unusual dishes I've ever encountered in China and delicious as well. A northern Chinese inspired recipe, the tender goat meat was coated with spiced cornmeal and gently steamed, then served in a bamboo steamer lined with linen cloth. On my return home I was surprised at its ease of preparation. I have, used lamb in place of the rather more robust goat meat, although I wish everyone could also taste it made with goat.

60 g/2½ oz yellow cornmeal
2 teaspoons five-spice powder
2 teaspoons ground roasted Sichuan peppercorns
1 teaspoon salt
450 g/1 lb lean lamb (fillet or leg)
3 tablespoons finely chopped spring onions
2 teaspoons finely chopped garlic
2 teaspoons finely chopped peeled fresh
    ginger root
1 tablespoon rice wine or dry sherry
1 tablespoon light soy sauce
2 teaspoons sesame oil

In a medium-sized bowl, combine the cornmeal, five-spice powder, ground Sichuan peppercorns, and salt. Mix well and set aside.

Cut the lamb into thin strips, about 6 mm/¼ in thick by 7.5 cm/ 3 in long. In a large bowl, combine the lamb with the onions, garlic, ginger, rice wine or sherry, soy sauce, and sesame oil.

Lay the lamb in a large baking tray and toss with the cornmeal mixture to coat evenly. Arrange the lamb on a plate.

Set up a steamer or put a rack into a wok or deep pan. Fill the steamer with about 5 cm/2 in of hot water. Bring the water to a simmer. Put the plate with the lamb into the steamer or onto the rack. Cover the steamer tightly and gently steam over medium heat for 30 minutes. Replenish the water in the steamer from time to time as needed.

Serve at once.

Serves 4 as part of a Chinese meal, or 2 as a single dish.

influences from within and without – recipes

CHAPTER 4
THE IMPERIAL LEGACY

To make sure that the emperor's food was not poisoned, two eunuchs were assigned to the imperial kitchen to taste the food before it was served to the emperor. I thought how nice it is to taste every dish and bowl before the emperor did. The job's really a delight for the gourmet!

Aisin Gioro Pu Jie, brother of Aisin Gioro Pu Yi
(the last Emperor of China)

The imperial court, like the forbidden city, was an isolated entity. Since the dawn of China's political history more than two thousand years ago, when the country was unified in 220 B.C., the Chinese have experienced severe constraints on their political freedom. The first Emperor, Qin Shihuang, and those who followed, repressed all dissent. Over the centuries, in order to survive, the people had to sublimate their political and other social energies. They channelled their creative powers into art, literature, religious philosophy, and finally, their cuisine. Chinese chefs were rewarded for displaying excellence in their profession. Those who were innovative, experimental, freely creative often rose to the highest levels of the Imperial Court, their unfettered, politically innocuous creativity radiating into Chinese society. Its influence is still to be felt.

For the two thousand years of its reign, the Empire always commanded overwhelming loyalty or at least obedience, even though Imperial influence was not always kindly. The Empire undertook extensive land reclamation works; it coerced people into constructing vast irrigation, flood control, and water transport facilities which eventually benefited most Chinese. Autocratic though it was, Imperial government was an improvement over the piracy and banditry that occurred during interregnums and civil wars. It provided a framework of order within which the masses of people, though constrained, could nevertheless peacefully carry on daily life with inventiveness in all areas left open to them.

Imperial rule lasted into the twentieth century, and there are Chinese living today who recall with pleasure and in great detail their experiences of "sharing the same table," that is, dining with the last Emperor. Clearly, there was much to remember. What transpired at the Emperor's banquets, feasts, and celebrations, as well as what graced the everyday Imperial table, were no state secrets. The foods, drinks, implements, and techniques employed by Imperial chefs were available outside the Forbidden City and news of their creations spread quickly to the kitchens and restaurants in China at large. Everyone also knew which particular chefs were in favour in the Court.

But the movement was not only outward. No matter how isolated and insulated from everyday reality the Imperial Court may have been, it nonetheless depended upon the outside world for a constant stream of livestock, produce, seafood, spices, poultry, rice, wine, and wheat which flowed into the Forbidden City on a daily basis. At the height of Imperial splendour and opulence, literally thousands of permanent servants were employed in the royal kitchen and as serving staff. Organised into efficient, specialised bureaucracies, the Imperial servants made sure that the best and the freshest foods were always at hand for the Son of Heaven, his court, and his guests. They relied upon the resources of all China and often of foreign countries for their culinary supplies. The practices of the Imperial kitchen were as

the imperial legacy

important as its armies and bureaucracies in commanding the allegiance of the masses. Offering of food to heavenly powers, as a sacrifice to placate the supernatural, and as homage to the ancestors, dominated the Imperial Court.

In the early days, tradition dictated that only the Emperor, as the Son of Heaven, could make these sacrifices. Rituals allowed for no deviation and often were public in the sense that the entire court might be involved. Successive Emperors spent much of their time in ritualistic observances and many of the rites they performed involved the presentation and consumption of food. Steps were taken to separate China's Emperors from the realm of mortal men. An Emperor's public, and to a large extent private, life demonstrated clearly his lofty, separate status and enhanced his elevated dignity and authority. Dwelling in the innermost recesses of the palace, he was sealed off from all mundane influences and existed like an earthly god, distant, unapproachable and all powerful.

Instead of ministering angels, however, he was served by mortals, many of them eunuchs. The Emperor's servants, eunuchs included, often held the highest palace offices and governmental positions. He was also served by aristocratic courtiers, military experts, staff scholars and technicians, philosophers, poets, bureaucrats of all sorts, and, of course, master chefs and their assistants. The Dowager Empress, the Empress, the other women of the royal family, and the Imperial concubines each had their own servants, eunuchs, and ladies-in-waiting. With such an entourage, and with so many permanent members of the royal household, it's difficult to imagine the work and organisation involved in the preparation of the daily menu.

An official taster sampled the Emperor's dishes first, to test for poisons, but also to ensure that everything tasted as it should. When Emperors ate alone or with a few intimates, they quite often preferred rather simple fare. But on special occasions, anniversaries, holidays, or ambassadorial receptions when the Emperor's presence was required, sumptuous meals were prepared. Attired in the finest silks and damasks, adorned with precious jewels, the Emperor presided over an intricate series of ceremonies whose centerpieces always consisted of enormous and enormously complex food offerings.

The Imperial rituals evolved over time; however, from the beginning the bronze cooking cauldron was one of the symbols of the state. In fact, during the earliest recorded dynasty, the Shang (c. 1480–1122 B.C.), the Emperor maintained two thousand personnel in the Imperial food service, and one of his prime ministers had originally been a cook.

During the Han Dynasty (200 B.C.–A.D. 220) Chinese agricultural production experienced significant advances. Low taxes, land distributions, and public works helped to bring about a dramatic rise in productivity. Agricultural knowledge was disseminated by the state bureaucracy. Useful plants, including alfalfa and grape vines, were introduced from abroad, and plowing ceremonies were led by the Emperor Wen himself. The wok and the technique of stir-frying were introduced during the Han period. Historians have favourably compared the elaborate food preparations and rituals of the Han court with the best found at Versailles in the heyday of the Sun King.

After a time of troubles, the Tang Dynasty established itself (A.D. 618–907), ushering in one of the golden ages of Chinese civilisation. It was a time when Near Eastern crops such as spinach, sugar beet, lettuce, almonds and figs were introduced into China. Dates, palm sugar, yams, cardamom, new varieties of rice, citrus, litchi, and other foods became more widespread. The trade routes were filled with commerce, and contacts made with foreign cultures rapidly expanded. Exotic foods became familiar in daily life: Tibetan kohlrabi, Manchurian millet, Korean pine nuts, and Indian pepper. Tea became the national beverage during this time.

We know, too, that the Tang period carried the rituals and celebrations of the Imperial Court to an even higher state of refinement. Official celebrations still made use of familiar rituals and familiar foods but both rituals and menus were enriched. Ancestors, especially Imperial ones, were venerated as before but the Emperors now took to fasting as an act of purification before indulging in ceremonial feasts. The details of all the rituals and sacrificial offices were spelled out at length and codified in law. The Emperor's participation in these rituals, his public ancestor worship, his elaborate ceremonies, became even greater and more showy.

ritual and the court

It is easy to understand why the Chinese elite believed they lived in the domain of the Son of Heaven. By the first millennium, the Chinese Empire extracted tribute from the entire world known to it at that time. Riches of all sorts flowed into the Inner Kingdom, and the tastes and flavours of all Asia and the Near East were commonplace in the diet of the Empire's leaders. China was open to the outside world on its own terms – after all, if one were not of the Han, one must be a barbarian.

The Song Dynasty, especially the era of the Southern Song (1126–1279), was famous for the refinements it brought to Imperial, aristocratic, and bourgeois dining habits. During this time trade shifted from the west and north to the south and east as goods from Korea, Japan, and southeast Asia began to dominate Chinese commerce. Trade along the ancient desert Silk Route had required huge capital investments; the new overseas trade was open to the less wealthy entrepreneur. Regional middle classes finally were able to get on their feet. Since those with discretionary income love indulgences as well as any emperor, the members of this new middle class spent money on food and demanded excellence.

The capital city of the Southern Song was Hangzhou (Hangchow), located in the Yangtze River delta not far from Shanghai, the richest agricultural area in China. Buddhism provided a great impetus to the adoption of ingenious and delicious vegetarian dishes. The vastness of Hangzhou's culinary resources was so renowned that one of the Song Emperors left his palace and visited the city's markets to see for himself all that was available. The banquets of the Southern Song era may never have been surpassed. An intricate system of food preparation and service was recorded; the number of dishes and the extravagance of the service indicate how ostentatious as well as innovative it all was.

These culinary displays were also political and religious in nature. There are records of spectacular Imperial feasts that included thirty courses and hundreds of dishes, presented and removed with military precision. Each stratum of the official hierarchy, each foreign ambassador, received the number and type of dishes prescribed by protocol. Fresh and preserved fruits, foods deep-fried in honey, preserved meats, food on skewers, rivers of wine, fifty different desserts, food in ice brought from hundreds of miles away; the palatial setting of marvellous fabrics, woods, bronzes, jewels, furniture, tapestries, silver and gold table settings – all of the accouterments of these public spectacles demonstrated the power and wealth of the Son of Heaven and his affirmation as the Imperial upholder of the grand traditions of China. Today, Mr. Xu Hairong, general secretary of the Chinese Cuisine of the Southern Song Dynasty Society, is trying to revive and preserve this aspect of Imperial legacy. In his Bagua Lou restaurant in Hangzhou, he offers many dishes of that era that he has re-created from ancient texts. Those who dine there get a glimpse of the glory of the Southern Song.

At the same time, alongside Imperial displays, and sharing in the general prosperity of the age, the new middle classes developed their own culinary style, influenced by the Court but never aping it. Instead of the baroque manner of the Imperial chefs, they adopted a hybrid style, utilising the wealth around them but developing simpler, more balanced dishes. It is here for the first time that the dynamic tension between richness and simplicity was clearly expressed with the suave and the harsh, the exotic and the commonplace that characterises Chinese cuisine.

By contrast, the Yuan (Mongol) Dynasty (1271–1378) was the dominant political force but its influence on Chinese life was largely ephemeral. Being originally nomadic people from the Asian steppes, their not terribly refined diet centred around mutton, sheep products, and dairy foods such as yogurt and mare's milk. These foods were not unknown to the Chinese diet even before the Mongol invasion but they were given, as it were, the Imperial stamp of approval and became a normal part of Chinese cuisine. In my travels through China, I observed that dishes such as mutton hot pot (thin slices of mutton cooked in seasoned boiling water and quintessentially Mongolian) are popular everywhere, including Guangzhou (Canton). The Mongol Emperors came, conquered, and departed, leaving their imprint mainly on the cuisine of China.

Having chased out the Mongols, the Ming Dynasty restored and stepped up the ancient traditions. The Ming Emperors had tens of thousands of servants maintaining their kitchens, preparing the

Imperial banquets and organising and staging spectacular sacrificial and commemorative feasts. As in the past, the major culinary efforts were as much political, religious, and ideological as they were mere occasions for culinary delight. When for one reason or another members of the Imperial kitchen left the royal household, they plied the trades they had performed for the Emperor. It has always been good public relations to have a former chef of the Emperor working for your restaurant.

By the time of the last dynasty, that of the Qing (the Manchus, 1644–1911), the Imperial culinary rituals were set in something more solid than concrete. The weight of more than two thousand years of history and the desire of these foreign emperors for acceptance determined that the Manchus would do things as the Han Chinese had done before. Imperial rituals, heavily involved with food, continued as before. This period was not one of great innovation but one of conservation, of compilation and codification, of historical analysis and interpretation; the entire history of Chinese cuisine in all of its aspects was assembled under the Manchus. It was almost as if they believed that by encompassing the past they could legitimise their regime and secure the future. For a time, all went on as before. The rituals of the Imperial court, including those of the kitchen, became ever more elaborate and spectacular, stylised, garish, more and more removed from the lives of most of China's people.

By the nineteenth century, change was in the air. The process of Westernization, or secularisation, with its move toward modernity, was begun, a revolutionary process that even today has not yet run its course. Today, though the Imperial dynasties are gone, their legacy is still apparent in Chinese cuisine.

Though there are creditable efforts to recapture some of the glories of the Imperial cuisine, it is clear that the days of the thirty-course, two-hundred-dish banquet are gone forever. Government decrees forbidding Imperial-style menus are really not needed. Any effort to re-create the Imperial style might work as a tourist gimmick, but that is all. What remains of the Imperial culinary legacy can be found only in techniques and recipes, the tastes and fragrances it has bequeathed to the greater canon of Chinese cuisine, and this is more enduring than any empire. Certainly, the technical ability to mount such extravagance exists, but the religious and symbolic elements of those banquets will never again be known.

doufu chai
cabbage with bean curd

From the Imperial banquet hall to the most humble peasant kitchen, vegetarian dishes have always been included in any special feast. This recipe has been traced to the Long Yin Si Temple in Hangzhou, the ancient capital city of the Southern Song Dynasty (1126–1279). Temple cooking was influenced by Buddhist and Daoist religious philosophy and by the availability of vegetables that lent themselves to subtly sweet but delicious combinations. The extraordinary versatility of bean curd can be seen here in its marriage to the venerable Chinese cabbage.

450 g/1 lb firm bean curd
450 g/1 lb Chinese cabbage
125 ml/4 fl oz peanut oil
1½ tablespoons peanut oil
3 tablespoons finely chopped spring onions
2 tablespoons coarsely chopped garlic
2 tablespoons rice wine or dry sherry
1 tablespoon light soy sauce
½ teaspoon salt
2 teaspoons sugar
1 tablespoon sesame oil

Cut the bean curd into 25-mm/1-in squares. Drain well and lay them on kitchen paper to drain for another 10 minutes.

Cut the cabbage into 6-mm/¼-in shreds and set aside.

Heat a wok or large frying pan until hot. Add the oil and when it is hot, stir-fry the bean curd on both sides until it is golden brown. Drain well on kitchen paper.

Drain and discard the oil. Wipe the wok or pan clean, reheat, and add the 1½ tablespoons of oil. Put in the onions and garlic and stir-fry for 30 seconds. Then add the cabbage and the rest of the ingredients except the sesame oil. Continue to stir-fry for 2 minutes. Return the fried bean curd pieces to the pan and cook over high heat for 5 minutes or until the cabbage has completely cooked. Add the sesame oil and give the mixture a final turn. Serve at once.

Serves 4 as part of a Chinese meal, or 2 as a single dish.

zha li rou
fried stewed country spareribs

One of the most cultured periods of Chinese history, and of Chinese cuisine, was that of the Southern Song Dynasty (1126–1279). The Imperial Court gave banquets with hundreds of dishes. Among them were delights such as hearty spareribs, marinated with honey, stewed and finally deep-fried. Re-created and very much enjoyed by me in a Hangzhou restaurant, the dish offers a glimpse into the gastronomic delights of the Song court.

700 g/1½ lbs meaty pork spareribs
350 ml/12 fl oz chicken stock
450 ml/16 fl oz peanut oil
MARINADE
1 tablespoon honey
1½ tablespoons rice wine or dry sherry
2 tablespoons light soy sauce
1 tablespoon Chinese black rice vinegar
1 tablespoon sugar
2 teaspoons ground roasted Sichuan peppercorns
1 teaspoon salt

In a large pot of boiling water, blanch the spareribs for 5 minutes. Drain thoroughly.

Mix all the marinade ingredients together. Rub the spareribs with

the imperial legacy

the marinade and let sit for 30 minutes at room temperature.

In a medium-size clay pot or casserole, combine the chicken stock with the marinated spareribs. Bring the mixture to a simmer, cover, and cook for 15 minutes. Remove the spareribs with a slotted spoon. Reduce the liquid in the pot for 15 minutes over high heat or until it is slightly thick and syrupy. Return the spareribs to the pot and coat thoroughly with the mixture. Remove and allow the sparenbs to dry, about 30 minutes to 1 hour.

Heat a wok or large frying pan until hot. Add the oil and when it is medium hot, deep-fry the spareribs until they are crisp and golden. Drain on kitchen paper and serve at once.

Serves 4 as part of a Chinese meal, or 2 as a single dish.

ji you cai xin
cabbage in "cream" sauce

Vegetarian dishes are common throughout China. Historic religious influences and rituals played a part, but the availability of so many different vegetables, especially soybeans, had a practical influence. In this traditional dish the Chinese cabbage is first stir-fried, then it is slowly braised in chicken stock. The stock would then be reduced, thickened, and finally enriched with chicken fat. I omit the chicken fat; the dish is tasty enough without it. The "cream" sauce is chicken stock thickened with a little cornflour. It's a humble dish, but one worthy of the Imperial banquet hall.

450 g/1 lb Chinese cabbage
1½ tablespoons peanut oil
2 peeled garlic cloves, crushed
350 ml/12 fl oz chicken stock
½ teaspoon salt
½ teaspoon freshly ground white pepper
1 teaspoon cornflour mixed with
  1 teaspoon water

Cut the Chinese cabbage into 6-mm/¼-in thick strips.

Heat a wok or large frying pan until hot. Add the oil and garlic and stir-fry for 30 seconds, then remove the garlic and discard. Put in the cabbage, stock, salt, and pepper and cook for 1 minute. Reduce the heat, cover, and cook slowly for 10 minutes or until the cabbage is tender. Remove the strips with a slotted spoon.

Over high heat, reduce the liquid in the wok or pan by half, add the cornflour mixture and continue to cook. Arrange the cabbage on a platter, pour the sauce over it, and serve at once.

Serves 4 as part of a Chinese meal, or 2 as a single dish.

leng yacai
bean sprout salad

What we call "bean sprouts" come from the mung beans, which are grown in almost every part of China. They are a popular delicacy – crunchy, subtly flavoured, and nutritious – as well as inexpensive. I rarely saw them in the many markets I visited because they require proper refrigeration which is uncommon in China. Fragile, they must be eaten very soon after they sprout or they will lose their fresh, lovely taste. Some of the best I sampled, as in this recipe, were elegantly served at the Bagua Lou restaurant in Hangzhou whose recipe is below. The management is dedicated to reviving and re-creating dishes from the Southern Song Dynasty (1126–1269), one of the most glorious periods in Chinese history. Their salad is refreshing, delicate, and sophisticated despite its apparent simplicity. It is quite easy to prepare and uncommonly delicious.

450 g/1 lb fresh brean sprouts
3 tablespoons white rice vinegar
1½ tablespoons sugar
1 teaspoon salt

Trim the bean sprouts at both ends. Rinse them well in cold water and blanch them for 20 seconds in a large pot of boiling water. Remove the sprouts with a slotted spoon, and immediately plunge them in cold water. Drain thoroughly.

Combine the white rice vinegar, sugar, and salt in a small bowl, stirring until the sugar and salt have dissolved.

Toss the bean sprouts in the dressing and serve at once, or cover the bowl with cling film and refrigerate for up to 2 hours.

Serves 4 as part of a Chinese meal, or 2 as a single dish.

leng donggua
winter melon salad

Winter melon has nourished Asians since earliest times. Today it's mainly used in soups, so this unusual salad made with slightly pickled winter melon was a delightful surprise for me when I first sampled it at the Bagua Lou restaurant outside of Hangzhou. Juicy and slightly bland, winter melons are large but you can buy them by the slice in Chinese grocers. Westerners sometimes confusingly call them Chinese bitter melon, a name that is also applied to a completely different kind of squash. Use watermelon if winter melon is unavailable.

700 g/1½ lb fresh winter melon
1 teaspoon salt
1 tablespoon sugar
1 tablespoon white rice vinegar

Halve the melon and remove the seeds and coarse fibers from the center. With a sharp knife, cut away the peel and rinse well under cold water. Cut the melon into long shreds.

Sprinkle the melon shreds with the salt and allow them to sit in a colander set inside a bowl for 10 minutes. Rinse them in cold water, blot them dry with kitchen paper, and toss with the sugar and white rice vinegar.

Refrigerate for 1 hour before serving.

Serves 4 as part of a Chinese meal, or 2 as a single dish.

recipes – the imperial legacy

yunnan kao ya
yunnan roast duck

Every region of China has its duck speciality, and Yunnan is no exception. In the Yunnan countryside, roadside restaurants display ducks, cooked and uncooked, hanging from poles outside. Brick and clay ovens are kept going day and night, cooking even more ducks. The Yunnan method of preparation follows the typical Chinese technique: the ducks are basted and hung out for hours to dry in the breeze, a necessary step before roasting to produce crispy skin and moist meat. What makes eating duck in Yunnan unique is the combination of condiments and seasonings used as dipping sauces: sweet bean sauce with chilli, a salt-and-pepper mixture which uses black instead of Sichuan peppercorns, and spring onion morsels are all served. To my surprise, no flour pancakes or steamed wheat buns came with the duck. Served simply with plain rice, I enjoyed excellent Yunnan roast duck at the Kang Le Xiao Wu restaurant, prepared by chef Wen Hongchun whose recipe I offer here. It makes an excellent centerpiece for a special dinner party.

1.6–1.8 kg/3½–4 lb whole duck,
    fresh or frozen
Salt and freshly ground black pepper
850 ml/1½ pt water
3 tablespoons dark soy sauce
3 tablespoons honey
2 tablespoons white rice vinegar
DIPPING CONDIMENTS
5 tablespoons hoisin sauce mixed with
    2 tablespoons chilli bean sauce
2 tablespoons salt mixed with
    2 teaspoons freshly ground black pepper
6 spring onions, cut into 5-cm/2-in pieces

If the duck is frozen, thaw it thoroughly. Rinse the duck well and blot it completely dry with kitchen paper and season the cavity with salt and pepper. Then insert a meat hook near the neck.

Combine the water, soy sauce, honey, and vinegar in a large pot and bring the mixture to the boil. Using a large ladle, baste the duck several times until all the skin has been completely coated with the mixture. Hang the duck in a cool, well-ventilated place to dry or, alternatively, hang it in front of a fan for about 4 to 5 hours, longer if possible. Once the duck has dried, the surface of the skin will feel like parchment.

Preheat the oven to 240°C/475°F/Gas Mark 9. Place the duck on a roasting rack in a roasting tin, breast side up. Pour 125 ml/4 fl oz water into the roasting pan. Put the duck into the oven and roast for 15 minutes, turn down the temperature to 180°C/350°F/Gas Mark 4 and continue to roast for 50 minutes. The skin will be a deep mahogany colour and very crisp when the duck is done. Meanwhile, prepare the dipping condiments.

Remove the duck from the oven and let it sit for 10 minutes, then cut it for serving. Using a cleaver or sharp knife, cut the duck into serving pieces by first dividing it into quarters, and then cutting the quarters into bite-sized pieces. Serve at once with the sauces.

Serves 6 to 8 as part of a Chinese meal, or 2 to 4 as a single dish.

CHAPTER 5
THE GLORIOUS CUISINE of GUANGZHOU

The food of contemporary southern China is, in the opinion of many, the finest in the world. It combines quality, variety, and a nutritional effectiveness that allows it to sustain more people per acre than any other diet on earth. South China may well cultivate more crops, at least on a commercial scale, than any other comparable region. Certainly it is well endowed with native (or long-cultivated) crops and has also been quick to add new importations to its roster. To pick a recent example, Taiwan has taken up cultivation of asparagus and European mushrooms. In addition to cultivated plants and animals – from microscopic yeasts to giant palms, and from carp to water buffalo – wild plants (especially herbs) and wild animal life (especially aquatic, but also including game) contributed much to the diet. South China . . . has the most diverse flora of any region outside the wet tropics. A complexly faulted and folded landscape blessed with abundant rain and warmth encouraged tremendous diversity, and the human inhabitants of the region were not slow to make use of this. Indeed, they increased it, by borrowing every easily adaptable crop from every major region on earth. With animals, the borrowing was less extensive, but even so a large number of domesticated strains is found. . . . the southern Chinese diet feeds more people, better, on less land, than any other diet on earth.

Food in Chinese Culture, Anderson and Henderson

There is a well-known Chinese saying: "To be born in Suzhou (famous for its beauty and beautiful women), to eat in Guangzhou (where the food is by general repute the best in China), to be attired in Hangzhou (home of the best silks and fabrics), and to die in Luzhou (where the best wood for one's coffin is found), these are the great wishes of one's life." I was born in the United States of Cantonese parents, nourished by my mother's delicious Cantonese food, and I grew up with the conviction that Cantonese cooking is the best in the world. Certainly, although I enjoy all of the many regional variations of Chinese food, the offerings of Guangzhou (Canton), the capital city of the thriving, teeming province of Guangdong, remain my favourite.

Those reasons may be briefly stated. No other cooks insist so emphatically on the freshest and highest quality ingredients. Nowhere else are the culinary arts and sciences, empirical and theoretical, and the mundane and the spiritual aspects of food so consciously and conscientiously joined. In no other cuisine is timing so important: a fraction of a second can make the difference between a delicacy and a disaster. Cantonese apprentice chefs must learn to "hear" when the shellfish, vegetables, or whatever must be whisked away from the flame and they must learn to "listen" when the wok "talks," with its sputtering noises.

Cantonese cooking is eclectic, experimental, and innovative. Thus, chefs draw upon the widest range of ingredients, traditionally from all over China and her neighbours, today from all over the world. Yet they maintain their traditions: whatever the food, it remains distinctively Cantonese. One can even find a beef and potato curry, but the stew will have been transformed into a Cantonese dish by using a more modest touch of curry spices, making it unrecognisable to anyone from India.

No other chefs are as expert in so many cooking techniques. Deep-frying, stir-frying, simmering, stewing, grilling, and their variations

the glorious cuisine of guangzhou

and combinations are but some of these methods. Even Western-style baking has been adopted. Cantonese restaurateurs will apologise at the sparseness of their menus, sometimes listing a mere five hundred offerings. I confess that perhaps the soups of Fujian (Fukien) are better in general than those of Canton and that Cantonese desserts reflect the region's lack of interest in that part of the meal. Otherwise, "to eat in Guangzhou" is indeed the wish of a lifetime.

In my travels throughout China, in talks with Chinese friends and relatives, in my chance encounters with Chinese workers, peasants, and teachers, I've been struck by the consensus that the food of Guangzhou is the best of all Chinese regional styles. From my first moments walking through the streets of the city, I could see, smell, and then taste why this is so. "Every five steps a restaurant" – the famous Cantonese saying is almost true.

The extensive open markets of Guangzhou are a marvel. Each day, they stock an enormous number and variety of fresh and dried foods. The restaurants, food stalls, meat and fish speciality stores, and pastry shops display their tempting and bountiful possibilities to passersby.

My favourite shops are those that sell condiments. It is a splendid experience to see the locals come to fill their bottles with their favourites: many varieties of soy sauces, chilli pastes, oyster sauce, plum sauce, and hoisin sauce, all as fresh as can be, all essential components of Cantonese cooking. Other market favourites of mine are the innumerable food stalls that line the always-jammed streets. The stalls offer quick and easy snacks and light meals, all satisfying dishes and some quite exceptional in their taste and delicacy. Walking along the streets and alleyways, one can peer into restaurant and family kitchens and constantly see food being prepared. There are no convenience foods and only a few processed foods in evidence.

Unlike many other places in China, it is easy to dine out at most times of the day in Guangzhou. There are a number of late-night restaurants, and many food stalls remain open until the early morning hours. These are usually filled with vivacious patrons, including children. The adults, in typical Chinese fashion, talk and joke vociferously, and the pleasure they take in their dining out is palpable. During an after-dinner stroll, travelers encounter street cart vendors offering deep-fried tidbits of shellfish, squid, or vegetables filled with minced fish. In my opinion, the whole scene makes Guangzhou the liveliest place in China, unrivaled even by Shanghai.

Friends and relatives could not wait to share with me the latest news about which restaurants and food stalls were the best or most inviting. With each visit, the sights and wafting odours took me directly back to my childhood, to my mother's kitchen. Talking with Cantonese friends about food and cooking techniques also reminded me of my family: these were always topics of conversation in our home. As a result, my visits to Guangzhou are like homecomings, full of the aesthetics and the sensual pleasures of Cantonese cookery.

It is no accident that Cantonese cuisine is superlative. Human ingenuity, history, and natural geography have combined to create this unique style. The city of Guangzhou is ancient, tracing its founding back almost three thousand years. This is certainly long enough to allow for cultural refinements, such as fine dining. Moreover, as the capital of Guangdong province, Guangzhou is a magnet for all sorts of people and products.

According to legend, in the year 887 B.C, during the Zhou Dynasty, five immortals flew to Guangzhou on clouds, riding five rams holding rice grains in their mouths. They blessed the residents and granted them abundant harvests forever, so that the people would never go hungry. Hence, Guangzhou is known as the City of Rice Grains, or the City of Rams.

Another legend has it that Guangzhou's (and Guangdong's) culinary reputation came about when, with the overthrow of the Ming Dynasty (1644), chefs of the Imperial household fled south, bringing with them their recipes and skills. According to some storytellers, they laid the foundation of Guangzhou's cuisine. History, and Cantonese pride, reject this fable.

THE BEGINNINGS

Beginning as an administrative center, the city quickly generated a bustling commercial, manufacturing, and trading economy, drawing increasing numbers of people from the inland areas. Guangzhou was soon an important stop on the so-called Silk Road of the Sea, the trade routes linking China with Southeast Asia and, later, Europe. By the year 1000, Guangzhou was China's southern trade center and a famous port. It remains so to this day.

This growth in wealth and population could not have occurred without the genius and energy of the people and the natural blessings of the area's climate and topography. The province has a 160-km/ 100-mile coastline with many natural harbours, bays, and inlets. There are hundreds of creeks, streams, and rivers in the province: "The water in and around Guangzhou is like a treasure waiting to be spent," says one local guide book; I interpret that to mean glorious fishing. The city itself is ideally situated at the confluence of three tributaries of the Pearl River. Rich soils, nurtured and husbanded for centuries; a mild, sunny, subtropical climate (perhaps twenty-five frosty days a year); well watered, with a twelve-month growing season; thousands of varieties of plants and trees; freshwater and saltwater fish in abundance; many wild animals and game birds – all of these are the foundation for Guangdong's bounty. Small wonder that Cantonese inventiveness and attention to technique, in combination with such natural resources as these, were able to perfect what is arguably the world's finest and most nutritious cuisine.

As with all great cuisines, a wealthy elite capable of affording and sustaining a passion for gourmet excellence is also a feature of Guangdong's history. Government functionaries, soon joined by an expanding commercial and industrial class, cultivated the fine art of dining. As the city and its surrounding territory grew in wealth and importance, the traditions of culinary excellence sent down deep roots. Chefs became celebrities; the restaurant trade flourished – culinary academies were established. By the mid-nineteenth century, Cantonese food was internationally known, and not just by reputation.

For centuries, Guangzhou's people have had extensive connections abroad. After the infamous Opium Wars in the late 1800s, Guangzhou was for a long time the *only* Chinese port open to outside trade. Even today, the vast majority of overseas Chinese living in some seventy different countries originally came from Guangzhou. It no doubt helped through all the years that the province was rather far removed from the political control of the Beijing under the Emperors. The stylised rigidity of the Imperial Court would have curbed Cantonese creativity.

My own experiences of the Cantonese cuisine accord with the views of scholars and food experts concerning its distinctive style. Beyond the factors I've already mentioned, there are other certain specific points that need emphasis. Simplicity is the first of them. Cantonese recipes extol the virtues of straightforward techniques: boiling, steaming, stir-frying. The point is, *always,* to trap the flavour of fresh, lightly cooked ingredients, predominantly fish, vegetables, or poultry – but also very little meat. Proper combinations of foods, textures, flavours, and colours are another essential. The rules for these combinations are many and subtle, and, as with most arts, they cannot be guessed at – they must be learned.

Cantonese chefs also introduced, and raised to a fine art, the use of fragrant and spicy sauces and dips. Condiments such as soy sauce, oyster sauce, chilli sauce, hot mustard, ground chillies, sesame oil, chopped chillies in soy, white pepper, and other flavourings are found on the Cantonese table. The diner, however, uses them according to his or her own taste. The condiments, along with sauces, are never used to cover or drown any dish; their purpose is to enhance, clarify, or complement the natural flavours of whatever food is served. Table salt, incidentally, has never been favoured by Chinese chefs; salt shakers have only recently made their appearance in Chinese restaurants to placate the Western palate or as an alternative to the ever-present bottle of soy sauce.

Authentic Cantonese style is best and most often displayed in its seafood dishes, with the emphasis on clarity, simplicity, freshness of taste, and a highly refined aesthetic. Chicken is relied upon for special occasions, then cooked simply and with due regard for the subtle tenderness of the meat. Pork is the standard meat of Cantonese cooking and one that has always brought out the best in Cantonese techniques: marinated and barbecued and glazed with honey or brown sugar; or diced and stir-fried; or minced and used as a filler or base for sauce – the variations are endless and all are tasty.

As for the more exotic meats, for example, dog, civet cat, bear's

expertise and adaptation

paw, tiger, snake, monkey, in my opinion too much has been written about a very narrow range of ingredients. These are, more often than not, used as medicinal brews rather than as food. My own view is that, because the Cantonese (and Chinese in general) have very few food taboos, they will try almost anything if it seems well prepared. This openness is reinforced by the common perception that food, medicine, and nutrition overlap if not coincide. Some foods are eaten for specific medicinal purposes and others, I was often told, "because they are good for you," but such exotica are in general exceptional to the basic Chinese diet.

Of all the foods that suggest Cantonese cooking, none is more famous than the "dim sum" dishes to be found throughout the province. All Chinese enjoy dim sum snacks and soups laden with noodles that can make up quite a substantial meal. It is in Canton, however, in restaurants renown for their boisterous atmosphere that dim sum dishes have been elevated to sophisticated heights. Minced shrimp and other ingredients wrapped in thin dough skin; chopped meat covered with taro dough; glutinous rice dumplings stuffed with fish or chicken or pork: the number of such dim sum dishes is almost countless, with new combinations of ingredients appearing all the time.

The Cantonese style in the capital city is so pervasive that its regional variations are obscured. There are areas of the province, however, whose cuisine is worth a detour. One is the Kaiping (Hoiping) area, the site of my ancestral home. It has a vast production of vegetables of all sorts but almost no animal foods. Its generally poorer population struggles to make the best of what is available and this translates into a cuisine in which vegetables and noodles are blended together in every imaginable way (ten vegetables in one dish is not uncommon). The scarce animal protein serves as a garnish or a base for sauces.

Making a virtue of their necessity, the Kaiping locals produced and enjoyed the best and freshest vegetables found anywhere in the world. Being poor, these were the people who emigrated whenever possible; in fact, most of the Cantonese immigrants to the New World, my parents among them, came from this region. These were people who survived, often by *creating* a Cantonese style of cooking for the countries they found themselves in. Fortunately, by the time my generation of "American Cantonese" was born, the chop suey-chow mein style of foreign Chinese restaurants once synonymous with Cantonese cooking was on the way out. Today, I would find this kind of menu distasteful, if not unrecognisable, having experienced one of the great wishes of life "to eat in Guangzhou!"

cong chao mian
fried noodle with onions

This is a recipe from one of my favourite restaurants in China – Bagua Lou, which specialises in culinary creations from the Southern Song Dynasty. Unfortunately I was unable to extract the history of this dish from the manager or the chef; however, their version reminded me once again of how good Cantonese food can be. Perhaps because I've enjoyed this dish several other times in Canton I have managed to reproduce it below rather effectively. The noodles are easy to cook and make a wonderful accompaniment or a splendid finale to any meal.

450 g/1 lb fresh thin Chinese
    egg noodles
8 spring onions, finely chopped
2 teaspoons salt
3 tablespoons peanut oil
Salt to taste
2 tablespoons Chinese black vinegar

Blanch the noodles in a large pot of salted boiling water for 3 minutes and drain thoroughly. Then scatter the noodles on a baking tin, mix in the chopped spring onions and sprinkle the salt over the top.

Heat a 30-cm/12-in frying pan, preferably nonstick, with half the oil. When hot, add the noodles, press down to make the noodles conform to the shape of the pan. Turn the heat to very low, and continue to cook for 10 to 15 minutes (sprinkling a spoonful of water from time to time, if the mixture seems to be drying too much), until the bottom is brown. Flip the noodles over in one piece, add more oil as necessary, and continue cooking them until the other side is brown. Sprinkle the noodles with salt and the black vinegar to taste. Slide onto a serving platter and serve.

Serves 4 as part of a Chinese meal, or 2 as a single dish.

gulao rou
sweet and sour pork made with fruit juice

This dish is often on menus in mediocre Chinese restaurants in the West where it invariably appears as a sweet, gluey, reddish concoction. This version, however, captures the virtues of the classic dish, "Gulao Pork." In China, gulao means venerable. In it, a sour taste was obtained from such fruits as plums, oranges, and berries, then combined with sweetened vinegar and other seasonings. Below I use fresh orange juice along with sugar and vinegar. The "sweets" and "sours" combine and penetrate the meat, while the shallots provide a rich and fragrant background.

700 g/1½ lb boneless pork neck on the fatty side
½ teaspoon salt
1 tablespoon light soy sauce
2 teaspoons rice wine or dry sherry
2 teaspoons sesame oil
1 egg, beaten
1 tablespoon cornflour
2 tablespoons peanut oil
225 g/8 oz whole shallots, peeled
2 tablespoons sugar
3 tablespoons Chinese red vinegar
275 ml/10 fl oz freshly squeezed orange juice
1 teaspoon cornflour mixed with 2 teaspoons water
Salt and freshly ground pepper to taste
75 g/3 oz unbleached plain flour
75 g/3 oz cornflour

450 ml/16 fl oz peanut oil

Cut the pork into 5-cm/2-in chunks and combine with the salt, soy sauce, rice wine or sherry, sesame oil, egg, and the tablespoon of cornflour. Mix well and let the mixture sit for about 30 minutes.

In a small saucepan, heat the oil and add the shallots and sugar. Cook over low heat until the sauce becomes a light caramel colour, about 2 minutes. Pour in the Chinese red vinegar and orange juice and simmer for 4 minutes. Gently beat in the cornflour mixture, and when the sauce thickens, season to taste with salt and pepper. Set the sauce aside and keep warm.

Combine the flour and 75 g/3 oz cornflour together in a large paper bag. Add the marinated pork pieces, close the bag, and toss well to coat each piece of pork. Shake off the excess flour.

Heat a wok or large frying pan until hot. Add the oil and a few pork pieces and deep-fry until cooked through, about 4 minutes. You will have to do this in several batches. Remove the pork with a slotted spoon and drain on kitchen paper.

Drain off all the oil from the wok or pan, wipe it clean, and reheat the sauce. Return the fried pork pieces to the wok and stir to coat well with the sauce. Serve at once.

Serves 4 as part of a Chinese meal, or 2 as a single dish.

chao sansi
three-shredded dish

I savoured this dish at a small restaurant, the Qing Hui Yuan, in the town of Shunde, a few hours by car southwest of Canton. My good friend Willie Mark, one of Hong Kong's leading food critics, insisted that I pay it a visit because the restaurant specialises in local dishes and its food is stunningly good. It was. "Three-shredded" refers to the roast duck, pork, and pork liver which are stir-fried in a savoury sauce. Then they are placed on a bed of crisply deep-fried egg shreds. Hmmm, perhaps the recipe should be called "Four-shredded."

225 g/8 oz fresh pork liver
2 teaspoons light soy sauce
1 teaspoon rice wine or dry sherry
Pinch of salt and pepper
1 teaspoon cornflour
1 teaspoon sesame oil
225 g/8 oz boneless lean pork
1 teaspoon light soy sauce
1 teaspoon rice wine or dry sherry
Pinch of salt and pepper
1 teaspoon cornflour
1 teaspoon sesame oil
225 g/8 oz cooked boneless duck or chicken
4 eggs
1 tablespoon cornflour mixed with 1 tablespoon water
½ teaspoon salt
1 teaspoon sesame oil
450 ml/8 oz peanut oil
1½ tablespoons finely chopped garlic
2 teaspoons finely chopped ginger
4 tablespoons finely chopped spring onions
125 ml/4 fl oz chicken stock
1 tablespoon light soy sauce
2 teaspoons dark soy sauce
2 teaspoons cornflour mixed with 1 tablespoon water
2 teaspoons sesame oil

Cut the liver lengthways into 5-cm/2-m wide strips, then cut them crossways into thin slices. Blanch them in boiling water for 40 seconds, remove with a slotted spoon, and plunge them immediately into cold water. Drain thoroughly and blot dry with kitchen paper. Combine the liver with the soy sauce, rice wine or sherry, salt, pepper, cornflour, and 1 teaspoon sesame oil and set aside.

Cut the pork into thin slices in the same manner as the pork liver, and combine it with the soy sauce, rice wine or sherry, salt, pepper, cornflour, and 1 teaspoon sesame oil.

Cut the cooked duck or chicken into slices the same size as the pork.

Beat the eggs in a small bowl and combine with the cornflour mixture, salt, and sesame oil. Heat a wok or large frying pan until hot and add the peanut oil. When the oil becomes hot, pour a small amount of the egg mixture into a strainer. When the egg drips through, rotate the strainer around the top of the wok to make a single layer of lace-like batter that covers the top of the oil. Deep-fry the egg shreds in batches until they turn a golden brown, about 15 seconds. Remove the shreds with a slotted spoon and drain them on kitchen paper. Arrange on a platter and keep them warm in a low oven.

Drain off all but 2 tablespoons of oil and reheat the wok or pan. When it is hot, add the garlic, ginger, and onions and stir-fry for 30 seconds. Then add the pork liver and pork. Continue to stir-fry for 3 minutes. Then add the cooked duck or chicken, stock, and soy sauces. Continue to stir-fry for 3 minutes. Thicken the sauce with the cornflour mixture, stir in the sesame oil, and give the mixture two final stirs. Serve this on top of the shredded fried egg.

Serves 4 to 6 as part of a Chinese meal, or 2 to 4 as a single dish.

qing zheng yu
steamed fish southern style

Having seen their fish swimming around in a tank or pond only minutes before they eat it, the Cantonese know how fresh it is. While few of us in the West are so lucky, we can best enjoy the flavour of fresh fish by cooking them whole. Steaming them this easy Cantonese way ensures that the delicate flesh remains moist and the result is an elegant main course.

900 g–1.1 kg/2–2½ lb firm, white-fleshed fresh fish such as a small cod, halibut, haddock, scrod or red snapper, or a sole, cleaned and left whole
1 teaspoon salt
3 slices of peeled fresh ginger root, cut into shreds
2 tablespoons light soy sauce

4 spring onions, finely shredded
2 tablespoons peanut oil

Make three or four shallow slashes on each side of the fish. Rub the fish on both sides with the salt and let it sit for 20 minutes. Blanch the fish in a large pot of boiling water for 2 minutes. Drain the fish well, and put it on a heat-proof platter. Scatter the ginger shreds evenly over the fish. Set up a large Chinese steamer or put a rack into a wok, fish kettle, or other deep pot. Fill it with about 5 cm/2 in of hot water. Bring the water to a simmer. Put the platter with the fish into the steamer or onto the rack. Cover the steamer tightly and gently steam over medium heat for 20 minutes.

Remove the platter and cooked fish from the steamer and pour off all the liquid. Pour the soy sauce over the fish and scatter the onions over and around the fish. Heat the oil until it just smokes, pour this over the fish, and serve at once.

Serves 4 as part of a Chinese meal, or 2 as a single dish.

bai zhuo jiwei xia
white-blanched prawns

Using the freshest possible prawns is essential for this dish. For finicky chefs in Hong Kong or Guangzhou, both close to the China Sea, this is not a problem. Another imperative is never to overcook the prawns; they must be plucked from the boiling water at just the right second to retain their unmatched flavour.

In Hong Kong, the prawns are served with a fresh chilli dipping sauce, but I prefer this version from Guangzhou's Liang Jing Ji restaurant. It's a simple mixture of soy, spring onion, and hot oil that makes an impressive start to any meal.

450 g/1 lb medium-sized fresh raw
   prawns, unpeeled
2 teaspoons salt

DIPPING SAUCE
1 tablespoon dark soy sauce
2 spring onions, finely shredded
1½ tablespoons peanut oil

Rinse the prawns well under cold running water. Blot them completely dry with kitchen paper and set aside. Mix the soy sauces and onion shreds in a small saucer. Heat the oil until it is smoking and pour this over the spring onion mixture. Bring a large pot of water to the boil and add the salt. Add all the prawns at once and cook for 4 minutes. Remove them immediately with a slotted spoon, arrange on a platter, and serve at once with the dipping sauce.

Serves 4 as part of a Chinese meal, or 2 as a single dish.

qing chao bai cai
stir-fried pak choi

Simple, dependable, tasty, and refreshing – this is the Chinese attitude to fresh seasoned vegetables, stir-fried immediately before they are served. All Cantonese cooks understand that by skillfully using the minimum amount of oil in their heated woks, a few select seasonings, and just a splash of water at exactly the right moment they can bring out all the natural flavour of the vegetable. One of the best illustrations of this technique is fresh bai cai (pak choi). Found throughout China, it has a truly wonderful flavour reminiscent of spinach or Swiss chard.

450 g/1 lb pak choi
1 tablespoon peanut oil
2 garlic cloves, crushed
½ teaspoon salt
1 tablespoon water

Prepare the pak choi by removing the stalks with leaves from the stem. If the stalks are wide, split them in half. Cut the stalks with leaves into

7.5-cm/3-in pieces. Peel the stem and cut it thinly at a slight angle. Wash the pak choi in several changes of cold water. Drain well and set aside. Heat a wok until it is hot. Add the oil and garlic and stir-fry for 30 seconds. Add the salt and pak choi and stir-fry for 1 minute over high heat. If the mixture seems dry, add 1 tablespoon of water. Continue stir-frying for 4 minutes. Serve at once.

Serves 4 as part of a Chinese meal, or 2 as a single dish.

hongshao ruge
crispy roast squab

Justly famed for their skill in cooking small birds, the Cantonese overcame the problem of there being so many small bones by cutting the birds into bite-sized morsels before serving them. Diners can then easily extract the meat.

In this recipe, the squab are not really roasted. They are quickly cooked in a flavourful liquid, dried, and then, just before serving, dropped into very hot oil to finish the cooking. Their skin becomes crisp, with a lacquered look, while the meat remains tender, juicy, and flavourful. The preparation takes a little time but the first steps may be done well in advance. The result is well worth the effort and makes a terrific first course.

2 squabs, each about 350–450 g/12oz–1 lb
BRAISING LIQUID
2 fresh ginger root slices
3 whole spring onions
3 tablespoons light soy sauce
2 tablespoons dark soy sauce
2 tablespoons rice wine or dry sherry
2 tablespoons sugar
1 tablespoon honey
1 teaspoon salt
700 ml/1¼ pt chicken stock
450 ml/16 fl oz peanut oil

the glorious cuisine of guangzhou

Blanch the squabs in a large pot of salted boiling water for 2 minutes and remove them with a slotted spoon. Drain well.

In a medium-sized pot, combine the braising liquid ingredients, and bring the mixture to a simmer. Add the squabs, cover, and simmer for 20 minutes. Remove the squabs and allow to dry thoroughly, about 1 hour. The recipe can be made to this point up to 4 hours ahead.

Just before serving, heat a wok or large frying pan until hot. Add the oil and when it is medium hot, deep-fry the squabs until they are crispy and brown. Dram them on kitchen paper, cut them into bite-sized pieces, and serve at once.

Serves 4 as part of a Chinese meal, or 2 as a single dish.

lianggua rouru he
minced bitter melon with rice noodles

The famous Sha He restaurant attracts visitors from all over China to taste what is reputed to be the ultimate rice noodles. Located just outside the port of Guangzhou in an area renowned for the quality of its rice and its water, the Sha He makes over one thousand pounds of rice noodles every day, serving them in forty different dishes. One recipe they shared with me marries the cool, tangy flavour of bitter melon with pork and the airy lightness of their delicate noodles. If you aren't able to buy fresh rice noodles in your local Chinese market, substitute dried ones but do try the recipe.

450 g/1 lb fresh rice noodles or dried, thin rice noodles
450 g/1 lb bitter melon
2 tablespoons peanut oil
2 tablespoons finely chopped garlic
225 g/8 oz minced pork
2 tablespoons light soy sauce
2 teaspoons sugar
1 teaspoon salt
150 ml/5 fl oz chicken stock

If you are using dried noodles, soak them in warm water for 20 minutes and drain well before using.

Slice the bitter melon in half lengthways. Remove the seeds and finely chop the melon. Blanch it in boiling water for 2 minutes and drain thoroughly. Heat a wok or large frying pan until hot. Add the oil and the garlic and stir-fry for 30 seconds. Put in the pork and stir-fry for 2 minutes, breaking it up. Add the soy sauce, sugar, salt, chicken stock, bitter melon, and rice noodles. Continue to stir-fry until the noodles are heated through and most of the liquid has evaporated. Turn onto a platter and serve.

Serves 4 as part of a Chinese meal, or 2 as a single dish.

fen xiang majian tang he
sweet sesame rice noodles

Another Sha He recipe, this unusual sweet dish excited my palate. Redolent of peanuts and sugar, it came as a refreshing counterpoint to some of the salty rice noodle dishes I was served. Although this is not served as a dessert in China, it could easily be enjoyed that way.

450 g/1 lb fresh rice noodles or dried wide,
   thin rice noodles
125 ml/4 fl oz chicken stock
SAUCE
5 tablespoons sesame paste or
   peanut butter
3 tablespoons sugar
5 tablespoons warm water. Garnish
3 tablespoons sugar

If using dried noodles, soak them first in warm water for 20 minutes. Heat the stock in a wok or large frying pan, add the noodles and cook them until they are soft and most of the liquid has evaporated. Turn them out on a warm platter. While the noodles are cooking, prepare the sauce. In a blender, mix the sesame paste or peanut butter, sugar, and water and blend until the sauce is smooth, adding more water if it is too thick. Pour it over the rice noodles, sprinkle with sugar. Serve.

Serves 4 as part of a Chinese meal, or 2 as a single dish.

haoyou sigua
silk squash with oyster sauce

Subtle flavours, delicate textures, the freshest ingredients, and just the right amount of the most appropriate seasonings, these are the virtues of classic southern Chinese cooking. The squash is so named because of its soft, spongy flesh which is markedly sweeter the younger the squash. It tastes like a cross between an aubergine and a cucumber. Aubergine can be used if you are unable to find silk squash. This recipe comes from the Qing Hui Yuan restaurant in Shunde, Canton, where silk squash was cut into larger pieces than I'd seen in the same dish elsewhere. The chef believes that the larger slices hold the flavour of the sauce better.

700 g/1½ lb silk squash or courgettes
2 tablespoons peanut oil
2 tablespoons finely chopped shallots
2 garlic cloves, sliced
3 tablespoons oyster sauce
125 ml/4 fl oz chicken stock

Peel away the tough outer skin of the silk squash and cut the flesh in half lengthways, then into 5-cm/2-in pieces.

Heat a wok or large frying pan until hot and add the oil. Put in the shallots, garlic, and silk squash and stir-fry for 2 minutes. Add the oyster sauce and chicken stock and simmer uncovered until tender, about 5 minutes. Serve at once.

CHAPTER 6
FAMILY TRADITIONS

The moon is especially bright in mid-autumn.

Traditional saying

Chinese cuisine reflects Chinese life itself. The grand design and profound richness of Chinese cuisine rests upon many centuries of dedicated application, splendid intuitions, accidental discoveries, and brilliant improvisations by millions of ordinary Chinese, usually women, working within countless family kitchens. Their skills and knowledge have been passed on through the centuries and spread gradually across villages and regions.

There is no other civilisation where eating plays so central a role in daily life and in festive occasions. No other cuisine has so many symbolic features, so many ritual and social aspects in the matter of dining. Much of the excellence and vitality of Chinese cuisine derives from its ancient role in family rituals and popular celebrations. Nowhere is this more evident than in the enduring traditions of family celebrations, almost every one of which centers around food.

These traditions fall into two separate but sometimes overlapping areas. The first comprises "private" feasts and celebrations. When I returned with my mother to our ancestral home, we were the cause of, and took part in, a family gathering. We were feted with an array of specially prepared foods symbolic of reunion and of reverence for our ancestors. Such a family feast might involve a birthday or anniversary, a wedding, or a funeral. The second, often similar, tradition consists of "public" national and regional celebrations such as the New Year festivities (also called the Spring Festival), the Autumn Moon feast, and the Dragon Boat Festival. Such private and public affairs are not peculiar to Chinese culture; however, other cultures commemorate them less frequently. Moreover, few others can compare with the rich symbolism of food in Chinese customs which conveys information, wishes, hopes, and even puns.

BIRTHS, WEDDINGS, DEATHS

Universally significant moments of individual and communal life are celebrated with food rituals. The birth of a child entails the preparation of special foods for the enjoyment of family and friends. This is especially so with the birth of a boy, for, historically a patriarchal society, China favours and honours males. In a mostly agricultural country, this was reinforced by the need for workers and the custom of inheritance.

Only sons could inherit family land and only sons could carry on the family name. Furthermore, given the once frightful rate of infant mortality an ancient saying becomes clear: "One son is no son, two sons is part of a son; only with three sons can you be sure of a son."

Nevertheless, there always was, and still is, a celebration of the birth of any child, daughters included. The occasion calls for special foods, each with its special meaning. At the baby's ceremonial first bath, for example, fruits such as jujubes are placed in the water and the women in attendance compete to pluck them out. The punning significance of this tradition is that the homonym for jujube (*tsao-tzu*) is "early son." Thus, the practice celebrates the birth of the child but, especially in the case of a female infant, the wish is for a son, and quickly. In a rite called *huantai* ("changing the womb") a woman who has just given birth to a daughter is given pig's stomach to eat "so that she will have a son next time."

In anticipation of childbirth, friends will send the expectant mother stalks of ripe grain, symbolising the ripeness of the time, and special steamed bread or dumplings called "share the pain." After the birth, the new mother must eat one poached egg every day and consume chicken soup with her other meals. Chicken represents health, strength, and fertility in Chinese medicine and folklore, and it's hoped that these attributes are transferred to the new mother. The new father's family distributes red-dyed boiled eggs to friends and neighbours, for red signifies the happiest and most auspicious events. These special foods are eaten in addition to the banquet to celebrate the birth. The normally frugal habits of the Chinese are put to one side, as much wine is drunk and no expense is spared.

Marriage also evokes a festive spirit. Although couples in urban China today have a freer choice in marriage, in the countryside – that is, among the vast majority of people – ancient traditions remain strong. Horoscopes of the prospective bride and groom are cast; the advice of matchmakers is sought; premarital contracts are drawn up between the heads of the families. "Wealth" and "well-being" remain synonymous among the Chinese masses and at the wedding feast, chicken and fish, whose homonyms in Chinese are, respectively, "good luck" (*ji*) and "riches" (*yu*), are always prominently included on the menu which always reflects the symbolic richness of the occasion.

Traditionally, both families provide separate banquets in celebration of the marriage. This custom is less evident today and instead families are combining to give one big affair. In the case of affluent families, however, wealthy relations may also provide banquets that might extend over several days.

The banquet provided by the groom's family has always been considered the more significant. Ideally, this banquet should be so extensive that the guests find it impossible to consume it all. Central to the menu are steamed cakes called "honey-harmonising-with-oil-cakes," signifying the happy and cooperative union of the two disparate family elements. The cakes are distributed to all relatives and friends according to strict traditional guidelines of seniority and family linkages. Exact protocol, understood by all, must be followed to secure harmony. Given immediately after the wedding, the "bridegroom banquet" represents the very public acceptance of the bride into the groom's family.

Death has its ceremonies and feasts. Ancestors long-dead are regularly revered and remembered with food placed before their shrines or at their burial sites. In the case of a recent death, the food rituals that would occur in life are initially continued at the grave. By treating the dead as one would the living reduces fear and anxiety and perpetuates family solidarity.

The belief that the dead are not dead and therefore, need food, helps explain the evolution, over thousands of years, of Chinese ancestor worship and of the funeral rituals. Furthermore, food offered to the dead is meant to ensure fertility among the living. Food, most notably cooked rice, is placed in coffins to nourish the deceased and to ward off hungry spirits. In some areas, coins and other material symbols of wealth are also put into the coffin. Such items are meant to induce the dead to give up their earthly possessions willingly. These are apportioned out among the family members and the deceased's rice bowl may be broken to symbolise the separation of living and dead.

The immediate family offer a banquet to the deceased on the day of burial. Though a relatively modest affair, it features many meat dishes. These high-status dishes are meant to honour the deceased and to placate any hungry spirits who might be lurking about. Oftentimes, when a chicken is prepared for this banquet the bereaved family eat the chicken but reserve the head for the deceased. A severed head, after all, graphically depicts separation. It is also believed that chicken signifies security and prosperity, welcome notions in a time of bereavement. It is probably no coincidence that the Hokkien word for chicken, *ke,* puns with and can sometimes stand for the word "family." Finally, wine is poured out at the grave site, as a libation for the deceased.

Soon after the funeral the family traditionally gives a great funeral banquet for the mourning relatives and friends. Certain traditional

births, weddings, deaths

guidelines are followed closely, and adhering to them is its own source of comfort in a time of emotion and sorrow. Offerings to the gods consist of meats only, each dish accompanied by wine. Offerings to ancestors consist of *caifan* dishes, that is rice (*fan*) with side dishes of meats and vegetables. (Ancestors, please note, are not ghosts. *Uncooked* rice is set out to placate ghosts; *cooked* rice is for ancestors.) However, during the course of the funeral banquet, meat dishes, usually reserved for the gods, are dedicated to the deceased. These often consist of a progression of four separate dishes, marking the transition of the deceased from the status of ghost to that of ancestor.

The aim of the living is threefold: to see that the deceased is harmoniously joined to both ancestors and the living; to placate gods, ancestors, and ghosts, ensuring prosperity and harmony on earth; and to reincorporate the deceased's family into the village life, which is accomplished by a satisfactory execution of the first two steps. In achieving each of these ends food plays vital roles as an offering, a message, and as a unifier.

The need to honour one's ancestors remains strong, and the continuation or re-emergence of many traditional values, practices, and beliefs can be seen throughout China. As state control over the countryside has loosened, these and many other customs are now being revived.

The line between public and private is quite vague among Chinese peasants, but there are many festive occasions that are by definition "public" in the sense that every household celebrates them at the same time and more or less in the same fashion. Of these, the most important is the Chinese Lunar New Year, since 1911 called the Spring Festival. Though the official government New Year falls on January 1st, the Lunar New Year falls, variously, between January 21 and February 19, marking the return of the sun and the beginning of the agricultural year. As such it is filled with meaning, hope, and desires as well as a fatalism which is normal among Chinese peasants. It is a holiday, then, that combines the significance of our Western Christmas, New Year's, and the more pagan aspects of our Easter holidays, and it is celebrated accordingly. Seen as a whole it has less religious foundation than in the festivals of the West.

Even under the austere government of the People's Republic, of the seven official public holidays the New Year holiday lasts for three days. The New Year holiday is everywhere seen as a time of clean slates, of fresh starts, of "out with the old and in with the new," of new resolutions and hoped-for auspicious omens. Many couples are married at this time. Old debts must be repaid. Homes are thoroughly cleaned as the dust of the past must not cling. Presents are exchanged, children are given small gifts of money, families get together. The gods and ancestors are propritiated: fathers and sons go to the family grave sites or shrines to invite the ancestral spirits into the home; pictures of the deceased are hung up, candles are lighted before them, incense sticks are lighted. Prayers are intoned for peace and prosperity. Above all, meals, feasts, and banquets featuring specially prepared foods are prepared and enjoyed.

In the northern areas, the weeks before the holiday are still devoted to the preparation of special foods for the festivities. Most typical of these are meat dumplings called *jiaozi*: chopped pork and cabbage, salt, ginger, spring onions, and ground white and black pepper in a thin wrapper of dough. Large households may prepare thousands of these dumplings; if refrigeration is lacking, they are simply allowed to freeze in special racks placed in unheated rooms as it gets very cold in northern China. They thaw and reheat nicely in boiling water, and are eaten with dipping sauces, soy sauce, and side dishes. In some southern areas the same dumplings are formed into the shape of the gold and silver ingots (*yuan bao*) that were used as money in ancient China; this augurs good fortune as well as good eating.

Dumplings are eaten as appetizers or side dishes. Most families slaughter a pig for the main New Year's feast and make bean curd, sausages, and special wine for the occasion. Regular markets are supplemented by hundreds of food stalls to satisfy the demand for *nian huo* or "New Year goods." The sumptuous main meal, on New Year's Eve, usually begins in the late afternoon. There will be lavish servings of vegetables (cabbage, turnips, dried mushrooms), pork, chicken, fish (the "trinity" of wealth, health, and luck), and shellfish, with every imaginable traditional condiment and delicacy such as thinly sliced jellyfish in vinegar and soy sauce. Wealthier families will serve sea cucumbers, shark's fin, bird's nests, and "lions' heads," made of giant pork meatballs. "Eight precious rice" is another traditional favourite: sweet sticky rice with lotus seeds, almond seeds, sliced red dates, candied fruits, sweet bean paste, and brown-sugar syrup. White rice is also served, as well as wine and other spirits. It all adds up to quite a feast. Small wonder that the mouths of the benevolent kitchen god icons are smeared with honey at this time of year.

The New Year's Eve feast is only the first of a number of sumptuous meals that follow, as distant relatives and close friends arrive over the next few days to help along the continuing celebrations. This is a time, too, to enjoy all sorts of snack foods: watermelon seeds, sesame candy, sliced salted eggs, and roasted peanuts as well as pears, oranges, and cakes. During this holiday the number of offerings to the gods and to one's ancestors are increased and made more substantial to give thanks for getting through another winter and to welcome in the New Year as auspiciously as possible. The hope is that the gods and ancestors, pleased and impressed by such bounty, will continue to send prosperity through the coming year.

In southern areas of China, where the seasonal changes are much less pronounced, the New Year is nonetheless celebrated. In the rice regions, rice is ritually washed clean over several days before the feasts begin. This is known as the "grain for ten thousand years" (*wan nian hang*); eating it during the New Year festivities is hoped to bring prosperity. More so than in the north, sweets like glutinous rice pudding and pastries of all sorts abound. A New Year cake, or *nian gao,* is an essential part of the celebration. Any self-respecting family will have several including a savoury steamed cake, a turnip cake, a nine-layer cake, and a "sticky cake." All through China at this time, dates and chestnuts are consumed together in abundance because the words for these treats sound like "early" and "coming of a son," one of all families' greatest wishes.

The regime in China has sanctioned the revival of a great number of ancient observances. The Lantern Festival, banned for years, is being celebrated again. At this extension of the New Year celebration, there are ingeniously decorated and brightly coloured lanterns, shaped like animals, and the fireworks which punctuate the ritual represent the return of the sun with its light and warmth. True, in northern China the lanterns may be made of ice, but even so, the sun is returning.

As always, food is central to the celebration. One custom calls for soft-boiled taro (a starchy root-like vegetable) to be eaten under the lantern lights. In the warmer cotton-growing areas, wheat flour is shaped into "cotton bolls" which are then placed in the fields. The villagers walk through the rows of seedling cotton plants with lanterns, burning incense to bring a good cotton crop. The "bolls" are then distributed among the children of the village, to protect them from all kinds of danger. In most areas, special treats, such as glutinous rice-flour balls filled with sweets, are prepared. Even though the lanterns may be electric-powered these days, the Lantern Festival seems destined to endure.

The names Spring Dragon Day, Clear and Bright Festival, Dragon Boat Day, Heaven's Gift Day, Double Seventh Night, Kitchen God's Day only hint at the variety and large number of other Chinese seasonal observances. Two of them are of such significance they must be noted.

The Mid-Autumn Festival, also called the Autumn Moon Festival, is a celebration of harvest time and a tribute to the declining sun. The idea is to give thanks for the bountiful food being stored for the long winter ahead and to say farewell to the sun, hoping that it will soon return. This is also the time of year when the full moon appears most luminous, the time when, as the Chinese say, "the moon is perfectly round." The core of this celebration features seemingly incessant family get-togethers, with, as always, a feast, but also the reciting of poetry, and the drinking of a bit more wine than usual. Ideally, this all takes place in the evening and outdoors, so that the moon may be properly seen and appreciated.

Melons and other round fruits are customarily placed outdoors as tributes to the moon. Yellow beans are also ritually offered to the rabbit which Chinese people see in the moon's features. But the most popular food, and the one specific to this holiday are mooncakes, a light-brown crusted cake of flour, with a sweet purée of red beans or lotus seeds as a filling. The cakes can be quite large and legend has it that Han rebels hid their weapons in such cakes before their successful revolt against the Mongols. Mooncakes, which come in round as well as square shapes, sometimes made with salted duck egg yolks, are still exchanged as gifts among family and friends to express wishes for a happy autumn and mild winter. It is a delightful custom, and a culinary adornment to this pleasant holiday.

In the spring, about the time of a late Western Easter or May Day celebration, the Qing Ming, "Pure Brightness," or "Tomb-Sweeping Festival," occurs. Clearly related to the renewal of life its emphasis is on proper reverence for the dead, whose influence in the next world can protect the living. At this time, ancestors' tombs, grave sites, and shrines must be cleaned, renovated, repainted, decorated, weeded, and otherwise refurbished. Just as the land in which the seeds are planted must be cultivated, so the tomb in which the ancestor has been "planted" must be cared for if good harvests are to come forth.

Solemn as the occasion is, the Chinese again turn duty into festival and naturally food plays its role. The expedition to the grave site is turned into an outing. After breakfast at home, the entire family treks to the site, carrying the tools and baskets needed to tidy up the area. Incense is also burned at the graveside and joss-paper is left behind to demonstrate publically that the family has attended to its duty. Offerings of food, tea, and wine are set up, and each member of the family makes three obeisances before the shrine or grave, then firecrackers mark the occasion. On returning home, the family feasts on a special meal commemorating the completion of their duties toward the ancestors. This meal must include at least one pork dish and grain. The pork is a tribute to the ancestors and a blessing to the living, the grain represents growth and renewal. The feast itself marks the separation of the living from the dead as well as their unity as a living or spiritual family.

From the most cheerful to the most solemn occasions, food unites people, the living and the ancestors, the native and the alien, families, friends, and strangers. It also serves to define the differences between them. The Chinese approach to food reminds us life is a banquet that deserves to go on as long as human civilisation endures.

ma po doufu
grandma chen's bean curd

Foodlore credits Grandma Chen as the creator of many traditional dishes in Sichuan. They show a genius for blending spicy, peppery, hot, tender, fresh, and fragrant ingredients so they can be tasted individually and as an ensemble in a kind of food fugue. Take this recipe for instance. Its essence lies in its seasonings and condiments, their quality, and the care taken in cooking them with the bean curd and beef. This achieves tenderness and contrasting spiciness, while adding garlic at the end of cooking enhances the balance of the whole dish.

450 g/1 lb fresh soft bean curd
2 tablespoons peanut oil
225 g/8 oz minced beef
2 tablespoons whole yellow bean sauce
2 tablespoons dark soy sauce
½ teaspoon salt
2 teaspoons ground red chilli powder
350 ml/12 fl oz chicken stock
2 tablespoons coarsely chopped garlic
2 teaspoons cornflour mixed with 1 tablespoon water
GARNISH
1 tablespoon Sichuan peppercorns, roasted and finely ground

Gently cut the bean curd into 4-cm/½-in cubes.

    Heat a wok or large frying pan until hot. Add the oil and beef and stir-fry for 2 minutes to partially cook. Put in the whole yellow bean sauce, soy sauce, and salt and continue to stir-fry for another minute. Add the chilli powder and continue to stir-fry for 30 seconds. Pour in the stock, add the bean curd and cook for 3 minutes. Stir in the garlic and cornflour mixture and cook for another minute. Ladle the mixture into a serving bowl, garnish with the Sichuan peppercorns, and serve.

Serves 4 as part of a Chinese meal, or 2 as a single dish.

family traditions – recipes

jing shao doufu
brown sauce doufu

Despite its simplicity, this was one of the most flavourful dishes I enjoyed at the Chen Ma Po Doufu restaurant in Chengdu. The soft texture of fresh bean curd is delightful to the palate, like chilled freshly baked custard. After braising it briefly in the sauce below, the bean curd takes on a brown colour and a quite delicious flavour. Serve the dish with rice.

450 g/1 lb fresh soft bean curd
1½ tablespoons peanut oil
1 tablespoon finely chopped peeled
    fresh ginger root
2 teaspoons finely chopped garlic
2 tablespoons dark soy sauce
1 tablespoon yellow
    bean sauce
1 teaspoon chilli
    bean sauce
1 teaspoon sugar
2 teaspoons sesame oil

Carefully drain the bean curd and cut it into 5-cm/2-in cubes using a sharp knife. Lay the cubes over kitchen paper and continue to drain for another 5 minutes.

Heat a wok or large frying pan until hot. Add the oil, ginger, and garlic and stir-fry for 10 seconds.

Then add the soy sauce, bean sauces, sugar, and sesame oil and stir-fry for another 10 seconds. Now add the cubed bean curd and gently heat it in the sauce, mixing thoroughly. Turn the heat to medium and continue to cook for 5 minutes.

Ladle the bean curd and sauce into a serving bowl and serve at once with rice.

Serves 4 as part of a Chinese meal, or 2 as a single dish.

chao qincai
stir-fried celery

Quick and simple, this family dish from Sichuan is also a good one to serve guests. You can use European celery or the Chinese variety, which is smaller, slightly tougher, and with a looser stalk than the European version. It is of the same species but the product of fifteen hundred years of oriental cultivation. In Chinese, European celery is inscrutably called "Western parsley." Certain traditionalists maintain that the European version is inadequate in Chinese recipes, but I cannot agree, just use the freshest celery you can find of whatever provenance.

700 g/1½ lb Chinese celery or European celery
2 tablespoons peanut oil
1 teaspoon salt
3 tablespoons finely chopped garlic
125 ml/4 fl oz chicken stock

Separate the stalks of the celery from the center and with a sharp knife, remove the strings from the tougher outside stalks. Then cut the celery into 25-mm/1-in lengths.

Heat a wok or large frying pan until hot. Add the oil, salt, and garlic and stir-fry for 20 seconds. Put in the celery and continue to stir-fry for 2 minutes. Finally, pour in the chicken stock and continue to cook until most of the liquid has evaporated. Serve at once.

Serves 4 as part of a Chinese meal, or 2 as a single dish.

qinggua fenpi
bean starch noodles with cucumbers

Although we rely on dried bean starch noodles in the West, in food markets around Beijing, fresh bean starch noodles can be bought to assemble a quick dish at home. My friends, the Qu family, made this refreshing vegetarian dish on one of my visits. So delicious and quickly made, the bean starch noodles provide a firm texture that contrasts beautifully with the thin, crisp slivers of cucumbers. The seasoning is inspired: soy sauce and vinegar with just a touch of sugar and sesame oil.

125 g/4 oz dried bean starch noodle sheets or
   dried bean thread noodles
450 g/1 lb cucumbers
1 tablespoon sesame oil
1½ tablespoons dark soy sauce
1 teaspoon light soy sauce
3 tablespoons white rice vinegar
2 teaspoons sugar

Soak the bean starch sheets or bean thread noodles in warm water for 15 minutes, then cut them into 12-mm/½-in strips. If you are using noodles, leave them whole.

Peel the cucumbers and discard the skin peelings. Then peel strips from each side of the cucumber, stopping when you reach the seeded center. You should have a pile of cucumber shavings.

Blanch the bean starch strips or noodles in boiling water for 2 minutes, remove and drain well. Toss immediately with sesame oil and place inside a large bowl. Add the cucumber strips, the dark and light soy sauces, vinegar, and sugar. Mix well and serve.

Serves 4 as part of a Chinese meal, or 2 as a single dish.

chun juan
spring rolls

These nutritious snacks, as their name suggests, symbolise and commemorate the coming oj the spring season. They are among the traditional foods eaten in China on New Year's Eve, which, by the Chinese lunar calendar, marks the end of the winter season; such foods as spring rolls and dumplings are always at hand then for family and for visitors.

The spring roll wrappers are thin and almost transparent, but they are firm enough to hold a substantial morsel of finely chopped meat, meat and vegetables, or just vegetables. In keeping with the Chinese tradition that maintains that for the first two days of the new year no work, including housework, should be done, they are especially useful because they can.be made ahead but retain their flavour when frozen. In northern China, where the below-freezing days of February allow it, the prepared rolls are easily kept on trays outdoors until ready for cooking.

Spring rolls are also enjoyed all year round. I helped with this particular recipe in the early summer months at the Qu home in Beijing. The wrappers are rarely homemade but purchased at a local store. In them, my hostess told me she used almost the same filling as for her dumplings. Although you'd think they would taste similar, the different cooking techniques make spring rolls quite different from dumplings in taste as well as texture. I ate and enjoyed far too many of Mrs. Qu's, dipping them into a zesty black vinegar sauce.

225 g/8 oz cabbage, finely chopped and blanched
125 g/4 oz minced pork
125 g/4 oz medium-sized uncooked prawns, peeled
   and finely chopped
25 g/1 oz dried black mushrooms, soaked, stems removed,
   and finely chopped
3 tablespoons dark soy sauce
1 tablespoon rice wine or dry sherry
1 tablespoon sesame oil
1 teaspoon salt
1 teaspoon freshly ground black pepper
1 egg, beaten and mixed with 1 tablespoon water
1 package spring roll skins, thawed if frozen
850 ml/1½ pt peanut oil

In a medium-sized bowl, combine the cabbage, pork, prawns, mushrooms, soy sauce, rice wine or sherry, sesame oil, salt, and pepper and mix thoroughly.Combine the egg and water in a small bowl. Place about 4 tablespoons of cabbage filling on each spring roll skin and fold in each side and roll up tightly. Use the egg mixture to seal the edge.

family traditions – recipes

Heat a wok or large frying pan until hot and add the oil. When the oil is quite hot, gently drop in as many spring rolls as will fit easily in one layer. Carefully fry them in batches until the spring rolls are golden brown on the outside and cooked inside, about 4 minutes. Adjust the heat as necessary.Remove the spring rolls with a slotted spoon and drain on kitchen paper. Serve them at once, while they are still hot and crispy.

Makes 15 to 20 spring rolls.

chao doujiao
stir-fried green beans with garlic

Crunchy, sweet green beans, stir-fried with gently pungent garlic is another speedy dish enjoyed throughout China. It exemplifies the Chinese ideal of simple but healthy, delicious food. Several varieties of fresh green beans can be used, the most dramatic being the famous Chinese yard long beans. Some do actually attain such a length, but are of course cut into stir-fry-size pieces.

450 g/1 lb Chinese long beans or any fresh green beans
1½ tablespoons peanut oil
½ teaspoon salt
2 tablespoons coarsely chopped garlic
1 teaspoon finely chopped ginger
125 ml/4 fl oz chicken stock

Trim the ends of the beans. If you are using Chinese long beans, cut them into 7.5-cm3-in lengths.

Heat a wok or large frying pan until hot, add the oil and salt, and the garlic and fresh ginger and stir-fry for 30 seconds. Add the green beans and chicken stock and continue to cook for 4 minutes or until the beans are just tender and most of the liquid has evaporated. Serve at once.

Serves 4 as part of a Chinese meal, or 2 as a single dish.

yang qiezi
stuffed aubergine

Of the many dishes I enjoyed in Beijing, this was among the most pleasing. Aubergine, of which there are many varieties, was introduced many centuries ago, probably from India. They are best eaten immediately after being picked as they can quickly become quite bitter. The ones that the Qu family served me were in season and at their peak of flavour. Stuffing added substance to the subtle aubergine taste and frying gave them a crusty exterior. Enjoy them straight from the wok, for they tend to soften up if they sit too long, though they remain delicious. The stuffing can be made well ahead of time, but dip the vegetables in the batter only when you are about to fry them.

BATTER
4 tablespoons cornflour
2 tablespoons unbleached white all-purpose flour
1 teaspoon baking powder
2 eggs, beaten
2 tablespoons beer or water
FILLING
125 g/4 oz minced pork
125 g/4 oz medium-sized uncooked prawns, peeled and
   finely chopped
3 tablespoons finely chopped spring onions
2 tablespoons dark soy sauce
1 tablespoon rice wine or dry sherry
1 tablespoon sesame oil
1 teaspoon salt
1 teaspoon freshly ground black pepper
450 g/1 lb Chinese aubergines (about 4 medium-sized)
850 ml/1½ pt peanut oil

In a medium-sized bowl, mix the batter ingredients until smooth and set aside to rest for 5 minutes.

In a medium-sized bowl, combine the pork, prawns, onions, soy sauce, rice wine or sherry, sesame oil, salt, and pepper and mix together thoroughly.

Slice the aubergines into 6-mm/¼-in rounds. (If you are using the larger variety, cut them into rounds, and then quarter them.) With a knife, spread a thin layer of the meat filling on one side of an aubergine slice and place another one on top and press together like a small sandwich. Continue this procedure until you have used all the aubergine rounds.

Heat a wok or large frying pan with the oil. Using cooking tongs and chopsticks, dip the stuffed rounds into the batter and then drop each gently into the hot oil. Be careful of splatters. Place as many rounds into the wok as will fit easily on one layer. Turn them gently and fry them until they are golden brown on both sides and cooked inside, about 4 minutes. Adjust your heat to keep the oil very hot but not enough to burn the rounds. Remove the rounds with a slotted spoon and drain on kitchen paper. Cook and serve the aubergine rounds in several batches so they are always hot and crispy.

Serves 4 as part of a Chinese meal, or 2 as a single dish.

leng pan
tomato and egg summer salad

Without a doubt, the Qu family cooked the best meals I had in Beijing. Made from the freshest ingredients, the dishes were simple and traditional, yet burst with flavour. We enjoyed them in a warm, friendly ambience, with a hospitality that comes only with homecooked food. One early, warm summer evening, Mrs. Qu prepared a quick and easy salad that was unusual but delightfully refreshing. It consisted of fresh tomatoes and two types of eggs, hard-boiled chicken eggs and preserved duck eggs, also known as thousand-year-old eggs. Buried in fine ash, salt, and lime for one hundred days, the eggs emerge with an aspic-like blackened jelly surrounding a greenish yolk, having been slow cooked by the action of the lime. Their distinctive, pungent flavour and aroma is reminiscent of strong cheese.

2 fresh eggs
2 preserved (thousand-year-old) eggs
450 g/1 lb ripe tomatoes
1½ tablespoons sugar

Boil the fresh eggs for exactly 10 minutes. Remove them from the pan with a slotted spoon, immerse them immediately in cold water, and crack them lightly with a back of a spoon. Let them sit for at least 10 minutes in the cold water, changing the water two or three times. Gently peel the eggs. With a sharp knife, cut them in half.

Rinse the preserved eggs in cold water, peel them, and cut them in the same manner.

With a sharp knife, cut the tomatoes into thin slices. Arrange them, slightly overlapping, in the middle of a large round platter. Sprinkle them evenly with the sugar.

Then arrange a boiled egg half alternating with a preserved egg half around the edge of the platter. Serve at once.

Serves 4 as part of a Chinese meal, or 2 as a single dish.

jiaozi-guotie
boiled and pan-fried meat dumplings

Boiled grains such as rice normally provide most of the calories in the modern Chinese diet. In the north, wheat is the preferred grain and dumplings, boiled or pan-fried, are a favourite food. Whole grain flour made from hard red wheat is the rule; freshly ground it makes delicious, healthy dumpling pastry.

Dumplings are made in Beijing restaurants and homes. Simple treats, I think they make a far better, more delicious meal than can be had at the more fancy restaurants that often cater to tourists. The best are said to be made in private homes, each family priding itself on its own version, its own savoury stuffings. This particular recipe is from the Qu family in Beijing. In their small kitchen we shared views on food and cooking as we prepared the dumplings, a family activity involving several generations of helpers and guests like myself. The family showed me the two basic ways of cooking them, boiling half for jiaozi and pan-frying the others for guotie in which they acquire a crisp brown crust on one side. Enjoyed throughout the year, these dumplings are also a traditional delicacy at New Year when families get together to make and eat hundreds of them. In keeping with the Chinese approach that dining is a sharing experience, the dumplings are always eaten with a variety of communal dipping sauces such as vinegar, soy sauce, and chilli bean sauce or chilli oil.

Once made, the uncooked dumplings freeze well; in fact Mrs. Qu tells me that during the long northern Chinese winters, she uses a window box as a freezer for them, thawing them thoroughly before cooking.

DOUGH SKIN
275 g/10 oz unbleached white flour
225-350 ml/8-12 fl oz very hot water
FILLING
225 g/8 oz cabbage, finely chopped
125 g/4 oz minced pork
125 g/4 oz medium-sized uncooked prawns, peeled
    and finely chopped
25 g/1 oz black mushrooms, soaked, stems removed,
    and finely chopped
1 tablespoon light soy sauce
1 tablespoon dark soy sauce
1 tablespoon rice wine or dry sherry
1 tablespoon sesame oil
1 teaspoon salt
1 teaspoon freshly ground black pepper
3 tablespoons peanut oil, for the wok
225 ml/8 fl oz very hot water, for the wok
DIPPING SAUCES
Chilli bean sauce
White rice vinegar
Dark soy sauce

Place the flour in a large mixing bowl. Add the hot water in a steady

family traditions

stream, mixing all the while with a fork or chopsticks until most of the water has been incorporated. If the mixture seems dry, add more water. The dough should be moist but not sticky. Remove the dough from the bowl and knead it on a floured board until it is smooth, about 5 minutes. Return the dough to the bowl, cover with a damp cloth, and let it rest.

In a medium-sized bowl, combine the cabbage, pork, prawns, mushrooms, soy sauces, rice wine or sherry, sesame oil, salt, and pepper and mix thoroughly. Set the mixture aside.

Knead the dough on a lightly floured board, dusting with a little flour if it is sticky. Form the dough into a roll about 45 cm/18 in long and about 25 mm/1 in in diameter. Take a sharp knife and cut the roll into 4 equal lengths. Cut each length into 8 pieces to make 36 equal segments.

Press each segment with the palm of your hand and then roll it into a 9-cm/3½-in round. Continue rolling out all the rounds, covering them with a damp cloth.

Pinch one side of the dough until you have four pleats along the side, and the dough is rounded and shell-like. Place 2 teaspoons of filling in the center of each round, making sure the filling fills the hollow. You may add more filling if necessary. Then fold the dough over the filling, pinching the two sides together until you have a half-moon dumpling. Continue until you have filled all the rounds. The dumplings can be frozen at this point until ready to use.

To fry the dumplings, heat a wok or large frying pan until hot. Add the peanut oil, then add the dumplings, pleated edge up, in a single layer. They should be crowded together. Cook the dumplings over medium heat until they are lightly browned on the bottoms. Pour in the very hot water, cover tightly, and cook vigorously for 2 minutes. Turn the heat down to a simmer and continue to cook for another 8 to 10 minutes or until most of the water has evaporated. Uncover the pan and continue cooking until all the moisture has evaporated and the pan is sizzling again and the dumplings are golden brown and crisp on the bottoms. Remove to a serving platter and serve at once with the dipping sauces.

If you are boiling the dumplings, drop them into a large pot of salted, boiling water for 2 minutes. Remove from the heat and leave them in the water for about 15 minutes. Remove the dumplings with

family traditions – recipes

a slotted spoon and serve them the same way as the fried dumplings.

Makes about 36 dumplings

guizhou lianai doufu
guizhou-style bean curd

Private homes are the places I remember best for eating in China. The Guan family of Kunming, in Yunnan, served a feast of twelve superb dishes, but the bean curd course captured my heart.

Vegetarians will delight in this dish as a main course or serve it as a side dish with or without meat. It can be prepared in advance, as it reheats nicely. You might want to reduce the chilli by half the first time you prepare it. I have a love for very hot foods.

450 g/1 lb firm bean curd
450 ml/16 fl oz oil, for deep-frying
FILLING
1 tablespoon peanut oil
3 tablespoons finely chopped fresh coriander
2 tablespoons finely chopped garlic
2 tablespoons finely chopped spring onions
1½ tablespoons finely chopped peeled fresh ginger root
1 to 2 teaspoons red chilli flakes or ½ to 1 teaspoon chilli powder
1 tablespoon dark soy sauce
1 teaspoon sugar
½ teaspoon salt
½ teaspoon sesame oil
SAUCE
1 tablespoon peanut oil
1 tablespoon finely chopped garlic
1 tablespoon finely chopped peeled fresh ginger root
1 tablespoon dark soy sauce
1 tablespoon rice wine or dry sherry
2 teaspoons light soy sauce

1 teaspoon sugar
225 ml/8 fl oz chicken stock
1 teaspoon cornflour mixed with 1 teaspoon water
2 teaspoons sesame oil

Drain the bean curd and cut it into 5-cm/2-in squares. Leave them to drain for 10 minutes on kitchen paper.

Heat a wok or large frying pan until hot. Add the tablespoon of oil and the rest of the filling ingredients and stir-fry for 1 minute. Transfer these ingredients to a bowl and allow them to cool thoroughly.

Heat a wok or large frying pan until hot. Add the oil for deep-frying and when hot, cook the bean curd on both sides until it is golden brown. Remove the bean curd squares from the wok, drain them well on kitchen paper and allow them to cool thoroughly. Discard the oil.

Take each bean curd square and split it open slightly with a knife on one side to form a pocket. Place a spoonful of cooked filling in each of the pockets. Continue to fill the squares.

Wipe the wok clean, reheat, and add the tablespoon of oil for the sauce. Then add the garlic and ginger, and stir-fry for 30 seconds. Then add the rest of the sauce ingredients except the cornflour mixture and sesame oil. Bring the mixture to the boil, return the fried bean curd pieces to the wok and cook over medium heat for 3 minutes. Add the cornflour mixture, stir gently, and then add the sesame oil. Give the mixture a final turn and serve at once.

Serves 4 as part of a Chinese meal, or 2 as a single dish.

mayi shang shu
bean thread noodles with pork

This classic Sichuan family dish has the rather fanciful name of "Ants Climbing a Tree". When mixed with bean thread noodles, the ground pork is said to look like ants climbing a tree. It is excellent, and made in minutes.

125 g/4 oz dried bean thread noodles
225 g/8 oz minced pork
1 tablespoon dark soy sauce
2 teaspoons rice wine or dry sherry
2 teaspoons sesame oil
1 tablespoon peanut oil
1 tablespoon finely chopped fresh ginger root
2 tablespoons finely chopped garlic
4 tablespoons finely chopped spring onions
2 tablespoons dark soy sauce
1 tablespoon chilli bean suace
½ teaspoon salt
2 teaspoons sugar
2 teaspoons sesame oil
450 ml/16 fl oz chicken stock

GARNISH
3 tablespoons finely chopped
   spring onions

Soak the noodles in. a large bowl of warm water for 15 minutes. When they are soft, drain them and discard the water. Combine the meat with the soy sauce, rice wine or sherry, and sesame oil.

Heat a wok or large frying pan until hot. Add the peanut oil and meat mixture. Stir-fry the mixture for 2 minutes. Then add the ginger, garlic, and onions and continue to stir-fry for 2 minutes.

Add the rest of the ingredients and the noodles. Bring the mixture to a simmer, mix well, and cook until most of the liquid has evaporated. Ladle into a large serving bowl, garnish with the spring onions and serve.

Serves 4 as part of a Chinese meal, or 2 as a single dish.

CHAPTER 7
CITY and COUNTRY FARE

O soul, come back! Why should you go so far?
All your household have come to do you honour; all kinds of good foods
are ready:
Bitter, salt, sour, hot, and sweet: there are dishes of all flavours.
            The Songs of the South, Ch'u Tz'u

The whole of China is vast, mysterious and seemingly unending. It would have taken me a dozen lifetimes to visit all of it, traveling up to the Tibetan highlands, and to the wastes of Inner Mongolia. But what I saw left me with an impression of people struggling against problems of poverty, lack of industry, sometimes primitive hygiene and other conditions, and barely functional kitchens. I had the luxury of a car and combination driver/guide, as well as the companionship of photographer Leong Ka Tai and his assistant. I also travelled by air. The planes were not exactly clean by Western standards and sometimes operated on a schedule I could not fathom. Still, like the trains, they carry a variety of Chinese people on the move including businessmen, people visiting relatives, and students going to Beijing. On one flight I saw a prosperous peasant grandfather going to visit his grandchildren on what was perhaps his first plane ride.

It constantly impressed me how tied to a common rural tradition of planting, harvesting, tending livestock, raising chickens, pigs, geese, and ducks most of the country seemed to be. Carts and trucks seemed constantly to be on the road bearing goods to sell at market or bringing other food home. Despite regional differences, such as between the minority peoples of southwest China and the majority Han Chinese, or the lush green of the south and the dried barren look of the north, there was nevertheless a sense of unity. There are foods and methods of transporting them that one finds everywhere in China, even in the most remote rural regions.

Most city dwellers are quite friendly, very willing to help or assist. The city style of dressing seems modern with touches of Western influence and yet uniquely Chinese. Conveniences and toys of the twentieth century such as radios, television, and refrigerators seemed to suggest a better material future. Yet food stalls and open markets harken back to China's ancient past. The country is full of these wonderful contrasts.

By far and away the best food I have eaten during my recent visits to China has been in private homes, whether in the countryside or in the cities or towns. All these meals were prepared with skill and care. They varied from place to place, and they reflected seasonal availability as refrigeration and processed foods are still generally the exception: only 10 percent of households have refrigerators. However, certain general patterns can be observed as one experiences Chinese family home cooking.

I was very fortunate in being able to spend time with family and friends, observing at first hand how they prepare and enjoy their "daily bread." Their food is quite different from what one sees in the "official," state-run restaurants or in the model families the government selects to demonstrate one or another aspect of the "new" China. My kind and generous friends and family shared not only their food with me but also their aspirations and yearning for a better future for their children.

The first impression of Chinese cities is that they are crowded, polluted, noisy, and chaotic. Unfortunately, this first impression is quite an accurate one. City life is one constant round of a huge number of busy people bustling about, making a living at a rather frenetic pace in the face of formidable obstacles. The only blessing is that China's delayed "development" has meant that almost none of the general population own automobiles. Otherwise Beijing would be as polluted as Mexico City.

China's population doubled from one-half billion in 1950 to one billion by 1985. Whatever government was in power during those decades would have faced enormous difficulties with such a huge population explosion. As agricultural mechanisation proceeded and as fewer hands were required in the fields, the cities became magnets to China's hundreds of millions of peasants. Compared with the rural areas, jobs are more readily found in the urban areas, more opportunities exist for entrepreneurial initiatives, the schools are better and more numerous, medical care is more available, and cultural life is more vibrant. It is thus understandable that the movement from countryside to city continues today, despite governmental efforts to control it.

One result of this influx is that there is an average living space of sixty-four feet per person in smaller Chinese cities and even less than that in the larger ones, or about one small room for every two persons. Most apartments have kitchens that must be shared with other families. While there is usually electricity, albeit with "brownouts," few places have bathtubs and less than half have indoor toilets. Even this standard of housing is horribly scarce; young couples intending to marry often must wait many years before obtaining accommodations necessary to start family life. Almost all housing is state owned and its shortage has been exacerbated by the fact that rents are artificially low, between one and five percent of the average worker's salary. Another problem is that much of the housing is in a very dilapidated condition. Only in the last ten years has the government shifted major resources to the housing problem.

It is not surprising, then, that urban dwellers in China live much of their lives outside the home. This is particularly true in areas with moderate or subtropical climates. People throng the tea shops, the public squares, the streets, the food stalls and restaurants – conversing,

chinese cities

playing mahjong and cards, walking, and, above all, eating; more than half of the average urban household budget is spent on food. By sunrise the markets are already selling fresh vegetables brought in from the countryside, so many families shop daily before going to work to secure the choicest foods. Working people have two-hour lunch periods and most prefer to eat at home. Because there are few modern conveniences, food preparation takes up much of the family's time. This is a chore, but I shudder at the thought that this might change, that the same time could be spent watching reruns on television while eating processed or prepared foods.

My friends, the Qus, exemplify urban life in China today. Mrs. Qu is a retired English teacher, while Mr. Qu works as the deputy director of the Chinese Academy of Fishery Sciences. Their son works in the electronics industry, while the daughter teaches. They live in a rather large, sparsely decorated three-bedroom apartment in Beijing. I would consider them rather prosperous with their colour television and small refrigerator. The family income is about two hundred yuan a month, supplemented by Mrs. Qu's private English classes, and they pay but *five* yuan a month for rent! The apartments in the building are rented from the municipal authorities.

Their separate but tiny kitchen is hard to imagine with more than one wok in it, but it's used to prepare most of their meals. The Qus are also fortunate because a small street market is a few minutes' walk away from their apartment complex. When we went there, stem lettuce, a popular vegetable, and aubergines were in season, fresh from the nearby countryside, and, as with most markets, we early shoppers got the best choice of vegetables. Their diet is varied, wholesome, and imaginatively prepared. I enjoyed some of the most delicate, subtly flavoured *jiaozi* (meat-filled dumplings) I've had anywhere in the world. Fish is eaten occasionally, but it is expensive and reserved for special occasions. Pork, they told me, has been much more available in recent years and they eat it regularly. However, vegetables and bean curd dominate the Qu family table, simply because they enjoy the freshness of seasonal vegetables.

I was also privileged to enjoy the hospitality of another family, the Guans, who live in the rather remote southwestern part of China, in

Kunming, Yunnan, a city of more than one million. I perceive the Guans as a typical contemporary family, their lives reflecting the social changes which have swept over China in the past forty years. Mrs. Guan was born in the city of Guiyang, county seat of Guizhou, on the border of Hunan arid Yunnan provinces. Forty years ago it was a rather sleepy provincial town; today it. bustles with almost one million inhabitants. Her husband, Mr. Guan Nafen, was originally from a peasant family in Yangguang in Guangdong province, not far, in fact, from the Hom ancestral home in Kaiping (Hoiping). His grandfather had emigrated to San Francisco, as did my great-grandfather. Returning after a few years with money he had saved, he was able to buy some plots of land for his impoverished family. The land was in the Pearl River delta, site of some of the world's richest and most efficiently worked farmland.

Although the Guan family were subsequently better off, conditions in China from the 1920s on were extremely unsettled. Civil wars, piracy, invasion, and again civil war characterised those decades. Mr. Guan himself spent some of the war years in Hong Kong, continuing his education as best he could. Like many young men he was disillusioned by conditions in China and, in 1949, at the age of eighteen, he joined the People's Liberation Army. He marched with the army from Guangzhou to Kunming. In 1954, he met his future wife and they were married in 1958.

During the Cultural Revolution, however, the Guan family suffered because of Mr. Guan's landlord status; it was because of Mrs. Guan's impeccable peasant credentials and Mr. Guan's military service and Communist party membership that he and the family escaped major duress. Today, he is one of a cadre of the Yunnan Medical Institute and a department leader; Mrs. Guan is a doctor and professor specialising in eye disorders. Mr. Guan described to me some of the recent changes that have benefitted the people of the area. Because of improvements in farm and manufacturing productivity and the rise of a profitable tourist trade, there is more – and more varied – food, clothing, and job opportunities. The relaxation of central controls has allowed for more local initiatives and innovations. The morale of the people, Mr. Guan said, is much higher than it has been for a long time.

urban life in china

The Guans are comparatively affluent by Chinese standards. They live in a roomy three-bedroom apartment with a small kitchen and a dining room. Their son, Guan Yuan, was recently married and he and his new wife live with them while awaiting assignment to their own place. Their daughter is a nurse and she too lives in the apartment along with her husband and their infant son. It means that three units of extended family in three bedrooms live together as the Chinese have for millennia. The working day begins at six a.m., with a lunch break from noon until two, and then back to work until six. They all bicycle to work, cars being out of the reach of most of the population. The buses are crowded and slow, and the Guans told me that except in heavy rain they all enjoy biking.

As the background of the Guans themselves might suggest, the population of the Kunming, Yunnan, area is a melange of different ethnic and regional minorites. Yunnan, in fact, has the most varied mix of ethnic minorities in all of China. In 1949, the area was rather sparsely populated and consisted mostly of Chinese ethnic minority, or non-Han, peoples. After 1949, the central government initiated a policy designed to induce people to migrate there from other parts of China, especially the crowded eastern regions. These migrants brought with them their own regional cuisines, which explains the amalgamation of food styles observable there today. The food prepared in homes and in restaurants is a combination of these different influences and this is one of the region's characteristics that appeal to me most.

In the Guan household, for example, Cantonese and Yunnan approaches to food are evident even though, or perhaps because, the mixture of the two has been smooth and in keeping with Chinese traditions and techniques. Both Mr. and Mrs. Guan do the family cooking in the home, depending upon whose schedule is least heavy. Kunming is surrounded by a very productive countryside whose cultivators keep the food preferences of all of the area's minority groups well supplied. This is particularly the case in recent years. Once the central government relaxed its rigid production controls and directives, enterprising peasants began growing the speciality crops for which they knew a profitable market existed.

I went shopping with the Guans several times and noted specialities such as fresh goat cheese, dried goat cheese in curled sheets, and so-called "stinky bean curd" that has been allowed to curdle and to acquire a strong cheese-like aroma and flavour. There were fresh vegetables in profusion. As I sipped smooth, delicious yogurt sold by a street vendor, I observed the distinct Muslim influence: goat meat and dried beef accompanied our goat cheese and fresh vegetables.

For one special occasion, Mrs. Guan prepared her version of Yunnan clay-pot steamed chicken. Most commercial or restaurant versions begin by adding water but Mrs. Guan's recipe develops the broth solely from the steam which condenses through the chimney of the clay pot. She allows the chicken to steam for four hours. Meanwhile, the dried goat cheese is soaked in water to soften it, then dried with towels before being deep-fried into savoury chips. Other members of the family helped by preparing savoury Yunnan mushrooms, rice, and the other foods which made up the *twelve*-course feast that was centred around the delicious chicken casserole.

Another time, Mrs. Guan made a regional speciality whose popular name is "Love Bean Curd of Guizhou." This delicious red-cooked bean curd is stuffed with a spicy blend of chilli pepper flakes, soy sauce, garlic, ginger, and a special herb called *yu dan chao*. Irresistible, tasty and satisfying, Mrs. Guan told me the dish is nutritious as well.

At other times, I enjoyed the Guans' version of mild goat cheese stuffed with Yunnan ham – another regional speciality. This was served with a delectable dish of minced pork and fresh local chilli peppers. For snacks there were fried goat cheese and some unusual chips made from chick pea flour. I found especially memorable a Cantonese dish of minced pork with Chinese yellow chives, and a dish of sliced beef with a kind of broccoli much more assertive than the broccoli of Guangdong. Mr. Guan told me he had never sampled goat cheese or developed a taste for spicy foods until he arrived in Yunnan. These are definitely not Cantonese preferences, but other dishes did evoke Guangdong memories for me: mangetouts and fresh water spinach stir-fried with garlic.

Our meals were always accompanied by Chinese beer, though I was a bit dismayed to see the younger people drinking cola. Beer does contain some alcohol, but it doesn't destroy the palate. Fresh fruit dishes ended our meals, the local watermelons being particularly sweet

a country of contrasts

and refreshing, and hot tea was always served after the food.

In the Guans' tiny kitchen there are only two gas rings on the stove. Consequently, every step of the meal is carefully thought out beforehand. Last minute stir-frying is kept to a minimum and cooking techniques are carefully plotted. The Guans have a small refrigerator, which sits in the dining room, and they have an electric rice cooker, the height of urban culinary sophistication in China. The first allows them to prepare some foods well ahead of time; the second frees up their gas rings for other dishes.

Even with these limitations, the Guans produce gastronomical delights. Their gracious hospitality and the excellence of their table made my visit memorable. I wish this level of urban life for all the Chinese people.

From Kunming, I travelled north to Sichuan, home of the fabled hot and spicy cuisine. Despite my Cantonese background, I have always enjoyed the fiery spices of Sichuan cookery. Whatever the reason, on my first trip to China years ago, as soon as I could, I travelled to Sichuan to sample the genuine taste of that cuisine. Visiting the markets, food stalls, and restaurants, I indulged my passion for its spicy food. One thing I noticed was how much more pungent and aromatic Sichuan peppercorns are in Sichuan: they lose so much in being shipped so far. There the peppercorns and freshly ground dried chillies have a richer, deeper dimension than the same spices elsewhere. I decided then that these two ingredients constitute the essence of the Sichuan style, and I have ever since tried to recapture it in my own attempts at Sichuan cooking.

Thus, early in 1989, when I returned to Sichuan, my Sichuanese friends helped me understand the elusive essence of their cooking. Their cooperation and guidance led me to a memorable birthday feast in the town of Baoguang, about an hour's ride from Chengdu, the largest city in Sichuan. It turned out to be quite an introduction to yet another facet of Chinese life, that of the countryside.

Despite 22 cities with a population of a million or more, China remains an overwhelmingly agrarian country. To generalize about so many people in so many and so varied regions and locales is inevitably going to be misleading. Nevertheless, there are certain patterns of rural life that in general characterize the Chinese peasant community.

Under the reforms that have been instituted over the past decade, the peasants have been given a more personal stake in the land they work. While they do not own the land, they have been guaranteed a form of tenure that allows them to plan realistically over several planting seasons and to gain materially from the labours they perform. The state permits peasants to produce whatever crops or products they wish once the state-required quotas of basic foods have been taken care of. This has allowed so-called "market forces" to come into play, meaning a vastly increased production of the fruits, vegetables, and speciality foods the Chinese have always loved. It has also meant improved transport and marketing practices and the emergence of a bustling trade from countryside to urban areas.

The center of village life has also shifted from the communal organisation back to the family as the key economic unit. Those families that are located near urban markets or seaports, that have sons to work the land, and have control of the better lands, or that are more industrious, frugal, innovative, and lucky, have been able to improve their material situation. This decade has also witnessed the rise of the so-called "ten-thousand-yuan households," the equivalent of Chinese millionaires. It does not appear that this economic-social process will soon end, although material ostentation may be officially condemned after the most recent political repression.

The majority of people anywhere, any time, will not be millionaires. And the majority of the Chinese peasants are impoverished and have limited opportunities for improvement. However, with the relaxation of central control traditional practices are reviving. The village, that middle ground between city and country, where peasant houses cluster closely together, is much as it was fifty years ago. People's lives are governed by the natural cycles of the seasonal requirements. Prosperity levels vary within the village, the province, and the region. Peasants will continue to pursue expedient sidelines in any and all trades, in order to eke out a better living than the preceding generation's. I couldn't escape seeing the poverty in the countryside alongside the compelling beauty of the land as a sad contrast. Infant mortality rates are higher; medical and education costs are higher there, too. Life is much harder for rural women than for their city sisters. There may be

kunming and sichuan

more physical living space in the countryside but the urban areas afford more room for the human spirit.

The standard of living in the countryside is evolving, but very slowly. The supreme test confronting the Chinese nation today is how to move from an overwhelmingly rural, traditional society to a more urban, innovative one. The enormity of the task is overwhelming. One can only hope that the inevitable trauma of such a profound transformation is as mild or as painless as possible for the Chinese people. They deserve good fortune.

Traveling with friends by rented car through the Sichuan countryside that morning, such thoughts went through my mind. On my lap I held the sweet cake I was to present to Mr. Huang Haijia, whose birthday it was. We passed by miles of rice fields before arriving at the gate of the family home, through which we were led into a large open courtyard in the front of the thatch-roofed house. It was immediately clear to me that this was a better-off household. (I learned later that the family possessed two televisions and an assortment of radios and cassette players.) The home was rather large, if modestly furnished, having three bedrooms, a roomy but primitive kitchen, and a small dining room. The courtyard served as the "family room." Mr. Huang and his wife, Ge Wenfeng, were from the Longhu area, Sichuan born and bred. I had some difficulty following their thick dialect, but they graciously welcomed us all and I soon felt right at home. The Huangs have five children, all of them in attendance that day, along with their eldest daughter's husband, who was a great help in preparing the meal.

In that task everyone had his or her duties assigned by Mrs. Huang, who was in charge of the enterprise. The kitchen was quite traditional – that is, primitive – and it reminded me of our Chinese relatives' kitchen in the Guangdong region. There was no refrigerator, everything had come from the market that morning, and was protected from sun and flies by draped cloths. Food was kept in a small screened pantry hung from the ceiling, which I speculated was to keep the food away from the rats. Everything was purchased fresh daily; sauces were served at room temperature. The room was illuminated only by a large skylight and a single low-watt bulb. The whole family seemed crowded into its confines, running in and out, preparing for the meal and attending to two large woks set in the stove, constantly stoking with chips of wood, rice stalks, and fragrant bamboo stalks.

As for the food, there were mounds of washed yellow chives, tomatoes, cloud ear fungus, already soaking, and the appropriate amount of rice, ready to be washed. Mrs. Huang told me that they usually ate mostly rice and vegetables with very little meat but because this was a birthday occasion they were having many pork dishes as well as fish. Many farms can raise their own pigs and carp but the Huangs got theirs from speciality markets nearby – Mr. Huang and his son, Kanze, had been assigned the task of bicycling to those markets to get the fresh pork and carp. The carp arrived very much alive, swimming around in red buckets, their freshness guaranteed.

During a quiet moment, I asked Mr. Huang why he did not raise pigs. He told me that he did not raise enough grain to feed any stock. Pigs are a wonderful animal, he said, but they eat what humans eat and he joked that his farm could not afford the competition. He actually specialises in raising chillies, garlic, and vegetables for urban markets, which are in great demand; in turn, he must buy his pork and fish from other specialists. It is clear that he finds it profitable to do so. A good example of the agrarian entrepreneur, Mr. Huang worked as a crane operator, among other jobs, before returning to the land twenty years ago. Now he and his wife are prospering, aided by their children, some of whom work on the farm, the others working in factories.

The Huang's version of the washing-of-the-rice ritual was one I had not seen before. The rice was first boiled in a wok in much water for about fifteen minutes; it was then drained in a bamboo sieve to separate out any impurities; then it was returned to the wok, covered, and steamed slowly until done. While the rice cooked, I helped Mrs. Huang string the crisp, fresh green beans, breaking them into bite-sized pieces. Everybody was bustling about. The family dog, Hei Shi ("black lion") was underfoot; the family cat, whose name I didn't get, looked on as if all the activity was in her honour. Someone brought plump pungent cloves of fresh garlic in from the garden to be peeled, crushed, and mixed for the chilli paste, used in many of the dishes. Mrs. Huang proudly showed me her earthen jar filled with red chillies she had pickled the year before. I watched her as she took some of

sichuan

these prizes and, using her ancient mortar and pestle, pounded them with the garlic into a chilli-garlic sauce. She then mixed it with freshly roasted ground Sichuan peppercorns. In those surroundings, so replete with natural, authentic touches, I felt I was witnessing a reenactment of the creation of Sichuan cuisine.

The meal, or rather banquet, included at least sixteen dishes. There was cold spicy chicken, fried peanuts with salt and Sichuan peppercorns, tender pork belly in a spicy sauce, fresh green beans stir-fried with mild chilli peppers, cooked smoked meats, Sichuan-style duck, stir-fried yellow chives with pork, stir-fried celery with minced pork, aubergine with pork, stir-fried oyster mushrooms, stem lettuce with 'cloud ears, stir-fried fresh chillies with pork, grass carp with chilli bean sauce, stir-fried cloud ears, a tomato soup, and, finally, cucumbers stir-fried with pork. Roasted Sichuan peppercorns were sprinkled on most dishes before serving. The meal was finished with a rice and cabbage dish, the cabbage having been boiled in water that the meats had been cooked in.

All of this we consumed in the courtyard, over a five-hour period of eating and drinking, in the warm haze of the Sichuan sun. Nature smiled beneficently down on a happy gathering of friends and family. It was so idyllic, I wished for such blessings on people everywhere.

As we reluctantly gathered in the courtyard to leave, I asked Mr. Huang to allow me to taste one last time the heart of the Sichuan style: an absolutely fresh peppercorn. He took me over to a scrubby bush I had barely noticed and plucked off one of its reddish, wrinkled berries. I bit into it; my tongue was startled and numbed at the same time, the pungent taste fixed on my palate.

I wish I could have similarly fixed that afternoon in time. Our parting was genuinely tearful; my memories of the day remain fresh and strong. As we drove off, I felt I had experienced a revelation, a discovery of the Sichuan touchstone, in the form of a berry on a modest shrub in the corner of a Sichuan courtyard.

donggu shaoji
mushroom – chicken casserole

*In the markets of Yunnan I saw more varieties of fresh mushrooms than in
any other region of China. I learned that the province produces over two
hundred edible varieties, many of which reminded me of the French cep.
Another kind I recognized, the oyster mushroom, is cultivated now even
outside China. But the most famous of the Yunnan mushrooms is the
Jizong, or the "chicken mushroom," so called because its shape resembles a
cock's comb and because its texture is like that of chicken. Not surprisingly, it
is often used in chicken recipes.*

*I enjoyed this dish in the Guan household, in the city of Kunming. With
fresh Yunnan mushrooms I had found earlier at a nearby neighbourhood
market, Mrs. Guan prepared this hearty, flavourful mushroom and chicken
casserole. For this recipe, I have substituted black mushrooms, since the
Yunnan variety is not often available outside of the Kunming area. The
rich smoky flavour of the mushrooms is quite delicious in this dish.*

450 g/1 lb boned chicken thigh meat, skin removed
MARINADE
1 tablespoon light soy sauce
2 teaspoons rice wine or dry sherry
1 teaspoon dark soy sauce
1 teaspoon sesame oil
½ teaspoon salt
1 teaspoon cornflour
25 g/1 oz Chinese dried black mushrooms
2 tablespoons peanut oil
6 slices fresh peeled ginger
1 tablespoon rice wine or dry sherry
1 tablespoon dark soy sauce
1 teaspoon light soy sauce
2 teaspoons sugar
225 ml/8 fl oz chicken stock
1 teaspoon cornflour mixed with 1 teaspoon water

Cut the meat into thin slices about 7.5 cm/3 in long. In a medium-sized bowl, combine the marinade ingredients and the chicken and let them sit for 20 minutes.

Soak the mushrooms in warm water for 20 minutes or until they are soft. Rinse under running water to remove any remaining sand. With a sharp knife, remove the stems and discard. Cut the caps in half and set aside.

Heat a wok or large frying pan until hot. Add the oil and ginger slices and stir-fry for 1 minute. Then add the chicken and stir-fry for 2 minutes. Pour the contents into a clay pot or casserole, together with the mushrooms, rice wine or sherry, soy sauces, sugar, and chicken stock. Bring the mixture to the boil, lower the heat, cover, and simmer for 15 minutes. Remove the cover, and pour in the cornflour mixture. Cook until the sauce thickens, about 2 minutes. Remove the ginger slices before serving.

Serves 4 as part of a Chinese meal, or 2 as a single dish.

lajiao shao sijidou
green beans stir-fried with chilli

Chinese who live in the countryside understandably enjoy a greater variety of fresh produce than those living in the city, with food from their back-yards or a few yards away in nearby fields. With no or little refrigeration, produce is eaten in season, the surplus being dried or pickled or salted. These preserving techniques have been perfected over the course of thousands of years, retaining the nutritional qualities of the foods and enhancing their flavours.

At one delightful feast I had at the home of the Huangs in Sichuan, my hostess retrieved from the ground an earthen jar she had filled with chillies to pickle the year before. She pounded the chillies into a paste, adding that to chopped garlic and then to stir-fried fresh seasonal vegetables, in this case, green beans. I successfully repeated the recipe, using fresh mild red chilles and adding a touch of vinegar. This is an appetising way to enjoy green beans when they are in season. They make a lovely side dish, authentically Sichuan in every way.

450 g/1 lb green beans
125 g/4 oz mild red or green chillies
1½ tablespoons peanut oil
1½ tablespoons finely chopped garlic
1 teaspoon salt
2 tablespoons rice wine or dry sherry
2 teaspoons white rice vinegar
2 teaspoons sugar
2 tablespoons water
1 teaspoon ground roasted Sichuan peppercorns

String the green beans and snap them in half. Split open the red or green chillies and chop them coarsely.

Heat a wok or large frying pan until hot. Add the oil, garlic, and salt and stir-fry for 10 seconds. Put in the chillies and stir-fry another 30 seconds. Then add the green beans, rice wine or sherry, vinegar, sugar, and water and continue to stir-fry until tender, about 5 minutes, adding more water if necessary. When the green beans are cooked, add the peppercorns, mix well, and serve at once.

Serves 4 as part of a Chinese meal, or 2 as a single dish.

qing jiao rousi
pickled chillies with pork

The pig, last of the twelve creatures in the Chinese zodiac calendar, is first in the hearts and palates of its people. It is the "red meat" of China, and the only portion of the animal not utilised in some way is its oink. The pig is the symbol for fertility, virility, and good luck, and during a birthday banquet at the home of friends in Sichuan, we were served several pork dishes. (I should note that the pork portions were small compared to the vegetables, for meat never dominates, even when it is a favourite one.)

Here again was a treasured family recipe served up in an at-home celebration. All of the adults took turns preparing and cooking the various parts of the meal. In other areas of China, chillies are often used as a garnish or decoration; in

Sichuan they are commonly used as a vegetable. In this case, the family's own homemade pickled chillies were used, but I have substituted fresh mild chillies with very good results.

450 g/1 lb lean boneless pork
2 teaspoons light soy sauce
1 teaspoon dark soy sauce
1 teaspoon rice wine or dry sherry
1 teaspoon sesame oil
½ teaspoon cornflour
125 g/4 oz mild red or green chillies
6 spring onions
1½ tablespoons peanut oil
1 tablespoon finely chopped garlic
2 teaspoons finely chopped peeled fresh ginger root
1 teaspoon chilli flakes or chilli powder
½ teaspoon salt
2 teaspoons light soy sauce
2 teaspoons rice wine
2 teaspoons white rice vinegar
1 teaspoon sugar

Cut the pork into thin slices, about 3 mm/⅛ in thick by 7.5 cm/3 in long. In a medium-sized bowl, combine the pork with soy sauces, rice wine or sherry, sesame oil, and cornflour and set aside.

Cut the chillies in half and remove the seeds and slice them into thin shreds. With the flat side of the knife or cleaver, crush the onions and shred them.

Heat a wok or large frying pan until hot. Add the oil, then the garlic, ginger, chili flakes, and salt and stir-fry for 10 seconds. Then add the pork and continue to stir-fry for 1 minute. Now add the chillies and onions, stir-fry for 1 minute, and add the soy sauce, rice wine or sherry, vinegar, and sugar. Continue to stir-fry for 2 minutes or until all the liquid has evaporated. Serve at once.

Serves 3 as part of a Chinese meal, or 1 as a single dish.

qing sun shao rou
stem lettuce with cloud ears

Stem lettuce is a Chinese original, found most often in the north and west. It has a quite unusual if not bizarre form, which is why it is also called "celtuce" or "asparagus lettuce." The top is in the shape of a thin oval, with wilted-looking lettuce-like leaves, while the stem is thick and crunchy, like asparagus or celery. Because raw greens are rarely eaten in China because of hygiene as well as taste, the leaves are generally eaten in soup. The stem is often pickled. I have enjoyed it this way as well as fresh and stir-fried. It can be found seasonally in Chinese food markets, though fresh broccoli stems are an acceptable substitute.

In their Sichuan country kitchen, the Huangs peeled the fresh lettuce stems, then sliced and stir-fried them with cloud ear mushrooms. The contrasts in taste and texture were memorable, and the flavour was enhanced by the touch of roasted ground Sichuan peppercorns tossed in at the last moment of cooking. This is a unique vegetable treat and a fine accompaniment to any meat dish.

450 g/1 lb stem lettuce or broccoli stems
12 g/½ oz cloud ear fungi
1½ tablespoons peanut oil
1 tablespoon finely chopped peeled fresh ginger root
1 tablespoon finely chopped garlic
2 tablespoons finely chopped spring onions
2 teaspoons chilli bean sauce
1 tablespoon rice wine or dry sherry
1 tablespoon light soy sauce
2 teaspoons dark soy sauce
1 teaspoon sugar
½ teaspoon salt
3 tablespoons water
1 teaspoon ground roasted Sichuan peppercorns

Peel the stem lettuce or broccoli stems and cut the stems into thin slices diagonally.

Soak the cloud ear fungi in warm water for at least 15 minutes. Rinse them several times in cold running water to remove any sand. Drain thoroughly and set aside.

Heat a wok or large frying pan until hot and add the oil. Add the ginger, garlic, and onions and stir-fry for 30 seconds. Put in the cloud ears and stem lettuce and stir-fry for 1 minute. Now add the chilli bean sauce, rice wine or sherry, soy sauces, sugar, and salt. Stir-fry for 1 minute, and then pour in the water. Continue to cook over high heat, uncovered, until the vegetables are tender, about 3 minutes. Add the peppercorns, mix well, and serve at once.

Serves 4 as part of a Chinese meal, or 2 as a single dish.

liang ban rou
twice-cooked pork

This dish is often served in Sichuan-style restaurants in the West. Rarely is it served properly because the authentic cut of meat, namely pork belly, is fatty. Westerners usually avoid it, thinking it's unpalatable. This is unfortunate because pork belly, properly prepared, is meltingly tender and rich.

To achieve this, pork belly requires a good bit of cooking. The Huangs simmered pieces of pork belly in water with spring onions and ginger in enormous woks for what seemed like hours. When removed, the meat was allowed to cool and sliced thinly, blanched again, and served with a homemade hot chilli sauce. The result was delicious, the pork tender without a trace of fat. I have changed the recipe slightly by stir-frying the pork instead of blanching it a second time. Because the dish reheats so well, much of the work can be done ahead of time. It is Chinese country cooking at its best.

900 g–1.1 kg/2–2½ lb fresh bacon or pork belly
6 whole spring onions
6 slices peeled fresh ginger root
1 tablespoon salt
6 spring onions
3 tablespoons peanut oil

2 tablespoons finely chopped garlic
1 tablespoon finely chopped peeled
   fresh ginger root
1½ tablespoons chilli bean sauce
1 tablespoon rice wine or dry sherry
1 tablespoon light soy sauce
2 teaspoons sugar
1 teaspoon salt

Add to a pot of boiling water, the bacon or pork belly, whole onions, ginger, and salt. Cover tightly and simmer for 1½ hours. Remove the meat with a slotted spoon and drain well. Discard the cooking liquid. When the bacon or pork belly has cooled thoroughly, cut it into thin 6-mm/¼-in pieces.

Cut the other spring onions into 7.5-cm/3-in pieces.

Heat a wok or large frying pan until hot. Add the oil and the meat slices and stir-fry for 10 minutes. Drain off any excess oil. Add the garlic and ginger and stir-fry for 10 seconds. Add the spring onions and continue to stir-fry for 3 minutes. Then add the rest of the ingredients and stir-fry for another 3 minutes, mixing well. Serve at once.

Serves 6 as part of a Chinese meal, or 3 as a single dish.

qing lazi chao roupian
pork stir-fried with chilies

Mrs. Guan Shouhua prepared this dish for me during one of my visits to Kunming. It reflects her origins, in Guizhou province, where she grew up enjoying the rather spicy foods of the neighbouring Hunan region. She thought, quite rightly, that I would enjoy this minced pork dish heavily larded with chillies which, while not so hot as the Sichuan varieties, nevertheless have plenty of bite. Kunming markets are well stocked with fresh produce from nearby farms, including various varieties of fresh chillies that are so plentiful they are regularly used as a vegetable in family meals.

city and country recipes

450 g/1 lb minced pork
2 teaspoons rice wine or dry sherry
1 teaspoon light soy sauce
½ teaspoon salt
350 g/12 oz fresh whole mild chillies
2 tablespoons peanut oil
1 teaspoon salt
2 tablespoons chopped garlic
1 tablespoon light soy sauce
2 teaspoons sugar
2 teaspoons sesame oil

In a medium-sized bowl, combine the minced pork with the rice wine or sherry, soy sauce, and salt.

Wash the chillies and pat them dry. Split them in half, remove the seeds, and then cut them into shreds.

Heat a wok or large frying pan over high heat. When hot, add the oil, salt, and garlic and stir-fry for 10 seconds. Then add the pork and continue to stir-fry for another 2 minutes. Now, put in the chillies and stir-fry for 2 minutes. Put in the soy sauce and sugar and continue to stir-fry until most of the liquid has evaporated. Stir in the sesame oil and mix thoroughly. Pour the mixture onto a serving platter and serve at once.

Serves 4 as part of a Chinese meal, or 2 as a single dish.

huang gua chao roupian
cucumbers stir-fried with pork

Yellow cucumbers, really large, heavy and firm melons, have a crisp, cool flesh and mild taste. They are often stir-fried or used in soup, where they give a distinctive flavour to the broth. If pickled, the cucumber is often eaten unpeeled. Being a "cooling" food, it is considered beneficial to the body during hot weather. Thus, I was not surprised to see it on the Huang family table one summer evening even though I personally consider it an equally excellent winter food. Served with pork and the family's own homemade chilli paste, yellow cucumbers made a good light stir-fried dish. They can be found at Asian markets; if unavailable, use the more familiar green cucumbers which come a close approximation in taste.

225 g/8 oz lean boneless pork
2 teaspoons light soy sauce
1 teaspoon dark soy sauce
1 teaspoon rice wine or dry sherry
1 teaspoon sesame oil
½ teaspoon cornflour
450 g/1 lb cucumbers
1½ tablespoons peanut oil
1 tablespoon chilli bean sauce
2 teaspoons finely chopped garlic
1 teaspoon roasted ground Sichuan peppercorns
½ teaspoon chilli flakes or chilli powder
½ teaspoon salt
2 teaspoons light soy sauce
2 teaspoons rice wine or dry sherry
2 teaspoons white rice vinegar
1 teaspoon sugar

Cut the pork into thin slices, about 3 mm/⅛ in thick by 7.5 cm/3 in long. In a medium-sized bowl, combine the pork with soy sauces, rice wine or sherry, sesame oil, and cornflour and set aside.

Peel the cucumbers, split them in half lengthways and with a spoon, scoop out the seeds, then finely slice the flesh crossways.

Heat a wok or large frying pan until hot. Add the oil, then the chilli bean sauce, garlic, Sichuan peppercorns, chilli flakes, and salt and stir-fry for 10 seconds. Then add the pork, and continue to stir-fry for 1 minute. Put in the cucumbers and stir-fry for 1 minute. Pour in the soy sauce, rice wine or sherry, vinegar, and sugar. Continue to stir-fry for 2 minutes or until all the liquid has evaporated. Serve at once.

Serves 4 as part of a Chinese meal, or 2 as a single dish.

xi hu cu yu
west lake carp in vinegar sauce

Carp have been domesticated and kept in ponds for many centuries in China. Valued for their golden scales as well as for their tasty flesh, they have a distinctive, rich, strong flavour. The Chinese use rice wine or vinegar or a combination to bring zest to the rich flesh. I enjoyed this dish in the Lou Wai Lou restaurant in the city of Hangzhou, famous for its West Lake where carp comes from, and also near Shaoxing, the rice wine area.

It is no accident that this recipe calls for rice wine and rice vinegar. Zhejiang province surrounding the city is famous for both but especially for its black vinegar. The vinegar is used by itself most often as a dipping sauce for the local freshwater hairy crabs. When used with wine, as in this recipe, the result is a subtle, sweet and sour, dark, rich sauce which makes a perfect complement for the carp. If carp is unavailable, catfish or trout make acceptable substitutes.

1.1–1.4 kg/2½–3 lb fresh whole carp or catfish or 3 fresh whole trout
2 tablespoons rice wine or dry sherry
3 tablespoons light soy sauce
1 teaspoon salt
2 tablespoons peanut oil
2 tablespoons finely chopped peeled fresh ginger root
3 tablespoons finely chopped spring onions
3 tablespoons black rice vinegar
2 teaspoons rice wine or dry sherry
2 tablespoons sugar
2 tablespoons dark soy sauce
125 ml/4 fl oz chicken stock
2 teaspoons cornflour mixed with 2 teaspoons water

Have the fishmonger clean and scale the fish. Rinse the fish under cold running water and then pat it completely dry. Make four diagonal slashes across each side of the fish. In a small bowl, mix together the rice wine or sherry, soy sauce, and salt, and rub evenly over both sides of the fish. Set aside for 10 minutes.

Heat a wok or large frying pan until hot, and add the oil, ginger, and spring onions. Stir-fry for 30 seconds, then add the vinegar, rice wine or sherry, sugar, soy sauce, and stock. Bring the mixture to a simmer and pour in the cornflour mixture. Pour the sauce into a saucepan and keep warm.

Clean the wok or pan, fill it with water, and bring it to a simmer. Carefully lower the fish into the water and simmer for 5 minutes. Turn off the heat and let the fish steep in the hot water for 5 more minutes. If you are using trout, reduce the cooking and steeping times to 3 minutes each. Remove the fish with a slotted spoon or spatula and drain well. Place the fish on a platter, pour over the sauce, and serve at once.

Serves 4 as part of a Chinese meal, or 2 as a single dish.

li yu
mandarin fish

With all of its rivers and lakes, China is blessed with a great variety of such fish as the Mandarin and the carp; the Mandarin is popular for its delicate taste. In this recipe, steaming preserves the delicate freshwater flavours. The Chinese speak highly of "sea-flavours," but freshwater fish are actually preferred by many. I sampled this recipe at a local restaurant in Shaoxing. The famous local rice wine provided the basis for the sauce, giving it a richness of flavour. With the mushrooms and bamboo shoots, this dish makes a substantial and flavourful meal, a centerpiece for any family gathering. In the presence of the Mandarin this recipe works well.

25 g/1 oz Chinese black dried mushrooms
450–700 g/1–1½ lb firm, white-fleshed fish such as a small cod, halibut, haddock, scrod or red snapper, or sole, cleaned and left whole
1 teaspoon salt
3 tablespoons dried rice wine or dry sherry
2 teaspoons light soy sauce

2 teaspoons sugar
25 g/1 oz finely shredded canned bamboo shoots
3 slices of fresh ginger, shredded
1 teaspoon cornflour mixed
  with 2 teaspoons water

Soak the mushrooms for 20 minutes in warm water. Remove the stems and finely shred the caps.

Make three or four slashes on each side of the fish to help it cook faster and allow the flavours to permeate. Rub the fish on both sides with the salt. Set on a heatproof platter.

Combine the rice wine or sherry, soy sauce, and sugar and pour over the fish. Scatter the bamboo shoots, mushrooms and ginger over and around the fish.

Set up a steamer or put a rack into a wok or deep pan. Fill the steamer with about 5 cm/2 in of hot water. Bring the water to a simmer. Put the plate with the fish into the steamer or onto the rack. Cover the steamer tightly and gently steam the fish until it is cooked. Flat fish will take about 6 minutes. Thicker fish such as sea bass will take about 15 to 18 minutes.

Remove the plate of cooked fish and pour all of the liquid into a small saucepan. Bring this to a simmer and stir in the cornflour mixture. When the sauce has thickened, pour it over the fish and serve at once.

Serves 4 as part of a Chinese meal, or 2 as a single dish.

mati jiding
spicy chicken with fresh water chestnuts

Famished one day while on a train trip from Hangzhou to Suzhou, I had to risk the dining car's offerings. To my surprise, I savorer a dish of bits of chicken and water chestnuts in a spicy, very pleasing sauce. It is easy to make, as befits a dining car specialty, and I was delighted to acquire a new recipe from my train ride.

225 g/8 oz boneless chicken breast, skinned
1 egg white
1 teaspoon salt
2 teaspoons cornflour
225 g/8 oz water chestnuts,
    fresh or canned
125 ml/4 fl oz peanut oil
1 tablespoon finely chopped garlic
2 teaspoons finely chopped peeled fresh
    ginger root
1 tablespoon chilli bean sauce
2 teaspoons dark soy sauce
2 teaspoons rice wine or dry sherry
2 teaspoons sugar
½ teaspoon salt
2 teaspoons sesame oil

Cut the chicken into 12-mm/½-in dice. Combine it with the egg white, salt, and cornflour in a small bowl and put the mixture into the refrigerator for about 20 minutes.

If you are using fresh water chestnuts, peel them. If you are using canned water chestnuts, drain them well and rinse in cold water. Coarsely chop the water chestnuts.

Heat a wok or large frying pan until hot and add the oil. When it is moderately hot, add the diced chicken and stir well to keep it from sticking. When the chicken pieces turn white, about 2 minutes, quickly drain the chicken and all the oil into a stainless steel colander set in a bowl.

Clean the wok or pan and reheat. Return 2 tablespoons of oil to the wok, add the garlic and ginger and stir-fry for 30 seconds. Then add the water chestnuts, chilli bean sauce, soy sauce, rice wine or sherry, sugar, and salt and continue to stir-fry for 1 minute. Return the chicken to the wok and continue to cook for another 2 minutes. Add the sesame oil, give the mixture a final stir, and serve at once.

Serves 4 as part of a Chinese meal, or 2 as a single dish.

163

you bao xia
oil-exploded prawns

*I enjoyed this austere but elegant dish at Shanghai's Lao Fandian restaurant.
It is usually made with unpeeled freshwater prawns that almost literally
"explode" when they come into contact with the very hot oil in the wok.
Quick cooking and light seasonings preserve and enhance the natural flavours
of the prawns. Native freshwater prawns may be difficult to find, as they are
not widely available commercially and the giant Asian varieties are only
rarely imported. Fortunately, saltwater varieties, whether native or imported,
are a good substitute.*

450 g/1 lb medium-sized raw prawns with
  shells but without heads, or
  350-375 g/12-13 oz peeled, raw prawns
1 teaspoon salt
2 teaspoons cornflour
2 tablespoons peanut oil
2 tablespoons rice wine
  or dry sherry
1 teaspoon cornflour mixed
  with 2 teaspoons water

If the prawns are unpeeled, peel them by removing their shells, legs,
and tails. Devein them by making a surface cut down the back of the
prawns and removing the black, green, or yellow matter with the
point of the knife or cleaver. Rinse them well under cold running
water and pat them thoroughly dry with kitchen paper. Rub the
prawns evenly with salt and cornflour.

Heat a wok or large frying pan until hot and add the oil. Put in the
prawns and stir-fry for 1 minute.

Add the rice wine or sherry, stir, and then pour in the cornflour
mixture and continue to stir-fry another 2 minutes. Serve at once.

Serves 4 as part of a Chinese meal, or 2 as a single dish.

furu chao tongcai
chinese water spinach with fermented bean curd

Chinese water spinach is a very popular vegetable throughout south and southwest China in both restaurants and homes. Chinese water spinach differs from the European variety in that it has hollow stems and arrowhead-shaped leaves. (It is not the same as the vegetable called simply Chinese spinach.) When properly prepared, Chinese water spinach offers a delightful contrast between the soft leaf and the still crunchy stem. It is available from some Chinese markets and supermarkets. European spinach does not offer the same textural contrast but may be usaed as a substitute. The fermented bean curd seasoning provides a zesty dimension; this makes a fine accompaniment to any meat dish and is perfect with rice.

700–900 g/1½–2 lb fresh Chinese water spinach or
   European spinach
2 tablespoons peanut oil
3 tablespoons chilli fermented bean curd or
   plain fermented bean curd
2 tablespoons rice wine or
   dry sherry
3 tablespoons water

Wash the Chinese water spinach thoroughly and drain. Cut off 5 cm/ 2 in from the bottom of the stem, which tends to be tough. Cut the rest of the spinach into 10-cm/4-in segments.

Heat a wok or large frying pan until hot and add the oil. Put in the fermented bean curd and crush it with a spatula, breaking it into small pieces.

Put in the water spinach and stir-fry for 2 minutes. Pour in the rice wine or sherry and water and continue to cook for another 3 minutes.

Place on a platter and serve at once.

Serves 4 as part of a Chinese meal, or 2 as a single dish.

city and country recipes

xiami baicai
cabbage with dried shrimp

Nothing evokes memories as sharply and as immediately as odours and tastes. In the middle of Sichuan, at the Chen Ma Po Doufu restaurant in Chengdu, I enjoyed a dish familiar to me from childhood. The fragrance and taste of this spicy dish is very much like a comforting meal my mother used to make for me. She stir-fried common Chinese cabbage, the most common and cheapest Chinese vegetable, and enlivened the taste with dried shrimp. Like many peasant dishes, it is both nutritious and sustaining.

25 g/1 oz dried shrimp
450 g/1 lb Chinese cabbage
2 tablespoons peanut oil
2 tablespoons finely chopped garlic
1 tablespoon finely chopped peeled fresh ginger root
1 tablespoon chilli bean sauce
2 tablespoon dark soy sauce
2 teaspoons sugar
125 ml/4 fl oz chicken stock

Soak the dried shrimp in a large bowl of warm water for 20 minutes, drain them thoroughly and coarsely chop them.
Cut the cabbage into long strips.
   Heat a wok or large frying pan until hot and add the oil, garlic, and ginger and stir-fry for 30 seconds. Then add the soaked shrimp, the cabbage, chilli bean sauce, soy sauce, sugar, and chicken stock. Cook over high heat for 5 minutes, stirring constantly. Turn onto a platter and serve.

Serves 4 as part of a Chinese meal, or 2 as a single dish.

CHAPTER 8
RESTAURANT COOKING

If one has the art, then a piece of celery or salted cabbage can be made into a marvellous delicacy; whereas if one has not the art, not all the greatest delicacies and rarities of land, sea, or sky are of any avail.
                                        Notes on His Cook, Yuan Mei

Restaurants appeared relatively late in Chinese history, having been in existence for a mere one thousand years. Monasteries probably began the custom of providing food to travelers and pilgrims, but secular establishments soon followed. Among them, wine shops generally offered food so customers would drink more and food stalls became commonplace in every urban setting. By the Tang Dynasty (618–907), they could be found throughout most of China but especially in cities, seaports, and larger towns along trade routes and the routes of religious pilgrims.

During the Song era (960–1279), recognizably "modern" commercial restaurants were well established, with business and religious travelers constituting a good portion of their clientele. The growing tourist trade among restaurants in urban areas was evidence that many people were able to move about freely during the prosperity and internal peace of the Song period. Until the present century, the restaurant tradition prospered, with regional speciality restaurants developing along with simple menus in urban areas. These appealed to officials, businessmen, pilgrims, and students who wanted "home" cooking that was familiar and comforting.

As if war, revolution, and the economic upheaval of the last thirty to forty years were not enough to rock the venerable traditions of restaurant cuisine, standards in the very quality of the raw ingredients and their preparation were made worse by many decades of official policy directed against the "decadent" or "bourgeois" practice of dining out. During the Cultural Revolution (1966–1976) especially, many restaurants were shut down, master chefs were forced into other trades or out of the country, and the entire custom of dining out was denigrated if not actually made illegal.

Because of this, when my travels through China first began, I expected to find inferior restaurants. I was indeed disappointed, but not in the way I had anticipated; they were much worse than I had expected. With some bright exceptions, dining out in China was a depressing experience. State-managed restaurants were, and still too often are, among the worst places I have ever encountered, summoning up nightmares out of Orwell's *1984*. The food was of poor quality, badly prepared and served, and for it foreigners paid a premium price. The dining rooms were often noisy, not very clean, poorly lighted, aesthetically repellent, and in general badly managed. Sometimes state-run restaurants were our only alternative to starving. After waiting in line to get in, I was usually seated at a table still heaped with the debris from the previous diners. Employees were often lackadaisical, discourteous, and even surly to travelers as well as local patrons. Known among the Chinese as the "iron rice bowl" treatment, it is based on the premise that public institutions, including state restaurants, exist not to serve people but to provide income and security for the employees. In my own experience, it often happened that as closing time approached, while we were still prudently picking our way through a meal, the employees would begin turning off the lights and fans, to hurry us on our way.

Are things improving? Fortunately, the answer is yes. Changes for the better are already apparent on two fronts. Government and the state-managed restaurants have in recent years begun to recognise the economic value of fine cuisine and excellent service. Today decent meals, decently served, can be found in some of these establishments. Excellence is still far off, however. Government policy now also encourages privately owned family and cooperative restaurants. The clear successes of these new businesses have stimulated the state-managed business to improve their performance. Moreover, for the past decade or so, official policy has authorised the revival of professional culinary and restaurant training. There are now over one hundred and thirty such academies and vocational centers for training chefs and support staff. Twenty thousand students are enrolled in these highly regarded schools.

As additional evidence of the new policy, the government has sponsored a massive publication project, a nine-volume series, *Authentic Chinese Cuisine*. Lavishly illustrated and drawing on expert scholarship and the knowledge of China's best chefs, the series represents a lasting testament to one of the world's great cuisines. The government has finally recognised that in resource-poor China, one of its greatest treasures is its cuisine. Further evidence of this is the regular publication of eight different magazines devoted to Chinese cuisine, with more specialised ones in several of the regions.

From what I've seen, most of the future health and glory of Chinese restaurant food will unfold within the family-run restaurant kitchens and in cooperative restaurants. In contrast to state-managed establishments, they are cleaner, more congenial, and more comfortable, being warm in winter and as cool as possible in summer. They feature clean plastic tablecloths, instead of soiled cloth ones. The menu is usually considerably more expensive than that of the state restaurants, but then their patrons are not served fish heads, gristle, and bones either.

As in the past, an adventurous traveller can find restaurants that specialise in one type of food. Chen Ma Po Doufu, in Chengdu, Sichuan, is one place I visited. Famous throughout China for its spicy

restaurant cooking

bean curd dishes, the restaurant was established toward the end of the Qing Dynasty (1644–1911). Its chefs passed their recipes down from father and mother to son and daughter but never outside the family. Jealously guarding the family recipes and determined to keep the quality of food which has made this restaurant famous, it has managed to maintain a high degree of excellence. I overheard gossip that a branch will soon open in Japan. Right now, the restaurant is thriving, catering to new Chinese and foreign patrons and expanding its repertory. War and the recent revolution seem far away, especially for those living in the interior of China.

One thing I noted was that the farther we travelled from Beijing, the better the restaurant food. In Yunnan, young chefs are busy reviving regional dishes, long forgotten or neglected. There, in the small remote village of Yi Liang Gou Jie, we discovered an unusual and unsung restaurant, more like an eating house or glorified food stall, with a patron's goat tethered outside. The food was basic but delicious. I was served a superb roasted duck, one of the tastiest dishes I have ever had anywhere, served hot from the fire outside. The setting was unpretentious, but the duck was cooked as it was meant to be cooked. I contrast this with my experience in one of the most famous Peking duck restaurants. There the duck was greasy, improperly cooked, and the entire meal was a disaster.

In some private restaurants, elaborate dinners are available. I experienced such a banquet in the Spring Happy restaurant, in Kunming. There we feasted on a fifty-four-course dinner with goat appearing in one form or another in almost every dish. The meal was an example of the cuisine of one of the ethnic peoples of the region, the Hui. They traditionally prepare such a meal and invite friends to enjoy it with them. The owners of the Spring Happy work conscientiously to preserve this impressive tradition.

On my latest trip I found the restaurants of Hangzhou to vary from the mediocre to the very good. In Shaoxing, I sampled delicious food served with the sauce made with the famous rice wine of the city. I was a bit disappointed in Shanghai. While there are some decent private eating places, the great and authentic Shanghai cuisine still awaits its true renaissance in the restaurants of that city. It is, however, alive and well in the kitchens of private homes.

When I consider the restaurant scene in China today, I sense that the improvements of recent years will continue. Chinese history is replete with sudden advances and just as sudden regressions, but I remain hopeful that today's improvements in restaurant cooking will be permanent. The state-managed restaurants are better than they were; the private ones are generally good and improving every day. Their combined success is good for tourism, for the government, and for the Chinese people. There is room for hope, even optimism, but only time will tell.

shen tui
"fantasy pork"

I was very encouraged when I tasted this dish because it catered to my ideal of Chinese cooking with its straightforward, careful preparation and attention to a balance of flavours. Friends took me to a privately-owned restaurant in Kunming, Yunnan, where I sampled this "fantasy pork." It was properly braised, with just the right enhancing seasonings that gave the meat a robust but not overpowering fragrance. The rich wine sauce and subtle sweetness of the other ingredients combined beautifully with the taste of pork. It was a true pleasure to partake of this meal, and, in memory, it remains a minor masterpiece. This dish is easy to prepare, and can be made ahead of time. It reheats well and is also very good served cold – perfect for a dinner party or large gathering.

Fresh ham, about 2.3 kg/5 lb
8 spring onions
3 tablespoons peanut oil
8 slices fresh ginger root
4 garlic cloves, peeled and crushed
BRAISING LIQUID
1.1 L/2 pt hot water
225 ml/8 fl oz dark soy sauce

225 ml/8 fl oz rice wine or dry sherry
3 tablespoons whole roasted Sichuan peppercorns
6 tablespoons rock or ordinary sugar
4 star anise
2 cinnamon sticks or bark
2 teaspoons five-spice powder
1 teaspoon salt

Dry the ham thoroughly with kitchen paper.

Cut the spring onions into 7.5-cm/3-in segments.

Choose a heavy casserole pot, large enough to hold the ham comfortably. Heat the pot and then add the oil, ginger, garlic, and onions, and stir-fry in the pot for 2 minutes. Push the aromatics to the side and brown the ham on each side until it has some colour, 10 to 15 minutes. Pour off the oil.

Add all the braising liquid ingredients to the pot and bring the mixture to the boil. Turn the heat down to a simmer, cover the pot tightly, and cook for about 4½ hours, turning the ham from time to time. When the ham is tender, remove it gently with a large spatula. The meat should be literally falling apart. Carefully place it on a serving platter.

Strain the sauce, skim off any surface fat, and reduce the liquid until it is slightly thickened. Pour this over the ham and serve.

Serves 8 to 10 as part of a Chinese meal, or 4 to 6 as a single dish.

jiaoyan pai gu
salt and pepper spareribs

Shanghai chefs especially know how to coax out all of pork's best qualities. Here it is marinated, fried, and then stir-fried in a savoury mixture of spices. I have modified the Lao Fandian restaurant's recipe for convenience but without detracting from its excellent taste. And I have used boneless spareribs.

450 g/1 lb boneless meaty spareribs or

pork shoulder
2 teaspoons light soy sauce
2 teaspoons rice wine or dry sherry
1 teaspoon salt
1 teaspoon sesame oil
2 teaspoons cornflour
350 ml/12 fl oz peanut oil
2 tablespoons finely chopped garlic
1 teaspoon salt
2 teaspoons roasted ground Sichuan peppercorns
1 teaspoon five-spice powder
½ teaspoon chilli powder

Cut the pork into 25-mm/1-in cubes and combine it with the soy sauce, rice wine or sherry, salt, sesame oil, and cornflour. Set aside for 15 minutes.

Heat a wok or large frying pan until hot. Add the oil, and when it is medium hot, deep-fry the pork until it is golden and crisp about 10 minutes. Remove the pork with a slotted spoon and drain off all but 2 tablespoons of the oil. Reheat the wok or pan and when it is hot, add the garlic and stir-fry for 10 seconds. Then add the salt, peppercorns, five-spice powder, and chilli powder and stir-fry for another 10 seconds. Return the fried pork to the wok or pan and continue to stir-fry over medium heat for about 3 minutes. Serve the spareribs at once.

Serves 4 as part of a Chinese meal, or 2 as a single dish.

guoqiao mixian
across the bridge rice noodles

Substantial, this very special Yunnan soup of rich chicken stock is served along with slices of pork, chicken, black mushrooms, blanched bean sprouts, cooked ham, rice noodles, and spring onions. The condiments include chilli oil, or chili bean sauce, salt, and soy sauce, for dipping. Legend has it that a scholar, preparing for the Imperial examinations, isolated himself on an island

restaurant cooking – recipes

connected to the shore by a long bridge. His devoted wife was dismayed that her carefully prepared meals were always cold by the time she delivered them to him. She finally hit upon the technique of keeping a stock for a soup very hot by topping it with a thin layer of vegetable oil. Crossing the bridge with the hot stock, she was then able to drop the other ingredients into the kettle, to be cooked on the spot. Her husband had hot food and passed his exams.

We can enjoy the same soup today. Serve scalding hot bowls of chicken stock. Allow diners to pick from numerous side dishes of chicken and pork, sliced wafer thin, vegetables in season, and fresh rice noodles. All are put into the stock and cooked to perfection. Needless to say, it is vital to serve the stock very hot. The condiments are used as dipping sauces to flavour the bits of meat and vegetables after they have been cooked.

175 g/6 oz boneless chicken breast, frozen
125 g/4 oz boneless lean pork, frozen
125 g/4 oz fresh bean sprouts, rinsed
25 g/1 oz Chinese dried black mushrooms, soaked,
  stems removed
450 g/1 lb fresh rice noodles or
  dried rice noodles
4 spring onions
850 ml/1½ pt rich chicken stock
DIPPING CONDIMENTS
5 tablespoons finely chopped
  spring onions
3 tablespoons chilli bean sauce
2 tablespoons salt mixed with 1 teaspoon freshly
  ground black pepper
5 tablespoons dark soy sauce

Remove the chicken and pork from the freezer and let them sit at room temperature for 30 minutes.

Cut them into the thinnest slices possible with a sharp cleaver or knife and arrange them on a platter.

Place the bean sprouts, mushrooms, and rice noodles on another platter. If you are using dried rice noodles, soak them for 15 minutes in hot water and drain thoroughly. Cut the spring onions into 5-cm/2-in diagonal segments and put into a small bowl. Arrange the condiments on small dishes.

Preheat the oven to 140°C/275°F/Gas Mark 1 and put in four large, heat-proof soup bowls. Leave them in the oven for 15 minutes.

Bring the chicken stock to the boil in a medium-sized saucepan. Turn the heat down and keep just simmering. Remove the bowls carefully from the hot oven. Pour in the hot stock.

Place all the meat, vegetables, and condiments in the center of the table. Let each diner cook the meats, the vegetables, and finally the noodles in the hot stock.

Serves 4 as part of a Chinese meal, or 2 as a single dish.

guo ba
sizzling rice

"Sizzling rice" is the term describing the miniature explosion that occurs when crisp hot rice collides with thick soup. The magic of having the rice sizzle as one pours the hot soup over it always delights diners. I enjoyed this popular Sichuan version of the well-known rice dish at the Guihu restaurant in Xindu. Although it is a Sichuan recipe, this dish is not spicy. It is, however, so thick and satisfying, it may well become a meal in itself. You may make your own crisp rice at home or buy the dried rice at a Chinese grocery.

50 g/2 oz Chinese dried black mushrooms
225 g/8 oz lean pork
1 tablespoon light soy sauce
2 teaspoons dark soy sauce
1 tablespoon rice wine or dry sherry
2 teaspoons cornflour
225 g/8 oz boneless chicken breast
1 egg white
½ teaspoon salt

2 teaspoons cornflour
225 g/8 oz Chinese cabbage
850 ml/1½ pt chicken stock
1 teaspoon salt
2 tablespoons rice wine or dry sherry
2 tablespoons light soy sauce
1½ tablespoons cornflour dissolved in 2 tablespoons water
3 tablespoons finely chopped spring onions
1 tablespoon sesame oil
450 ml/16 fl oz peanut oil
1 rice cake (page 201) or 10 crusts of dried rice cakes

Soak the mushrooms in warm water for 20 minutes, squeeze out the excess liquid, cut off the stems, and quarter the caps.

Cut the pork into slices about 6-mm/¼ in thick by 5 cm/2 in long. Combine them with the soy sauces, rice wine or sherry, and cornflour.

Cut the chicken into slices about 6 mm/¼ in thick by 5 cm/2 in long. Combine the chicken with the egg white, salt, and cornflour and set in the refrigerator for 20 minutes.

Wash and shred the Chinese cabbage.

Bring the stock to a simmer, add the mushrooms, cabbage, salt, rice wine or sherry, soy sauce, and cornflour mixture. Simmer for 5 minutes and add the onions and sesame oil. Meanwhile, bring another pot of water to a simmer, and add the pork and chicken. Cook for 30 seconds, turn off the heat, and let the meat sit for 2 minutes. Remove the meat with a slotted spoon and add to the soup mixture.

Heat a wok or large frying pan until hot and add the oil. When the oil is very hot, deep-fry the rice cake or crusts and drain on kitchen paper. Quickly place it or the crusts in a soup tureen or deep bowl, and pour in the soup. Serve at once.

Serves 4 as a part of a Chinese meal, or 2 as a single dish.

dong po rou
tung po pork

This delicious dish is named for Su Dongpo, a famous poet, statesman, and gourmet of the Song Dynasty, a combination of talents not uncommon in Chinese history. I certainly admire him for his many culinary skills, and especially for inventing this savoury dish. Dong Po pork is a house speciality in several restaurants in Hangzhou since Su Dongpo was a governor of the city. Gentle, long, slow simmering renders the meat into a melting, buttery, tender gastronomic experience. The cut used is pork belly, referred to as "five-flowered" pork in Chinese. There seem to be many versions of this popular dish in restaurants throughout China, but my favourite is this one in which the skin is first browned; in addition, simmering the pork in a whole piece keeps the meat moist. Although this is a time-consuming preparation, it is relatively simple, and it reheats well. It is wonderful served with plain rice and stir-fried vegetables.

900 g–1.1 kg/2–2½ lb fresh bacon
3 tablespoons peanut oil
6 spring onions
6 fresh ginger root slices
125 g/4 oz rock sugar, crushed or 4 tablespoons sugar
125 ml/4 fl oz dark soy sauce
2 tablespoons light soy sauce
125 ml/4 fl oz rice wine or dry sherry
125 ml/4 fl oz water

Blanch the bacon in a pot of boiling water for 10 minutes. Remove with a slotted spoon and blot thoroughly dry with kitchen paper.

Heat a wok or large frying pan until hot. Add the oil, turn down the heat, add the fresh bacon, skin side down. Slowly brown the skin until it is golden and crispy. This should take about 10 to 15 minutes. Remove the meat and wipe off any excess fat with kitchen paper.

Cut the onions into 7.5-cm/3-in pieces. In a large heavy casserole pot, combine the onions, ginger, rock sugar, the soy sauces, rice wine or sherry, water and meat together. Bring the mixture to a simmer, cover tightly, and cook slowly over low heat for 3 hours or until the pork is very tender and much of the fat is rendered. Drain off the liquid, remove the onions and ginger. Skim off any surface fat. Cut the pork into thin slices, arrange on a platter, pour the sauce over and serve. *Serves 6 as part of a Chinese meal, or 3 as a single dish.*

long jing chao xia
prawns in dragon well tea

I sampled this well-known dish at the renowned Lou Wai Lou restaurant, on the shores of Hangzhou's West Lake. I have heard about this dish since I was a child: freshwater prawns stir-fried and uniquely flavoured by the legendary Long Jing (Dragon Well) teas of Zhejiang province. Connoisseurs of Chinese tea regard Dragon Well as the finest. The leaves of this green tea are prepared in a complex process that avoids fermentation. The best quality leaves are picked before the spring rains fall and when the young stems have but one tender sprout. These fragile sprouts are the basis for the tea's delicate and refreshing fragrance and taste. In the recipe, the tea leaves themselves combine with the prawns to make an exquisite and quite unusual combination with an almost fresh taste. Even more common Chinese green teas will produce wonderful results.

450 g/1 lb medium-sized raw prawns, unpeeled
   with heads removed, or 350–375 g/12–13 oz peeled,
   raw prawns
2 teaspoons salt
1 tablespoon Long Jing (Dragon Well) Tea or any green tea
225 ml/8 fl oz boiling water
1½ tablespoons peanut oil
1 tablespoon rice wine or dry sherry

If the prawns are unpeeled, peel them by removing their shells, legs, and tails. Devein them by making a surface cut down the back of the prawns and removing the black, green, or yellow matter with the tip of the knife or cleaver. Rinse them well under cold running water and pat them thoroughly dry with kitchen paper. Rub the prawns evenly with salt and set aside.

Put the tea leaves in a heatproof measuring jug and pour in the hot water. Let the tea steep for 15 minutes.

Heat a wok or large frying pan until hot and add the oil. Then add the prawns and rice wine or dry sherry and stir-fry for 30 seconds. Pour in the tea and add about half of the tea leaves and cook for 1 further minute.

Remove the prawns with a slotted spoon to a serving platter and reduce any liquid in the wok by half.

Pour this over the prawns and serve at once.

Serves 4 as part of a Chinese meal, or 2 as a single dish.

zhima haizhe
sesame jellyfish

Sea cucumbers, limpets, sea slugs, barnacles, sea snakes – all the creatures of both fresh and salt water that are big enough to eat and not outright poisonous are welcomed in Chinese cooking. This includes jellyfish, which is always bought dried. It is a textured, fat-free, protein food that makes a refreshing and crunchy appetiser.

Salty and mild-tasting by itself, marinated jellyfish takes on another dimension with the sesame flavours permeating the slightly salty jellyfish to produce a cooling treat. This is traditionally served by itself and is a a very easy dish to prepare because the jellyfish comes already partially soaked and shredded in the package. This dish will stay fresh for hours in the refrigerator.

225 g/8 oz prepared shredded jellyfish
2 teaspoons light soy sauce
3 tablespoons sesame oil
2 teaspoons white rice vinegar
2 teaspoons sugar

3 tablespoons white sesame
  seeds, toasted

Rinse the jellyfish well in cold running water and drain. Put it in a stainless steel bowl and cover with boiling water. Let the jellyfish sit in the water for about 15 minutes or until it is tender.

Drain the jellyfish and continue to soak at least 6 times in several changes of cold water. Drain thoroughly and blot dry with kitchen paper and set aside.

Mix together the soy sauce, sesame oil, white rice vinegar, and sugar in a small bowl. Toss the jellyfish well in this sauce and let it sit for at least 30 minutes.

Just before serving the jellyfish, garnish with the sesame seeds.

Serves 4 as part of a Chinese meal, or 2 as a single dish.

zao liu yu pian
stir-fried fish fillets with cloud ears and cucumbers

Students of Chinese cuisine know, and countless of its recipes illustrate, that China could be called the land of mushrooms. The commercial cultivation of mushrooms began in China around the mid-seventh century, about one thousand years before European cultivation began in France. There are about three hundred kinds of mushrooms to be found in China; eighty-three of these varieties are known to be poisonous. Since it is impossible to identify with certainty some of the poisonous mushrooms except by their effects, one hesitates to speculate on how the Chinese managed over the centuries to differentiate them so successfully. In any event, mushrooms are among the most popular foods in China with enough production to export more mushrooms than any other country.

In this recipe, which I learned from the proprietor of a small restaurant in Kunming, Yunnan, "cloud ears", a smaller version of the popular wood ear fungus, lend their subtle earthy flavour and distinctive texture to the dish.

The crunchy cucumbers add another texture and complement the delicately flavoured fillets. In China, I enjoyed this dish made with fresh carp fillets but any firm, white-fleshed fish will work as well.

700 g/1½ lb thick-cut fillets of any firm, white-fleshed fish
   such as cod, halibut, scrod or red snapper, or
   800 g/1¾ lb fish steaks on the bone
2 teaspoons salt
2 tablespoons light soy sauce
1 tablespoon rice wine or dry sherry
2 teaspoons cornflour
25 g/1 oz cloud ear fungus
225 g/8 oz cucumber, about 1
3 tablespoons peanut oil
½ tablespoon finely chopped peeled garlic
1 tablespoon finely chopped peeled fresh ginger root
1½ tablespoons rice wine or dry sherry
2 tablespoons light soy sauce
1 tablespoon dark soy sauce
225 ml/8 fl oz chicken stock
2 teaspoons cornflour mixed with 1 tablespoon water

Cut the fillets into 5 cm/2 in long and 25 mm/1 in wide pieces. Put them into a bowl with the salt, soy sauce, rice wine or sherry, and cornflour and mix well. Let the fillets marinate for 1 hour.

Soak the cloud ear fungus in warm water for at least 15 minutes. Rinse them several times in cold running water to remove any sand. Drain thoroughly and set aside.

Peel the cucumber, slice it in half lengthways, and remove any seeds. Cut the halves into 5 cm/2 in long and 25 mm/1 in wide pieces.

Heat a wok or large frying pan until hot and add 2 tablespoons of oil. Put in the fish pieces and fry them until they are lightly browned, about 2 minutes. Remove them with a slotted spoon and drain thoroughly on kitchen paper.

Reheat the wok or pan and add the remaining oil. When the oil is hot, add the cloud ear fungus, cucumber, garlic, and ginger and stir-

restaurant cooking – recipes

fry for 1 minute. Add the rice wine or sherry, soy sauces, and chicken stock and cook for 3 minutes. Add the cornflour mixture and stir. Return the fish pieces to the wok and cook gently until the fish is heated through. Ladle onto a platter and serve with rice.

Serves 4 as part of a Chinese meal, or 2 as a single dish.

ban doufu
tofu salad

In the middle of a Shanghai heat wave, my appetite was as languid as the weather, but I longed for some of the local specialities, especially something light and simple. A friend directed me to a small private restaurant where the quality was uneven but this cold appetiser made from fresh bean curd was a delectable treat. China is the place where soybeans were first cultivated over three thousands years ago. By the first millennium B.C., the soybean was already enshrined as one of the five sacred grains, the others being millet, glutinous millet, wheat, and rice.

This recipe involves no cooking. Extremely nutritious, but rather bland, soft and silky-smooth bean curd needs only a touch of taste and texture. Here the dried shrimp and preserved vegetables turn it into a truly delightful first course. Very fresh bean curd is essential. Serve it cold.

450 g/1 lb fresh soft bean curd
2 tablespoons dried shrimp
2 tablespoons Sichuan preserved vegetables, rinsed
    and finely chopped
1 tablespoon chilli bean sauce
1½ tablespoons sesame oil
GARNISH
1-2 chopped spring onions

Gently drain the bean curd and soak in several changes of cold water. Drain it again thoroughly and cut it into 25-mm/1-in cubes. Place the bean curd on a serving platter and refrigerate.

Soak the dried shrimp in warm water for 20 minutes and drain thoroughly. Finely chop the shrimp and place in a small bowl with the preserved vegetables and chilli bean sauce. Arrange this mixture evenly over the bean curd and drizzle with the sesame oil. Garnish with the spring onions and serve at once.

Serves 4 as part of a Chinese meal, or 2 as a single dish.

ganbian kugua
stir-fried bitter melon with fresh mild chillies

Most often used in soups and stir-fried dishes, bitter melon was originally deemed a medicine and was supposed to clear the blood. Eating it without blanching to reduce its bitterness one can well understand its reputation, especially with children. Like other edible medicines, it worked its way into the culinary repertory and is now a popular food item. The ones I sampled had just been harvested, fully grown but quite green. Even with blanching, the meat retains its firm texture. Riper melons are somewhat less bitter and softer in texture.

700 g/1½ lb bitter melon
225 g/8 oz fresh mild chillies
1½ tablespoons peanut oil
Pinch of salt
1½ tablespoons chopped garlic
225 ml/8 fl oz chicken stock
2 tablespoons light soy sauce
2 teaspoons sugar

Wash, then cut the bitter melon in half lengthways and remove the seeds. Cut the melon into fine slices and blanch them in a pot of boiling water for 2 minutes. Remove with a slotted spoon and drain well on kitchen paper.

Cut the chillies in half and remove the seeds. Finely slice the chillies. Heat a wok or large frying pan over high heat and add the oil. When

restaurant cooking – recipes

hot, add the salt and the chillies and stir-fry for 10 seconds. Put in the bitter melon, garlic, chicken stock, soy sauce, and sugar. Turn down the heat and simmer the mixture for 3 minutes. Serve at once.

Serves 4 as part of a Chinese meal, or 2 as a single dish.

leng oing gua
cold cucumbers with garlic

Recently, the loosening of state controls have encouraged a number of family-run private enteprises, among them new restaurants. A knowledgeable friend led us to one such place in Shanghai, a simple but increasingly popular restaurant. There, we enjoyed this delightful cold dish, a refreshing starter on a humid summer night. I have modified the recipe slightly, since I found the bits of raw garlic in the original version too strong. A quick browning of the garlic in the wok gives off a wonderful aroma.

1½ tablespoons peanut oil
1 tablespoon coarsely chopped garlic
450 g/1 lb cucumbers
2 teaspoons salt
2 teaspoons sugar
1 tablespoon white rice vinegar

Slice the cucumbers in half lengthways and, using a spoon, remove any seeds. Cut the cucumber halves into 7.5-cm x 12-mm/ 3 x ½-in pieces.

Combine the cucumber pieces with salt and allow to sit in a colander set inside a bowl for 10 minutes. Rinse them in cold water, blot them dry and toss with the sugar and vinegar.

Heat a wok or large frying pan until hot and add the oil and garlic. Stir-fry for 15 seconds until it is lightly brown. Mix with the cucumbers and serve.

Serves 4 as part of a Chinese meal, or 2 as a single dish.

CHAPTER 9
SNACKS and STREET FOODS

One often sees in the streets of China what are known as "street kitchens,"
to which a labourer, after a day's toil, will resort with a choice piece of meat,
instructing the cook, on the spot, to cook it to his own liking.
                                   Musings of a Chinese Gourmet, F.T. Cheng

Between-meal snacks are an important component of Chinese cuisine.
As far back in time as archeological records take us, it seems the
Chinese had three broad categories of food: *fan* (grain foods, such as
rice), *cai* (meat, fish, and vegetable dishes), and *xiao chi* (snacks, or small
eats). In southeastern and western China, where the large majority of
Chinese people live, two main meals a day – midday and evening –
are the norm, but in fact five meals a day are consumed, because three
smaller *xiao chi* meals, are eaten. In northern China, village people
usually have three large meals a day during the season of long days (late
spring to early autumn) and two main meals a day the rest of the year.
But at all times of the year snacks during the day and substantial late
evening snacks are the rule. One reason for this is that many Chinese

eat only a light breakfast, and people are hungry for more food long before the midday meal.

From my own experiences in China, some of my favourite "commercial" foods (that is, not prepared at home) have been those served in snack shops, street food stalls, and roadside food carts. Many Chinese I spoke with seem to agree that the most satisfying foods outside their own homes were found in places offering *xiao chi*. The streets and alleyways of China's cities and villages are redolent with the fragrance of mouth-watering aromas drifting from the many food vendors that line them. Many of the markets I visited were filled with these vendors. Some people eat their snacks while shopping or simply buy the snacks as supplements to their meals, perhaps to keep the children quiet while it is being prepared.

Soup noodles, prosaic perhaps but satisfying, constitute one of the most popular snacks throughout China. These are easy for food vendors to prepare and there is never a lack of customers for them. Of the many other popular snack dishes, some of the most cherished throughout China are *jiaozi* dumplings. These are wonderful snacks which are sold boiled, fried, or less often, steamed. Filled with meats, vegetables, garlic, spring onions – each region has its regional touches and variations. Really a well-balanced, light meal, I have eaten more of these dumplings than I care to count and enjoyed every one.

I've eaten thick noodles in rich soup in a market in Hangzhou, light, satiny rice noodle pastries in a street stall in Guangzhou, and spicy noodles from a tiny food cart in Chengdu, all quickly and simply prepared, and delicious. Techniques used to cook them range from boiling to stir-frying and steaming. Variations also exist in what I thought were purely southern-style Chinese foods. For example, I enjoyed a rice porridge with fresh corn that had a topping of chilli sauce at several market villages in Sichuan. Wontons, dumplings in a thin noodle wrapping, are found in numerous regional forms. I have even had blanched noodles with wontons stuffed with minced pork in a hearty broth, and enjoyed the famous "congee" rice porridge of southern China on many street corners all over China.

Perhaps this habitual and substantial "snacking" started because for so many centuries officials and workers in the cities kept such long hours that restaurants stayed open and vendors hawked their goods until late at night, even until dawn. The account of life written in the Northern Song Dynasty (960–1126) says, "Right up until that time, there were those who brought forth their jars and sold tea,... even in the winter months, though there were great winds, snow, and rain."

In a thirteenth-century drama, *Baihu Ting,* there is a character, a fruit vendor, who hawks delicacies from five different provinces. These include "juicy-juicy sweet, full-full fragrant, sweet-smelling, red and watery fresh-peeled, round-eye lychees from Fuzhou; from Piguang some sour-sour tart, shady-cool, sweet-sweet, luscious yellow oranges and green tangerines with the leaves on; and some supple-supple soft, quite-quite white, crystal-sweet, crushed-flat candied persimmons from Songyang." It is clear from the text that the audience found nothing extraordinary about this catalog of delights. Even today, dried, candied, and pickled fruits are eaten as snacks everywhere in China. While traveling in China, I made sure I had a cache of wonderful dried plums before I set out on any day trip. Fresh fruits have always been expensive and in the past often available only to the wealthier classes. Today, however, fruits in season can be relished and enjoyed as a popular snack or dessert by everyone.

During the Song era, wine shops and so-called noodle shops were well-established snack food outlets. Some of them were located in permanent buildings, but most of them were quite movable, little more than thatched shacks. The two most popular snacks sold seem to have been *you bing,* sugared oil pastries filled with bean paste and steamed, and *hu bing,* the same pastries deep-fried. These pastries still exist in different versions, several of which I sampled throughout China. Other prepared snack foods popular in the Song Dynasty were *man tou* (steamed bread buns), cooked pork, preserved meats and fish, and sweetened fruits and thick slices of sweetmeats.

Food stalls were often production centers, wholesale suppliers to the hawkers who circulated throughout the cities and larger towns of the Song Dynasty. A thousand years ago, the sight of such street vendors was commonplace. Written records indicate that even then such street food was highly regarded and eaten with gusto. By the time of the Qing Dynasty, still hundreds of years ago, an elaborate "take out" or

soup noodles

"take away" system was in place. Either a restaurant or its licensed concessionaires, each with a shed next to the restaurant, would fill orders for snacks and light meals from the establishment. Nearby were other food stalls that specialised in "small eats" such as salted or pickled vegetables and rice, peanut and sugar candies, pastries, and plain or fancy rice porridge. For those who wished to cook their own, hot water was on sale.

Paintings and prints from almost four hundred years ago illustrate that many stalls, booths, and shops satisfied the "small eats" appetite of the masses in Beijing. Some of the places were quite elaborate, along the lines of a mobile restaurant. Most of the others were quite small affairs, featuring one or two popular specialities in season. These might be spring cakes, green dumplings (probably made from fresh cabbage or chives) in the late spring; summer wines, sea scallops, mustard green, salt eggs in the early summer; heavy dumplings for the Dragon-Boat Festival in the summer; watermelon at the autumn solstice. There would have been glutinous rice dumplings with sweet red bean stuffing for the kitchen gods' festival; river crabs in the early winter/late autumn (when the roe is most delicate); and all sorts of delicacies for the New Year festival. Being sensitive to their clients' tastes, which were often the vendors' own, was more than just a service. It was also smart business.

These traditions remained intact until the People's Republic of China was established in 1949. Then it was decreed that private entrepreneurial initiatives were too "bourgeois" or individualistic to be allowed to continue. Food stalls, street vendors, hawkers, and indeed even most restaurants disappeared. The policy reforms of the last decade have allowed the re-emergence of these valued institutions. Already many have recovered their previous levels of culinary skill and service. I think that given time and social stability, they will indeed once again become an important aspect of Chinese cuisine.

In western China, I walked around the so-called night markets. Open until the wee hours of the morning, they serve night-shift workers and hungry people in general. Delicious smoked pork treats are a speciality including almost every identifiable part of the pig. Wine shops sold bowls of what is called "white wine," actually a strong potion more like vodka, which is brewed from a type of millet. I watched with fascination as the local people strolled into the shops for a quick drink, while others entered with jars and bottles to have them filled for home consumption. It was evident that everyone appreciated the convenience of these night markets.

In Beijing, long famous for its "small eats," night markets and street stalls have sprouted like mushrooms since the government rescinded its ban on them. I was struck by the carnival atmosphere of the street scenes, crowded with people sampling the assortment of local and regional favourites. Clearly, these colourful markets and snack places are fulfilling a long-latent social and culinary need. That one eats better at the sidewalk food stalls in Beijing than at most of the fancy tourist restaurants is a common opinion with which I concur. Freshly made pulled noodles are boiled and served, as are homemade *jiaozi* dumplings, Beijing sausage, Sichuan cold noodles, Tianjin turnovers, Lanzhou noodles, Wenzhou fishball soup, and Xinjiang mutton barbecues – I sampled *all* of these at the Wangfujing street market in Beijing.

Far away from Beijing, in Chengdu, Sichuan, a different sort of "small eats" is consumed. There a friend took me to a place which specialises in typical Sichuan snacks, such as *dan dan mian,* spicy noodles tossed with chilli and minced pork, which I ate in two minutes amid the street traffic. We then had "pearl balls," a sweet glutinous rice pastry, and the famous *Chengdu huntuns,* dumplings known in the West as wontons, but tossed there in a marvellously spicy sauce with a good sprinkling of roasted ground Sichuan peppercorns. I also sampled a light egg crepe filled with meats and steamed pork dumplings – all of these in the most appropriately named snack restaurant, Long Chao Shou, "The Dragon's Eating Place," home of fiery and assertive snacks.

The best and most famous of snacks are in the south of China in the Guangzhou (Canton) region, where, in E.N. Anderson's words, "the Chinese fondness for snacks and small eats reaches a kind of apotheosis." This is the home of dim sum (literally meaning "heart's delight" or "to touch the heart"), famous beyond China's borders because they were carried by Cantonese emigrants around the world.

dim sum

And the region is also the home of the ultimate in "small eating," the tea house, serving only dim sum snacks and different teas. Guangzhou's relative affluence and the balmy subtropical climate of the region, with its long summery days and calm nights, create an atmosphere of sociability. The Cantonese, with great reason, believe that their cuisine is the best in China and they make the most of it as often as they can. Dim sum are available from early morning until the late afternoon, with the busiest times in the midmorning and midafternoon hours. Substantial breakfasts of fancy rice porridge with peanuts, meat, fish and sauces are served.

Noodle soups are to be had here as elsewhere in China. But in this region meat is almost always included along with noodles, and dumplings in soups are common. And the portions are as large as an equivalent light meal. Foreign foods, especially Western-style baked breads, rolls, and pastries, have been added to the lists of selections. In the Canton region, these so-called snacks are really more than that: they comprise a very substantial late breakfast or heavy lunch. Elsewhere in China, however, dim sum remains just that, "small eats."

The number and variety of the Cantonese regional snacks defy description. In one tea house, more than two thousand dim sum dishes are offered on a rotation basis. Among the exquisite savoury dishes were steamed dumplings with minced pork and shrimp, chicken soup with dumplings, steamed rice flour filled with assorted meats, deep-fried bean curd filled with pork and shrimp, steamed minced meat balls, and sliced beef liver with steamed shrimp dumpling. The equally impressive menu of sweet dishes included such items as crisp and sticky sweet cake topped with almonds, bean-filled cakes, sesame balls in sweet syrup, custard tarts, and sweet red bean paste soup. In northern China, these types of snacks are known as *dian xin,* a mandarin form of dim sum, the name referring more to sweet dessert snacks than to the savoury ones in the south.

Drinking tea is the norm when enjoying *dim sum.* And in the tea houses, where the pace is noisy, leisurely, and informal, it is interesting to watch the social interaction. People sit with their friends at a table and the waiter brings the desired teas. This is no casual choice. The five-thousand-year-old Chinese acquaintance with teas has led to a reverential attitude toward the beverage. "Tea tempers the spirits, calms and harmonises the mind; it arouses thought and prevents drowsiness, enlightens and refreshes the body, and clears the perceptive faculties," so wrote the great authority on tea, Luk Yu, over a thousand years ago. Whether one prefers Iron Goddess of Mercy, Dragon Well, or White Peony, or any other of a great number of teas with special flavours, strengths, and fragrances, the choice is thoughtfully made.

Once the tea is selected, it is followed by the dim sum dining ritual. As the carts containing the various delicacies are wheeled around, the diners, alerted by the servers' cries on the foods available, point to the desired dishes, which are then placed on the table. Such eating is a leisurely affair. There is no rush; business and social conversation is one of the main reasons for the tea house. And, given the din of the place, the conversation seems to take place at the top of everyone's lungs. All the foods and beverages served are totalled up at the very end; the servers, with unerring memories, recall everything that has been placed on your table. The trick to their seemingly magical calculation is that they count the empty plates on your table, keeping a sharp eye to see that none has been moved to a neighbouring one!

There are many true tea houses in China, places that don't serve dim sum but serve just tea and another of its familiar accompaniments, sweets. I've enjoyed the atmosphere of such houses from Hangzhou, where I sampled the famous local Dragon Well tea which was freshly picked, to Suzhou, where I enjoyed the tea and pastries of that region. One of my most interesting experiences was in the Chengdu Chengbei Shenxi Chashe tea house in Sichuan. On Sundays and holidays especially, but really just about on any day, mainly older male patrons come to relax. Most of the tables are outdoors, under shady trees. The tea house is next to the Hu Chen He moat, whose cool waters afford some relief during the warm muggy months of summer. The house features the local teas and is a very popular place. I was most amused by customers carrying around their caged pet birds. The men smoke, play cards and chess, read newspapers, even have their hair cut or face shaved, as they engage in animated conversation, drinking their tea.

Many tea houses provide entertainment as well – musicians, singers, and storytellers. In Huangzhou, I spent one long, languid, hot afternoon in a shady tea house that spilled outdoors, listening while a storyteller entertained us with ancient tales. Patrons pay a small cover charge that entitles them to a place to sit, a cup of tea, and as many refills as desired. They are like social clubs, traditionally for men, but on my last trip I noticed a few women as well.

One of the most delightful detours I took in China was a day trip to Shaoxing, the home of the famous yellow rice wine. Wine shops there still play a key role in Chinese social life. Akin perhaps to cafes and bars in the West, these places are quite informal, conducive to conversation lubricated by one's favourite beverage, and sometimes offering basic snack foods. The wines were, as the Chinese say, those which "go down with snack foods."

Wines and beers, like many of China's teas, tend to be locally produced, though there are some whose reputations transcend their regions. Shaoxing yellow wine, a name known throughout China, has been celebrated in stories and poems for hundreds of years. It also is used in the finest cooking of China. Until recently, Shaoxing wine was unavailable in local wine shops, as almost all of its production was exported. However, some of it now remains in China. Today, wine shops continue their contribution to Chinese social life.

dan dan mian
spicy sichuan noodles

Everywhere noodle dishes, xiao chi, or "small eats" are found in hole-in-the-wall restaurants, food stalls, and places selling snacks. This is a typical Sichuan dish that is now popular throughout China, especially in the north. There are many versions of it and they are all easy to make, tasty, and quite filling, but this is an exceptionally delicious one I sampled at a tiny street restaurant in Chengdu, Sichuan.

225 g/8 oz minced pork
1 tablespoon dark soy sauce

1 teaspoon salt
225 ml/8 fl oz peanut oil
3 tablespoons finely chopped garlic
2 tablespoons finely chopped peeled fresh ginger root
5 tablespoons finely chopped spring onions
2 tablespoons sesame paste or peanut butter
2 tablespoons dark soy sauce
2 tablespoons chilli oil
2 teaspoons salt
225 ml/8 fl oz chicken stock
350 g/12 oz fresh Chinese thin egg noodles or dry Chinese thin
   egg noodles
1 tablespoon Sichuan peppercorns, roasted and ground

Combine the pork, soy sauce, and salt in a small bowl and mix well.
Heat a wok or frying pan until hot. Add the oil and deep-fry the pork,
stirring with a spatula to break it into small pieces. When the pork is
crispy and dry, about 4 minutes, remove it with a slotted spoon and
drain on kitchen paper.

Pour off the oil, leaving 2 tablespoons in the wok. Reheat the wok
or pan and add the garlic, ginger, and onions and stir-fry for
30 seconds. Then add the sesame paste or peanut butter, soy sauce,
chilli oil, salt, and chicken stock and simmer for 4 minutes.

Cook the noodles in a large pot of boiling water for 2 minutes if
they are fresh or 5 minutes if they are dried. Drain the noodles well in
a colander. Divide the noodles into individual bowls or put them in a
large soup tureen. Ladle on the sauce, garnish with the fried pork and
Sichuan peppercorns and serve at once.

Serves 4 to 6 as part of a Chinese meal, or 2 to 4 as a single dish.

snacks and street foods – recipes

wangfujing leng mian
tasty cold noodles

Among the freshest culinary delights in Beijing today are the so-called night markets. These are recently opened groups of private enterprise food stalls located in busy sections throughout the capital. They serve quite delicious, simple food, representing the tastes and flavours of all regions of China. The markets are a little like pavement cafes, but without tables and chairs. People sample dishes standing up or walking along, and it is fun to go from stall to stall. The food is easy to prepare, savoury, and satisfying. I found that the night markets offer far better food than most of the state-owned eating establishments. Among my favourites is one near Wangfujing (the name derives from a fifteenth-century well), the major shopping area in the capital. It was there I enjoyed this recipe, a delicious platter of noodles, perhaps inspired by Sichuan cooking, that contrasted nicely with the refreshing cucumbers just then in season. Like most of the food stall offerings, this dish is very easily made, can be served at room temperature, and is a pleasure to eat.

450 g/1 lb fresh or dried Chinese egg noodles
1 tablespoon sesame oil
450 g/1 lb cucumbers
175 g/6 oz fresh bean sprouts
SAUCE
1 tablespoon finely chopped garlic
1 tablespoon finely chopped peeled fresh ginger root
2 teaspoons light soy sauce
1 tablespoon dark soy sauce
1 tablespoon sugar
2½ tablespoons sesame paste or
   peanut butter
1 tablespoon sesame oil
1 tablespoon white rice vinegar
2 teaspoons chilli oil
2 tablespoons granulated sugar

If you are using fresh noodles, boil them for 3 to 5 minutes, then drain thoroughly, rinse in cold water and toss immediately in sesame oil. If you are using dried noodles, cook them according to the package instructions or boil for 4 minutes, drain thoroughly, rinse in cold water and toss them in sesame oil.

Peel and slice the cucumbers in half lengthways, and, using a teaspoon, remove the seeds. Cut the cucumber halves into fine long shreds. Rinse the bean sprouts and drain thoroughly.

Mix the sauce ingredients together in a bowl or in a blender. When you are ready to serve, toss the noodles with the sauce, cucumbers, and bean sprouts. Sprinkle with sugar and serve at once.

Serves 4 as part of a Chinese meal, or 2 as a single dish.

chengdu huntun
chengdu wontons

Huntuns are simply dumplings, well-known in the West mostly by their Cantonese name, wontons. The skins (usually made from wheat) are filled with meat or fish or vegetables in a seasoned sauce. They are in the xiao chi *("small eats") repertory but are also found as part of complete menus. The filling and sauce will vary with the region and the season. I discovered this version at a delightful shop in Chengdu, Sichuan, that specialises in dumplings. The authentic taste requires these wontons to be hot and spicy, but you may tone this down a little bit by reducing the amount of chilli oil.*

1 package Wonton skins
   (about 30 to 35 skins)
FILLING
350 g/12 oz minced pork
1 egg, beaten
1 tablespoon sesame oil
2 teaspoons salt
½ teaspoon freshly ground black pepper

1 tablespoon finely chopped garlic
4 tablespoons finely chopped
   spring onions
3 tablespoons dark soy sauce
1 tablespoon sugar
1 tablespoon chilli oil
2 teaspoons Chinese black vinegar
¼ teaspoon freshly ground
   black pepper
GARNISH
1 tablespoon Sichuan peppercorns,
   roasted and ground

Combine the pork, egg, sesame oil, salt, and pepper in a large bowl and mix well.

Then, using a teaspoon, put a small amount of the filling in the center of each wonton skin. Bring up two sides, dampen the edges with a little water, and pinch them together to seal. Continue until you have used up all the filling or wonton skins.

In a large serving bowl, combine the garlic, onions, soy sauce, sugar, chilli oil, vinegar, and pepper. Stir to mix well.

Bring a large pot of water to the boil. Put in the wontons and simmer for 4 minutes. Remove them with a slotted spoon to the serving bowl.

Mix gently with the sauce, garnish with peppercorns, and serve at once.

Serves 4 as part of a Chinese meal, or 2 as a single dish.

chao liangyu zhusun mian
noodle soup with catfish and bamboo shoots

Fish provides much of the animal protein in the traditional Chinese diet. Whenever possible, a family or certainly a cooperative farm will have its own fish pond. While many varieties are raised, a very popular variety is catfish.

One evening in Hangzhou, I particularly enjoyed this hot soup of catfish with bamboo shoots in a sauce over noodles. It is a perfect quick meal and is a standard item in food stalls: the chicken broth is already prepared, the noodles are ready for blanching, and the fish quickly stir-fried. In minutes, every taste bud was satisfied, just the type of nutritious light meal or snack that the Chinese relish.

Catfish has a sweet delicate taste. It is bony but lends itself to stir-frying and braising. The texture is slightly flaky when cooked. If catfish fillets are unavailable, substitute any white fish fillets. With a vegetable or salad and some rice, this will make a substantial meal.

450 g/1 lb fresh catfish fillets or any firm, white-fleshed fish fillets
    such as cod, halibut, haddock, scrod or red snapper, or sole
2 teaspoons salt
1 egg, beaten
2 teaspoons cornflour
25 g/1 oz Chinese dried black mushrooms
450 g/1 lb fresh Chinese noodles
850 ml/1½ pt chicken stock
3 tablespoons peanut oil
1½ tablespoons peanut oil
2 tablespoons finely chopped spring onions
1 tablespoon finely chopped peeled fresh ginger root
125 g/4 oz bamboo shoots, finely shredded
2 tablespoons dried rice wine or dry sherry
1 tablespoon dark soy sauce
2 teaspoons sugar
1 teaspoon salt
1 tablespoon sesame oil

Cut the catfish or fish fillets into 7.5-cm × 25-mm/3 × 1-in strips and combine with the salt and egg. Sprinkle the strips evenly with the cornflour and set aside.

Soak the mushrooms in warm water for 20 minutes or until they are soft. Rinse under running water to remove any remaining sand. With a sharp knife, remove the stems and discard. Finely shred the mushroom caps.

snacks and street foods – recipes

Blanch the noodles in a pot of boiling water for 2 minutes. Drain thoroughly and set aside.

In a large pot, bring the stock to a simmer.

Heat a wok or large frying pan until hot. Add the oil, and when it is hot pan-fry the fish until it is golden brown. Remove the strips and drain on kitchen paper. Pour out the oil, wipe the wok or pan clean, and reheat. Add the 1½ tablespoons of oil, onions, and ginger and stir-fry for 15 seconds. Then add the mushrooms, bamboo shoots, rice wine or sherry, soy sauce, sugar, and salt. Mix the ingredients together well, and stir-fry for another minute. Return the fish to the wok and combine well.

Place the noodles in a very large bowl, add the stock and the fish, and drizzle the sesame oil over the top. Serve at once.

Serves 4 as part of a Chinese meal, or 2 as a single dish.

zong bao
deep-fried glutinous rice cakes

In China, almost any edible ingredient can be turned into a quick meal. Snacks vary according to the region, local preferences, and the season. Still, wherever you wander in China, you are sure to find something tasty for a quick bite to keep you going, whether shopping, working, or strolling along. The smells from the food stalls are always so tempting.

While exploring the fascinating markets of the remote village of Yi Liang Gou Jie, I happened upon an elderly woman selling these glutinous rice cakes. She wrapped the cakes in bamboo leaves and boiled them. When a customer ordered one, she unwrapped the cake and dropped it into hot oil. It quickly puffed up and turned golden brown and crispy. She then scooped it out, drained it, and sprinkled it with sugar. Glutinous rice is sweet and has a sticky texture that makes it easy to mould into any shape. In this recipe, I have slightly altered the method, by cooking the rice in a pot and then pressing it into a cake tin, bamboo leaves not always being available. The final results are the same. It's a delicious snack but also makes a rather unusual dessert.

450 g/1 lb glutinous or sweet rice
450 ml/16 floz water
1 tablespoon peanut oil
450 ml/16 fl oz peanut oil
sugar for dipping

In a large bowl, combine the rice with enough cold water to cover it at least by 5 cm/2 in. Soak for 8 hours or overnight. Drain well.

In a medium-sized pot, combine the rice and water. Bring the mixture to the boil, reduce the heat, cover, and cook for 40 minutes.

Using kitchen paper, rub 1 tablespoon of oil on all sides of a 20-cm/ 8-in square cake tin. Press the rice into the tin, cover it with aluminium foil, and press down on all sides until the rice is compressed as much as possible. Allow the rice to cool thoroughly.

Turn the rice onto a chopping board. It should fall out in one piece. Cut the rice into 7.5 x 4-cm/3 x 1½-in pieces.

Heat a wok or large frying pan until hot. Add the oil, and when it is hot, drop in the rice squares, a few at a time, and deep-fry until they are golden and crispy. Drain the squares thoroughly on kitchen paper. Serve warm with a dish of sugar for dipping.

Serves 6 to 8 as snacks or as dessert.

chao manli xiaren mian
stir-fried eels with prawns in noodle soup

All noodle soups in China use fresh ingredients, and this desire for freshness might disturb Western sensibilities. Eels, for example, harvested from nearby rivers are kept alive at food stalls until ready for cooking. High in protein and inexpensive, eel adds a great deal to the humble noodle soups that the Chinese so love. This is my version of a dish I had at the Gui Yuan Guan restaurant in Hangzhou. If fresh eel is not available, use white fish fillets.

225 g/8 oz fresh eel fillets or any firm, white-fleshed fish fillets
   such as cod, halibut, haddock, scrod or red snapper, or sole

1 teaspoon salt
1 teaspoon sesame oil
1 teaspoon cornflour
225 g/8 oz medium-sized raw prawns, peeled
450 g/1 lb fresh Chinese noodles
850 g/1½ pt chicken stock
1½ tablespoons peanut oil
2 tablespoons finely chopped spring onions
1 tablespoon finely chopped peeled fresh ginger root
2 tablespoons rice wine or dry sherry
2 teaspoons light soy sauce
2 teaspoons sugar
1 teaspoon salt
1 teaspoon cornflour mixed with 2 teaspoons water
1 tablespoon sesame oil

Cut the eel or fish fillets into long, thin 7.5-cm × 6-mm/3 × ¼-in strips. Combine the eel with the salt, sesame oil, and cornflour and set aside.

Blanch the prawns in a pot of salted, boiling water for 45 seconds. Drain thoroughly and set aside.

Blanch the noodles in a pot of boiling water for 2 minutes. Drain thoroughly and set aside.

In a large pot, bring the stock to a simmer.

Heat a wok or large frying pan until hot. Add the oil, onions, and ginger and stir-fry for 15 seconds. Then add the fish and prawns, and gently stir-fry for 2 minutes. Add the rice wine or sherry, soy sauce, sugar, and salt and stir-fry another minute, making sure to combine them well. Pour in the cornflour mixture and when it has thickened, remove from the heat.

Place the noodles in a very large bowl, add the stock, then the fish and prawn mixture and drizzle over the sesame oil. Serve at once.

Serves 4 as part of a Chinese meal, or 2 as a single dish.

huntun mian
wonton noodle soup

The taste of China comes through most clearly in the simplest dishes, and nowhere more clearly than in foods which rely heavily upon classic rich chicken stock, as does this simple recipe. Wonton dumplings and noodles are at their best in this context, and the result is a refreshing, quite satisfying meal, quick and easy to make. Small wonder it is a popular item at fast food stalls throughout southern China where people eat it at all hours of the day or night. There are probably as many variations on the basic theme of this recipe as there are cooks. Noodle soups outside of Guangdong tend to be a bit heavier than this Cantonese version, which relies upon good, light, clear, rich chicken broth. The thin wheat noodles supply a firm texture to the treat.

FILLING
125 g/4 oz fatty minced pork
125 g/4 oz raw prawns, peeled, deveined, and coarsely chopped
1 teaspoon rice wine or dry sherry
2 teaspoons light soy sauce
½ teaspoon salt
Freshly ground black pepper to taste
1 teaspoon sesame oil
1 package thin square wonton wrappers
225 g/8 oz fresh thin wheat or egg noodles
850 ml/1½ pt chicken stock
Salt
GARNISH
3 tablespoons finely chopped spring onions

Mix the filling ingredients together in a medium-sized bowl. Place 2 teaspoons of filling in the center of a wonton square. Pull up the sides and pinch them together to seal. The moisture from the filling should be enough to seal the wontons.

Bring a large pot of water to the boil and blanch the wontons for 3 minutes, drain well, and set aside. Then blanch the noodles for 3 to 5 minutes and drain well.

snacks and street foods – recipes

Bring the stock to a simmer, and season if necessary with salt. Add the noodles and wontons, and simmer for 1 minute. Garnish the soup with the spring onions and serve at once.

Serves 4 as part of a Chinese meal, or 2 as a single dish. Makes 25 wontons.

hua ji fan
chicken cooked with rice

When my mother and I returned to our ancestral village of Kaiping (Hoiping), we were impressed to hear that my cousin's son, Tan Songfa, was operating a successful food stall in town. The twenty-four-year-old and his two partners had a thriving business and when I visited the place I could see why. It is a modest shop, with a few chairs and tables set up. It has a pleasant river view, and the air is cool, and above all, the food is cheap, simple, and deliciously satisfying.

The limited menu included spareribs with rice and yellow eel with rice, both cooked in clay pots over charcoal. The young chefs also offered quail soup, chicken soup, stir-fried preserved vegetables, and braised pig tail, all cooked on a wok heated by propane gas. It was simple fare at its best. I was especially impressed by this chicken rice dish.

225 g/8 oz long-grain white rice
225 g/8 oz boneless chicken thighs with skin removed
1 tablespoon light soy sauce
2 teaspoons dark soy sauce
2 teaspoons rice wine or dry sherry
1 teaspoon salt
2 teaspoons sesame oil
1 teaspoon cornflour
1½ tablespoons peanut oil
2 teaspoons finely chopped, peeled fresh ginger root
GARNISH
1 tablespoon dark soy sauce

2 tablespoons finely chopped spring onions

Put the rice in a clay pot or medium-sized pot. Pour in enough water to cover the rice about 25 mm/1 in. Bring the rice to the boil and continue to cook until most of the water has evaporated. Reduce the heat to the lowest point possible and cover tightly.

Coarsely chop the chicken and combine it with the soy sauces, rice wine or sherry, salt, sesame oil, and cornflour.

Heat a wok or large frying pan until hot. Add the oil and ginger and stir-fry for 10 seconds. Then add the chicken and stir-fry for 2 minutes. Then pour the mixture on top of the rice, cover, and continue to cook for 10 minutes.

Just before serving, drizzle the soy sauce on top of the chicken and rice and garnish with the spring onions.

Serves 4 as part of a Chinese meal, or 2 as a single dish.

rousi chuan mian
pork and preserved vegetable noodle soup

It seems that every region in China is chauvinistic about its version of pork and vegetable noodle soup. Sichuan prefers to use preserved vegetables with chillies; in the north, red-in-snow cabbage, another style of preserved vegetables, is used. Whatever the variation, it is a dish common to many food stalls. Once the pork and vegetables are stir-fried, it is a simple matter to place them on the blanched noodles, then to quickly ladle clear broth over all. Of the many versions I tasted throughout China, I prefer the Sichuan version. It's easy to make for a delightful lunch or light supper dish.

450 g/1 lb minced pork
2 teaspoons rice wine or dry sherry
2 teaspoons light soy sauce
2 teaspoons dark soy sauce
1 teaspoon sesame oil
125 g/4 oz Sichuan preserved vegetables

450 g/1 lb fresh Chinese noodles
850 ml/1½ pt chicken stock
1½ tablespoons peanut oil
2 tablespoons finely chopped garlic
1 tablespoon finely chopped peeled
   fresh ginger root
2 teaspoons chilli bean sauce
1 teaspoon chilli powder
1 teaspoon sugar
GARNISH
2 tablespoons finely chopped
   spring onions

In a medium-sized bowl, combine the minced pork with the rice wine
or sherry, soy sauces, and sesame oil and set aside.

Rinse the Sichuan preserved vegetables in cold running water and
finely chop.

Blanch the noodles in a large pot of boiling water for 3 to 5 minutes.
Drain the noodles and set aside.

In a large pot, bring the stock to a simmer.

Heat a wok or large frying pan until hot. Add the oil, garlic, and
ginger, and stir-fry for 10 seconds. Then add the minced pork and
preserved vegetables. Stir-fry for 3 minutes, then add the chilli bean
sauce, chilli powder, and sugar. Continue to stir-fry for 2 minutes,
mixing well.

Place the noodles in a large bowl or in individual bowls. Add the
contents of the wok or pan and then ladle over the soup. Garnish with
the spring onions and serve at once.

Serves 4 as part of a Chinese meal, or 2 as a single dish.

shuijiao
dumplings in soup

These popular snacks are also called "water dumplings" because they float in a wonderfully clear broth. I have enjoyed them in all parts of China but my favourites are to be found in the street stalls of Guangzhou where the cooks have the knack of making them just right every time. Fine quality, thin pastry wrappers and a good filling are essential, but a good rich, clear chicken stock is also a basic requirement. Use thin round wrappers for these dumplings if they are available. Otherwise use square wonton wrappers instead. This dish could serve as a soup course or as a substantial snack.

FILLING
25 g/1 oz Chinese dried black mushrooms
225 g/8 oz fatty minced pork shoulder
225 g/8 oz raw prawns, peeled, deveined, and coarsely chopped
2 tablespoons finely chopped spring onions
2 teaspoons rice wine or dry sherry
1 teaspoon light soy sauce
1½ teaspoons sugar
½ teaspoon salt
Freshly ground black pepper to taste
1 teaspoon sesame oil
1 package round or square wonton wrappers
850 ml/1½ pt chicken stock
Salt
GARNISH
3 tablespoons finely chopped
    spring onions

Soak the mushrooms in warm water for 20 minutes or until they are soft. Rinse under running water to remove any remaining sand. With a sharp knife, remove the stems and discard. Finely chop the caps. Combine the chopped mushrooms with the rest of the filling ingredients in a medium-sized bowl.

Place 2 teaspoons of filling in the center of a wonton round. Fold over the round into a half-moon shape. If you are using a wonton square, fold over to make a triangle. Pinch the edges together to seal well. Fill all the wonton wrappers.

Bring a large pot of water to the boil and blanch the dumplings for 3 minutes. Remove the dumplings, drain well, and set aside.

Bring the stock to a simmer and season with salt if necessary. Add the dumplings, and simmer for 1 minute. Garnish with the onions and serve at once.

Serves 4 as part of a Chinese meal, or 2 as a single dish. Makes 40 to 50 dumplings.

CHAPTER 10
FOOD FOR THE BODY AND SOUL:
THE MEDICINAL AND THE VEGETARIAN

If you do not eat vegetables for three days, your eyes will catch fire.
Yangzhou folk saying

Every culture has some saying equivalent to: "eat this – it's good for you." And every cuisine has foods that are held to cure ailments: "Not feeling well? Have some chicken soup – or some tea with lemon; or some warm milk with honey; or some dry toast." (There are as many remedies as there are ailments.) What makes the Chinese equivalent of this practice so remarkable is that it has, through its history, raised the medicinal qualities of food to the level of a science and of a fine art. Certainly, in my own childhood experience, I *knew* that specific foods were cures for specific complaints. Instead of patent medicines for my early colds and "flu," I was plied with medicinal foods. Most were familiar items in our diet: pak choi, Chinese broccoli, cabbages, bitter melon (a favourite), or various meats and sauces; some were rather exotic herbs and roots with names unfamiliar to me. All had specific uses, depending upon whether my body needed heating or cooling, whether I had an appetite or not, whether I had a stomach ache or a headache, whether I was apathetic or hyperactive. There was an edible concoction for every complaint. Instead of a prescription from the doctor, I was fed a specially prepared, always flavourful dish.

All these foods had a beneficial effect, even if it was only because my mother said they did. Even so, all of my life I've esteemed the Chinese practice of respecting the medicinal qualities of foods as well as their nutritious and delectable ones. Certainly I absorbed the Chinese attitude toward not eating too much meat, because *fan* foods (grains) and *cai* (vegetables) are the foundation of good and wholesome diets. I think it proper, too, to explore food as medicine for the body, and food for the soul as in the case of Buddhists.

FOOD AS MEDICINE

It is quite remarkable that the first treatise on the medicinal qualities of foods was compiled in China about the second century B.C. Of the book, *The Inner Classic of the Yellow Emperor,* the Chinese scholar Cai Jingfeng wrote, "The foundations of the etiology, pathology, pathogenesis, treatment, and prevention (of disease) are laid down, (along with) the theoretical basis for dietotherapy." The Chinese, therefore, were among the first to link health with diet: you are what you eat. Even earlier, some time during the Zhou Dynasty (100–480 B.C.), nutritionists were made permanent members of the court's highest medical staff. The guiding model for the treatment of disease was by then well established: proper food and drink form the basis for curing illness.

As the noted Chinese scholar Frederick W. Mote has written, "It is perhaps not surprising that a civilisation preoccupied with food, and confronted with the greatest range of food products and ways of preparing them known to history, should seek to define the medical properties of foods. All material things were considered part of an organic cosmos in which all the parts belonged, interacted, and responded to the same dynamism … From one point of view, then, all foods are medicines." Thus, from the beginnning, Chinese scholars and scientists developed the empirical and theoretical bases of nutritional medicine. He continues: "It is hard to find a dish in the Middle Kingdom that is not based upon the recipe of some sage who lived centuries ago and who had an hygienic principle in mind when he designed it." That's an exaggeration, but it remains true that Chinese cuisine makes no sharp distinctions between "health foods" and other foods.

There are innumerable foods and dishes in the Chinese diet which nevertheless function at specific moments as therapy. By this I mean that many common foods can serve as medicine when necessary, and many specifically medical prescriptions are commonly used foodstuffs. Among these foods of a dual nature are such items – some familiar – as ginger, cinnamon, Chinese prickly ash, Chinese onion, garlic, Chinese yam, vinegar, egg, sesame, mung bean, and rice. Wine, too, is both a beverage and a medicinal agent, and was seen as such in ancient days: the words "wine" and "medicine" share the same linguistic root in Chinese. Indeed, they had the same Chinese character at one time. We "moderns" are understandably enthralled by the benefits of medicines and medical therapies and impressed by medical theories of diseases and their treatment. Yet food and medicine were almost indistinguishable worldwide before the twentieth century. Where the Chinese differed from most cultures is that they recognised food as essential to good health. They saw, too, that deficiencies, excesses, and inappropriate choices of foods would also lead to pathology.

It took many generations in China for strictly medicinal food, prescribed for specific ailments, to become defined as such and to be placed in a special category. Many still overlap and exist both in the kitchen and in the sick room. This is why, even today, foods such as those mentioned above and many others, like Chinese dates, pepper, crystal sugar, hawthorn, and seed of Job's tear, can be bought either in a grocery shop or from a herbalist to use as food or medicine or both.

The point of food as medicine is to attain and maintain harmony between the body and its nutritional needs. Historically, this is done

food as medicine

by the careful consideration of the "four natures" of both food and the body: cold, hot, cool, and warm. Then they are carefully complemented by the "five flavours": salty, sour, sweet, pungent, and bitter.

Chinese doctors (who are also nutritionists) have always attempted to rectify the pathological imbalances a patient manifests. Thus, for a fever, "cool" foods (which are also medicines) are prescribed; for chills, warm or hot remedies are in order. In matching the four natures to the five flavours, a salty food (also medicine) softens lumps, a bitter one eradicates dampness, a sour treats diarrhea, and so forth. In all cases, combining the various ingredients is carefully controlled, dosages are of supreme importance, and proper harmonising effects are always the goal. The best medicinal cook, like my mother, prepares a delicious dish tempting to the palate, easily digestible, and richly nutritious; the patient should neither know nor care that medicine is being administered.

Dietotherapy is the modern name given to the treatment of disease by using common foods. Its practitioners consider each patient's age, sex, and special circumstances. Over the centuries, specific foods and the recipes for the most common ailments were written about, discussed, and of great interest to healers and lay people alike. There are precise formulations for the preparation of medicines for such pathologies as the common cold, influenza, bronchitis, infectious hepatitis, insomnia, and the mumps. The list covers every known ailment, including "insufficiency of postpartum milk secretion," and the Chinese have always been masterful diagnosticians.

We should not smile too quickly or patronizingly at what might seem an entire country's quaint attitude concerning the relationship between diet and health. In fact, the current Western trend is to recognise precisely this connection. While Chinese theory may seem unpersuasive to many, consider that the mass of empirical data on which its attitudes and practices are based is indeed impressive and valuable to us today; it has a long, carefully developed history.

The varieties of medicinal foods are familiar even to Western eyes. There are porridges and thick soups made with meat, fish, or eggs; soothing broths, mild herbal teas, juices, mild alcoholic drinks; and staple dishes such as sweet cakes, pancakes, sweet or salty steamed stuffed buns, dumplings, and steamed rice (bitter and puckery residues are rarely prescribed). Clearly, the main purpose of dietotherapy is nourishment. In the absence of "miracle drugs," these foods – medicines, administered by mothers with tender care – produced their own miracles.

The strength of these traditions is evident even today in modern China. It is no denigration of either the people or their practices to note that China is overwhelmingly a nation of peasants. One may consequently expect that traditions are tenacious and not easily changed. In fact, the relaxation of centralised control over production has led to a resurgence of the medicinal herb market. In many areas, as much as one fifth of the land may be devoted to the raising of herbs. Profits are higher for these speciality crops than for either wheat or millet. Moreover, little land is needed to produce enough for a good living, given the demand. "Traditional" medicine, Chinese style, is as popular as it ever was. In Nanjing, a compilation of more than 100,000 medicinal food prescriptions is being assembled, the largest ever compiled for publication in one volume. In Jiangsu province, the number of hospitals devoted to herbal or "traditional" medicine, including acupuncture/pressure, has doubled in the last five years. A center for training doctors and nurses in this field of medicine was opened there in 1984.

During my visits, I encountered repeatedly the nutritious and the medicinal, side by side in shops and food stalls. Sichuan, in the far west of China, has long been famous for its medicinal foods, no doubt because of the overwhelming profusion of its plant and herbal flora. In the province's main city, Chengdu, I visited its largest herbal market, Chengdu Henhua Chi Zhongyaocai Schichang. This newly established (1984) market is a consolidation of several smaller ones. Even so, the large, sheltered area is insufficient to cater to all its customers, and many vendors spill out to the surrounding sidewalks and alleys. odours emanating from the area are strikingly pungent and pleasing. Bundled into hessian sacks are heaps of dry herbs, roots, tree bark, dried fungi, seeds of all sorts, dried fruit, and other speciality items which overflow all available bins and display counters.

resurgence of herb markets

At first count, it all appears to be one huge spice market, but closer inspection reveals its medicinal emphasis. The day I was there, the market was crowded, with a bazaar-like quality, and the dimness of the poorly lighted interior, so typical of China today, made for an exotic ambience. I watched the vendors, both wholesalers and retailers, haggling amid dried carcasses of snakes and skeletons of monkeys, cattle, and goats. All around were mounds of dried citrus fruits, wasp hives, dried starfish and sea cucumber, dried crab and scallop shells. I began counting the various mounds and sacks of plants, roots, and herbs but stopped when I reached two hundred.

Another day I attended a medicinal food banquet, sort of a Pritikin feast run wild, at the Tongrentang Dietotherapy Restaurant. I drank bitter wolfberry liqueur, which is good for kidney troubles; I also sampled some honeysuckle tea, rabbit with black sesame seed, buns made with a special fungus stuffing, ginseng soup, black chicken broth, and many others of their twenty-course offering. Every dish was good for some ailment or other. I found it more fascinating than gastronomical, but when I left the restaurant, I felt very healthy.

At another time, I talked with Mr. Song Rongcan, a knowledgeable young man and manager of a highly regarded medicinal and gourmet restaurant, Bai Cao Yuan, "the house of a hundred herbs" in Chengdu. He told me of his family's three generations in growing and preparing herbal medicinal foods. Although only twenty-eight years old, he is head of a medical herbal production center, after having spent two years as manager of the Tongrentang Dietotherapy restaurant nearby. His foods contain no monosodium glutamate or salt or any other additives. His herbs, when properly apportioned, comprise the five flavours to complement the four natures.

Mr. Song ordered four dishes for me, enlightening me during each course about their specific medicinal properties. *Long ma tongzi ji* consists of a young rooster, double-steamed with dried seahorses for four hours, then steamed again for forty minutes just before serving in a rich tasty broth; it is good for one's kidneys and for one's sex life. *Zi kou niurou* is a cold beef appetiser; the beef is braised in two types of herbs which are the basis for the distinctive flavour of the beef slices. The dish is supposedly good for the skin and the stomach lining; it tasted good. Next, I sampled *fu ling baozi,* a bun stuffed with minced meat. Instead of yeast, a fungus called in English "tuckahoe" was used to help the dough rise. The fungus, always found near pine trees, was prescribed for renewing youth, or as an anti-aging medicine. It tasted like a good savoury bun, or *baozi,* with the medicinal element barely discernible. (Mr. Song told me that minced snake and turtle meat had these qualities as well.) Finally, I sampled *du zhong yaohua,* a stir-fried dish of pig's kidney and a special tree bark. This was good especially for one's own kidneys, the human organ which is, in Chinese dietotherapy, the "door to life." It is the part of the body subject to abuse caused by poor or excessive eating and drinking and therefore most in need of protection and restoration. The recipe is two thousand years old, having been concocted by Zhang Zhongjing, a famous court doctor during the Han Dynasty.

All in all, I found my experiences of Chinese dietotherapy and medicinal foods fascinating. Whatever the actual medical benefits, there is no doubt that in the case of most of the prescriptions, the doctor's orders were a pleasure to follow.

VEGETARIANISM

"Vegetablism," to coin a term, is as old as Chinese civilisation, at least four thousand years old. The enormous variety of plant foods in China made vegetables, along with grains, the most central and most prominent element in the diet of the people. Much of the celebrated cuisine of Sichuan, an area of extraordinary vegetation, is strictly vegetarian without being Buddhist. No teachers, no government decrees nor religious injunctions were required to maintain and encourage the consumption of vegetables of the most varied sorts. Meats were used sparingly, and often just for broths.

Vegetarianism, on the other hand, is a relative newcomer. Only with the rise of Buddhism in China in the first six centuries A.D. did this culinary practice gradually emerge. Today, it remains a minority option, followed by relatively few Chinese. The number of Buddhists and their fewer Daoist co-religionists in China today is estimated to be merely twenty million, hardly even one percent of the population.

Nevertheless, Buddhism's reverence for all forms of animal life led to the introduction of new styles of cooking, new recipes, and new foods that have enriched the dietary and culinary heritage of all Chinese. The religion is not responsible for the introduction of nonanimal sources of protein – the Chinese have always relied upon such foods as legumes, especially mung and soy beans, for example. But Buddhism *did* give added prestige to such foods, and its adherents presented them in such new and palatable versions that many Chinese essentially forswore any animal flesh in their diets.

Buddhist chefs created the illusion of the rich, savoury succulence of pork, beef, chicken, and duck in many of their dishes. Their mock-meat dishes are so beguiling that diners often forget (or are fooled) that they are not having real beef, pork, chicken, abalone, and other meats. (I have heard that some Buddhist restaurants cheat a little by using chicken stock in some of their recipes.)

An ancient tale tells of a Daoist believer who was invited to dine with people who, it turns out, were alchemists. Confronting the two main dishes, which appeared to be a hairless dog and the body of a human infant floating in a clear broth, the Daoist recoiled in horror. His hosts encouraged him to at least sample each of the dishes of "special vegetables," as they called the food. But, as a devout vegetarian, he would not. Only later, when the meal had been entirely eaten, did his hosts tell him that the objects he found so repellent were in reality the curiously shaped roots of medical plants. Had he partaken of them he would have gained eternal youth and immortality. The point of this rather cruel story is that vegetarian foods can so simulate meat that one may always enjoy good vegetarian food without a sense of deprivation and so gain health and happiness.

Whatever the moral of the story, we know that Buddhism led to the development of a large variety of legume, wheat gluten, and especially soy bean substitutes for meat. Wheat gluten, high in protein and a most malleable food, is used in a variety of mock-meat dishes. Perhaps the most important element in the Buddhist repertory of meat substitutes, however, is bean curd, made from soy beans. Long before Buddhism took hold in China, soy beans were an essential part of Chinese cuisine. However, Buddhism certainly hastened the spread of their use throughout all of China. The Buddhist versions of the general Chinese practice of eating special dishes on holidays also helped to spread the vegetarian message.

One such offering was already famous in Song Dynasty times, the "Seven Treasure, Five Taste" rice porridge eaten on the eighth day of the twelfth moon. It was soon adopted by all Chinese, of whatever religious persuasion. Buddhism, and poverty, can share responsibility for the generally low repute and limited appearance of beef dishes in Chinese cuisine.

In China today, vegetarian food and vegetarian restaurants are still very much in evidence. I have sampled Buddhist temple food in various places, and I have to give their offerings uneven ratings. In Hangzhou, at the Lingyin Si temple, my bean curd dish was not fresh and it was swimming in an unidentifiable brown-coloured sauce. However, just across the city, in the Long Xiang Qiao market, bean curd in twelve different forms was being served in food stalls along the street: every one of these dishes was well prepared and delicious.

In Shanghai and in other large cities, I have especially enjoyed dining at a number of restaurants that have quite decent vegetarian menus, particularly when they include some imaginative dishes made from wheat gluten and bean curd. It remains true nevertheless that while the "taste of China" is redolent of vegetables in myriad forms, strict vegetarianism is the exception rather than the rule.

feicui ji pian
emerald chicken "meat"

For many centuries in China, wheat gluten has been separate from the starch category and made into imitation meats for vegetarian styles of cooking. The Buddhist influence here is unmistakable. Wheat gluten is a nutritious, high protein food with a texture that lends itself to imaginative uses. It has a delicate flavour of its own but readily absorbs sauces and condiments. I savoer this version in Shanghais Gongdelin restaurant, the mild green chillies imparting the "emerald" touch. One can make wheat gluten at home, but it is time-consuming.

225 g/8 oz fresh or canned wheat gluten
225 g/8 oz mild chillies or green peppers
1½ tablespoons peanut oil
1½ tablespoons finely chopped garlic
½ teaspoon salt
¼ teaspoon freshly ground white pepper
125 ml/4 fl oz chicken stock or water
1½ tablespoons rice wine or dry sherry
2 tablespoons light soy sauce
½ teaspoon cornflour mixed with 1 teaspoon water
1 tablespoon sesame oil

Rinse the wheat gluten in several changes of cold water. Cut it in slices and set aside. Seed the chillies or peppers and cut into similar sizes.

Heat a wok or large frying pan until hot. Add the oil, garlic, salt, and white pepper. Put in the chillies or peppers and stir-fry for 30 seconds. Add the wheat gluten slices and continue to stir-fry for another minute. Pour in the chicken stock or water, rice wine or sherry, and soy sauce and simmer for 3 minutes. Add the cornflour mixture and mix well. Lastly add the sesame oil and give the mixture several good stirs. Serve at once.

Serves 6 as part of a Chinese meal, or 3 to 4 as a single dish.

yuxiang gesong
minced chilli "fish"

The recipe mimics a well-known fish dish, and it certainly fooled and delighted me. The gluten is cut up as if it were fish and with the Chinese dried black mushrooms, pine nuts, and the traditional chilli sauce, it resembles and tastes very much like a real fish dish.

225 g/8 oz fresh or canned wheat gluten
25 g/1 oz Chinese dried black mushrooms, soaked, stems removed
1½ tablespoons peanut oil

2 tablespoons finely chopped garlic
3 tablespoons finely chopped spring onions
1 tablespoon finely chopped fresh ginger root
3 tablespoons pine nuts
2 tablespoons light soy sauce
2 teaspoons Chinese white rice vinegar
2 teaspoons sugar
2 teaspoons chilli bean sauce
½ teaspoon salt
½ teaspoon freshly ground black pepper
6 tablespoons water
½ teaspoon cornflour mixed
  with 1 teaspoon water

Rinse the wheat gluten in several changes of cold water, drain, and cut into small dice. Do the same with the mushrooms and set aside.

Heat a wok or large frying pan until hot. Add the oil, garlic, onions, and ginger and stir-fry for 30 seconds. Put in the wheat gluten, mushrooms, and pine nuts. Continue to stir-fry for 1 minute, then add the rest of the ingredients except the cornflour mixture and cook for another minute. Pour in the cornstarch mixture and cook until the sauce thickens. Turn the dish onto a platter and serve at once.

Serves 4 as part of a Chinese meal, or 2 as a single dish.

jin gu yin liu
stir-fried bean sprouts with lily buds

Lily buds are quite edible, nutritious, and inexpensive. They come dried, softening nicely when soaked and stir-fried. The bean sprouts cooked with them contribute a chewy texture which adds up to a simple but splendid dish, just like the one I enjoyed at the Gongdelin vegetarian restaurant in Shanghai.

50 g/2 oz dried lily bud stems
450 g/1 lb fresh bean sprouts

1½ tablespoons peanut oil
½ teaspoon salt
Pinch of freshly ground black pepper
3 tablespoons rice wine or dry sherry
1 tablespoon light soy sauce
2 teaspoons sesame oil

Soak the lily bud stems in warm water for 20 minutes. Drain them thoroughly and cut off the hard ends. If you wish, snap off the ends of the bean sprouts for a more finished presentation.

Heat a wok or large frying pan until hot. Add the oil and salt, then the lily bud stems, and pepper. Stir-fry for 30 seconds, add the bean sprouts, and continue to stir-fry for 1 minute. Then add the rice wine or sherry and soy sauce and continue to stir-fry for 3 minutes. Stir in the sesame oil and serve at once.

Serves 4 as part of a Chinese meal, or 2 as a single dish.

huangyou xie fen
mock crab

Another Gongdelin restaurant vegetarian dish masquerading as animal protein, this time including diced potatoes and carrots. The egg whites and shreds of yellow yolks simulate the colours of crab meat, hence the name of the dish. This is a quite flavourful simple-to-make vegetarian dish.

225 g/8 oz potatoes, peeled and cut into small dice
225 g/8 oz carrots, peeled and cut into small dice
2 tablespoons peanut oil
2 tablespoons finely chopped garlic
1 tablespoon finely chopped peeled fresh ginger root
1 teaspoon salt
½ teaspoon freshly ground white pepper
6 eggs, beaten
1 tablespoon sesame oil

Blanch the potatoes and carrots in a large pot of boiling salted water for 2 minutes and drain thoroughly.

Heat a wok or large frying pan until hot. Add the oil, garlic, ginger, salt, and pepper and stir-fry for 30 seconds. Put in the carrots and potatoes, and continue to stir-fry for 1 minute.

Combine the eggs with sesame oil and pour this over the vegetables and stir. Let the mixture cook much like an omelette. When the bottom has turned to a golden brown, turn over and allow the top to brown. Slide the mock crab onto a platter and serve at once.

Serves 4 as part of a Chinese meal, or 2 as a single dish.

bu xue yang yan tang
soup for the blood and skin

Chinese medicinal herbalists believe that this soup is a potent tonic for one's blood and the skin which is the mirror of inner health. The ingredients illustrate the ancient Chinese theory that beef, being naturally sweet and "warm," strengthens vital energies in the blood and nourishes the spleen and stomach. It holds that beef's powers are enhanced when peanuts are added to the soup.

The soup also includes red jujube dates. These have been used in China since early times as a tonic nutrient and a purifying food when combined with certain other ingredients. They are believed to build strength, improve circulation, and extend life. Moreover, since they are naturally sweet and contribute a honey flavour to the soup, they make this particular medicine go down very easily. While the peanuts give the soup its milky-white colour, dried tangerine or orange peel adds a pleasant tart element.

125 g/4 oz raw peanuts
2 dried tangerine or orange peels
12 dried red jujube dates
1.7 l/3 pt water
4 slices fresh ginger root
1.1 kg/2½ lb shin of beef

2 teaspoons salt

Grind the peanuts coarsely in a blender or food processor and set aside. Soak the tangerine or orange peels in hot water for 20 minutes or until they are soft and drain. Soak the red jujube dates in warm water for 20 minutes, drain, and set aside.

Bring the water to the boil in a large pot. Add the ground peanuts, tangerine or orange peels, ginger, and dates. Add the beef and bring back to the boil, skimming the surface continually. Lower the heat to a simmer, cover, and cook for 3 hours or until the beef is tender. Add the salt to taste.

Serves 4 as part of a Chinese meal, or 2 as a single dish.

huo zhong dun ji tang
stewed chicken with smoked ham knuckle

Here is another example of how the nutritious, the medicinal, and the flavourful are so often joined in Chinese cuisine. Pig's trotter and chicken are both believed to be good for the blood and circulation. Supposedly also endowed with curative powers they are prescribed for women after childbirth. I say that the warming richness of this stew is good for whatever may ail you including hunger. It can be made ahead of time as it reheats perfectly.

700 g/1½ lb smoked ham knuckle
4 slices fresh ginger root
4 whole spring onions
2 tablespoons rice wine or
   dry sherry
1 teaspoon salt
1.7 1/3 pt water
1.6–1.8 kg/3½–4 lb chicken
450 g/1 lb Chinese cabbage
4 slices fresh ginger root
4 spring onions, white parts only

3 tablespoons rice wine or
  dry sherry
1 teaspoon salt
Salt and pepper

Have your butcher cut the ham knuckle in 4 pieces. Wash the pieces in cold running water until cleaned. Place them in a bowl, cover completely with cold water, and soak for 8 hours or overnight.

Place the pieces of ham knuckle in a large pot of boiling water and blanch for 5 minutes. Remove them and drain well. Discard the water and wash the pot thoroughly.

Put the ham, ginger, whole onions, rice wine or sherry, salt, and water in the pot and bring the mixture to the boil. Turn the heat to low, cover, and slowly cook for 1 hour.

Cut the chicken into quarters and blanch them in a large pot of boiling water for 5 minutes. Drain well and set aside.

Cut the Chinese cabbage into thick 25-mm × 7.5-cm/l × 3-in strips. When the meat is tender, add the chicken and cabbage, then add the second batch of ginger, onions, rice wine or sherry, and salt. Cover and cook over low heat for another hour.

Skim off all the fat from the surface and remove the ginger and onions. Season to taste with salt and pepper. Ladle into a large bowl and serve at once.

Serves 4 to 6 as part of a Chinese meal, or 4 as a single dish.

qiguo ji
yunnan steamed pot chicken

This soup was prepared fry chef Wen Hongchun at his restaurant the Kang Le Xiao Wu. To make it I use a Yunnan ceramic steam pot, a squat, round, lidded vessel with an internal spout that allows steam to circulate but not to escape. Steaming in a covered heatproof casserole for 2 hours will do almost as well. Chicken steamed this way produces a superior clear soup

food for the body and soul – recipes

enriched by condensation of the natural juices of the bird. Serve the soup accompanied by a platter of chicken with dipping sauces.

1.8 kg/4 lb chicken, cut
   into pieces
1 teaspoon salt
6 slices of fresh ginger root
2 spring onions cut into
   5 cm/2 in pieces
700 ml/1¼ pt chicken stock
2 tablespoons rice wine
DIPPING SAUCES
Light soy sauce
Chilli bean sauce
Chopped spring onions

Blanch the chicken for 3 minutes in a large pot of boiling water. Remove the chicken and rinse thoroughly in cold running water.

Place the chicken pieces around the Yunnan pot or on a rack set into a heatproof casserole. Sprinkle the chicken with the salt, and scatter the ginger pieces and spring onions over the top. Pour in the chicken stock and rice wine or sherry. Cover and steam gently over low heat for 2 hours, replenishing the hot water from time to time if needed. Remove the ginger and onion pieces. With a spoon, skim off all the surface fat. Ladle the soup into a tureen, and pass the chicken on a platter with the selection of dipping sauces.

Serves 4 to 6 as part of a Chinese meal, or 4 as a single dish.

zhujiao jiang cu
pickled pig's trotters and ginger

I can remember living in Chicago when my mother's friends gathered in our living room to celebrate the birth of a child. The food for such a party always included boiled red-dyed eggs, a rice wine herbal brew, and pickled trotters and ginger. This dish makes a delightful appetiser. Lovers of trotters will readily appreciate its virtues, and those who try it for the first time will be impressed by how such lowly ingredients become so palatable. It is the ginger that mellows the vinegar. When you buy the pig's trotters, get the more meaty hind pair. Enjoy this dish hot or at room temperature, and it may be made a day or two in advance.

1.4 kg/3 lb pig's trotters, preferably from the hind legs
850 ml/1½ pt Chinese red or black rice vinegar
6 slices fresh ginger root
6 tablespoons sugar

Blanch the trotters in boiling water for 30 minutes. Drain well.

In a medium-sized pot, combine the vinegar, ginger, and sugar. Bring the mixture to the boil and add the trotters. Turn the heat to low, cover, and gently simmer for 2 hours or until tender. Serve hot or at room temperature.

Serves 4 to 6 as appetizers.

huaqi shen dun ruge
squab soup with ginseng

Ginseng is the most celebrated medicinal herb among Chinese everywhere. Of ancient provenance, it has a rich history and is extensively used as a restorative and preventor of disease. After speaking with many herb doctors and specialists in China, I came away thinking the only thing it is not credited with is actually reviving the dead. No other natural product can match its reputed healing powers. Ginseng, they believe, imparts energy, assists the body's natural healing powers, increases one's efficiency, and tranquillizes the soul, so it is often prescribed to those suffering from mental disorders. It's mysterious to me how the price of ginseng is determined. Some ginseng costs only a few dollars a root, while another root, looking much the same and, I am sure, exactly the same chemically, will cost thousands. Geography does play a role because ginseng from northern China

food for the body and soul – recipes

and from Korea commands the most money. Widely accepted legends confirm that those at death's door who drank a brew of ginseng from the north (or from Korea) recovered immediately and lived long, healthy lives.

In any case, this aromatic relative of wild sarsaparilla imparts a certain je ne sais quoi to any dish, especially one like this which combines some rather hearty flavours. Whatever its medicinal properties, this is a delicious and traditional Chinese squab soup.

2 squabs, each about 350–450 g/
   12oz–1 lb
1.4 1/2½ pt chicken stock
2 slices fresh ginger root
4 spring onions, white part only
25 g/1 oz ginseng root
2 tablespoons rice wine or dry sherry
2 teaspoons salt
Freshly ground white pepper
   to taste
2 teaspoons sesame oil

Blanch the squabs in a large pot of boiling water for 3 minutes.

In a large pot, combine the chicken stock, squab, ginger, and onions and bring the mixture to the boil. Turn the heat down, cover, and simmer for 2 hours. Add the ginseng and cook for 1 more hour.

Remove the ginger and spring onions, and skim off all surface fat. Add the rice wine or sherry, salt, pepper, and sesame oil. Stir the soup and serve at once.

Serves 4 to 6 as part of a Chinese meal, or 4 as a single dish.

donggu chao cai
stir-fried cabbage with mushrooms

Buddhism greatly assisted in promoting vegetarianism among the Chinese. However, the religious element alone counted for little among them because the Chinese are almost without taboos when it comes to food. Rather, the Buddhist influence spread because China's chefs concocted imaginative, delicious, and satisfying vegetarian recipes and whole menus which captured the spirit of Chinese cuisine. Temple restaurants developed a large clientele, and their successes and dishes were quickly emulated by non-Buddhist restaurants. Thus was created the venerable tradition of vegetarian dishes in China, holding their own with meat and seafood dishes.

I found this delicious vegetarian dish at the Lao Fandian restaurant in Shanghai. Its ingredients combine delightfully in a typical Buddhist way. Simple and easy to make, it is perfect either as a vegetarian dish or as an accompaniment to meat dishes.

25 g/1 oz Chinese dried black mushrooms
450 g/1 lb Chinese cabbage
125 g/4 oz bamboo shoots
1½ tablespoons peanut oil
1 tablespoon finely chopped peeled fresh ginger root
2 teaspoons rice wine or dry sherry
2 teaspoons light soy sauce
1 teaspoon dark soy sauce
½ teaspoon salt
Water
2 teaspoons sesame oil

Soak the mushrooms in warm water for 20 minutes or until they are soft. Rinse under running water to remove any remaining sand. With a sharp knife, remove the stems and discard. Finely shred the caps and set aside. Chop the cabbage into long shreds about 6 mm/¼ in wide.

Rinse the bamboo shoots under cold running water and finely shred them. Heat a wok or large frying pan until hot. Add the oil and ginger and stir-fry for 20 seconds. Then add the mushrooms and bamboo shoots and continue to stir-fry for 1 minute. Add the rice wine or sherry, soy sauces, and salt and continue to stir-fry for another 3 minutes or until the cabbage is cooked. Add about a tablespoon of water if necessary to keep the mixture moist. Spoon onto a platter, garnish with the sesame oil, and serve at once.

CHAPTER 11
REFLECTIONS

The subtle changes that take place inside a cooking utensil are things that cannot be understood or told.
Lu Shi Chuan Qiao, Chin Dynasty 225–209 B.C.

For the last few decades, it has been lamentably true that if one wished to find the best and most authentic Chinese cuisine, mainland China was the *last* place to look. During my many visits to Hong Kong throughout the 1970s, word from the mainland concerning Chinese cuisine was invariably gloomy. In that period, the grand traditions and delectable experiences of Chinese cookery were preserved outside of its heartland, especially in Hong Kong and Taiwan, but also and increasingly in Chinese restaurants in London, New York, Melbourne, and San Francisco.

Under the administration of the People's Republic, farmers were managing to provide enough in the way of daily calories for a billion Chinese. This is an astonishing enough feat given China's history of recurrent famines and the fact that her population almost doubled between 1950 and 1975. Beyond that, however, the news was quite depressing. Tourists and business travelers returning from the mainland unanimously reported that restaurants served wretched meals which were badly cooked, usually made with poor quality ingredients; service was said to be sloppy. During this dark period, the Red Guards of the Cultural Revolution accelerated a process begun in the 1950s: culinary institutes were abolished, cooking schools were closed down, and master chefs fled or were forced into other, more politically acceptable, professions. The infrastructure that supported the grand tradition was destroyed; the specialised farms and gardens, the bakeries and kitchens, the innumerable private restaurants and food stalls were all abolished or cruelly reduced by centralised planning.

In the state-owned restaurants of those decades, the clientele ate what might charitably be called "functional" food. Staff members were deemed equivalent to factory workers. No grades of talent or expertise were recognised or allowed, a practice hardly conducive to the preparation of excellent cuisine. Elitist or not, some people *do* have a greater ability than others to cook and can do so superlatively. Moreover, with most restaurants closed at seven in the evening the fabulous banquets lasting late into the night became part of the past. Furthermore, since all restaurant workers were paid on an equal scale and the prices of meals were controlled, there were no incentives to strive for excellence in menus. Food was sustenance and certainly not an expression of social class, let alone an art.

I refrained from visiting the mainland during those years, although it is in sight of Hong Kong's "suburbs," the New Territories. I knew I would find it too appalling. But in 1976 the death of Chairman Mao brought an astonishing reassessment of many aspects of Chinese life – the arts, education, and, especially, economic matters – and the result was an accelerated modernisation of a country that had long resisted the world's influence. Among these changes was a reconsideration of the virtues and commercial potential of traditional Chinese cuisine. By the early 1980s, gastronomy and even epicurism were no longer considered counterrevolutionary. The People's Republic initiated a planned, officially sanctioned resuscitation of the venerable Chinese culinary traditions.

On one of my many visits to Shanghai, I discussed this period with Mr. Zhao Qiren, the principal of the city's leading cooking school. He told me that before 1949, foods were cooked, as tradition required, in good stock made from chicken and ham. In the "difficult decades,'" however, shortages of essential ingredients led to substitutions and awful expedients. For example, with the decline in the availability and freshness of ingredients, monosodium glutamate began to be added to everything. My constant refrain during my recent frequent visits to China was, "*Bu yao weijing!*" ("No monosodium glutamate, please!") Mr. Zhao also acknowledged the breakdown of the regional and local cuisines over that thirty-year period. This was part of a deliberate policy, to nationalise the spirit of the people, to make uniform what had been different and separate. How tragic for a rich culinary tradition which prided itself on recognizably regional specialities, however much each was an amalgamation of many styles. There was another factor, the government's need for hard currency. In the 1970s, high-quality Chinese food stuffs produced on the mainland were unavailable locally but were sold instead in Hong Kong, allowing the much-needed money to flow back to the mainland.

Private gardens today are again supplying fruits and vegetables in abundance; private restaurants and food stalls are becoming common-place; culinary institutes and cooking schools are flourishing. There is a long-pent-up demand for quality foods and ingredients, and this demand is slowly being met.

By the 1980s this long campaign to reestablish authentic Chinese cuisine in its homeland was under full sail. Since then I have spent months at a time in China, traveling thousands of miles throughout the enormous and complex country. I sampled literally hundreds of different dishes, from practically every regional cuisine. I visited the coastal areas of Shanghai and Guangzhou (Canton), the interior Sichuan and southwestern Kunming (Yunnan) regions, and northern China including the capital, Beijing. The quality of the food ranged from outstanding – on a par with the best Hong Kong offered – to simply dreadful.

It was hard to overlook the fact that the state-owned food stores were almost always empty, while customers patronised the free markets. Indeed, Chinese farmers have seized upon the opportunity to grow and sell any excess fruits, vegetables, or meats after they fulfil their required government quota. Such family and personal enterprises are thriving and fed by a rise in the disposable income of many Chinese. In urban areas, a notable increase in the demand for consumer goods has led in turn to the revival of private restaurants keyed to market demands rather than state directives.

A good example of how things are changing may be seen in the history of Shanghai's popular fried doughnut, readily available until the late 1950s. When the government set a retail price on the doughnuts, they disappeared simply because they were impossible to produce at that price. Today, their price is determined by the market and the doughnuts are once more plentiful.

I must emphasise, however, that things have not yet reached the point where anyone can find good food anywhere in China. You *must* have personal local contacts or *guanxi*, as the Chinese call them. Unfortunately, but perhaps necessarily, most tourists are served food which is not too exotic and certainly less flavorful than the real thing. Through the help of relatives and many Chinese friends, I have been able to dine in many different local restaurants, in all parts of China, and some of them were superb.

In Chengdu, Sichuan, for example, I ate in a restaurant collectively owned by its workers that opened three years ago. The staff is committed to the revival of authentic regional Sichuan food, and their efforts have succeeded so marvellously that I returned for a second visit. Among the dishes I enjoyed there were the best aromatic tea-smoked duck I've ever tasted, a strikingly unusual stir-fried bitter melon with fresh chilli, and a delicious fragrant hot and spicy chicken with stem lettuce. In Guangzhou, where late dining is common, I enjoyed an excellent supper meal with local friends at a *dai pai dong*, the Cantonese term for street restaurant. The restaurant was festooned with cages containing various live wild animals – all ready for the pot. I rather timidly selected a pigeon, already partially cooked and swinging in the sultry evening heat to dry. It shortly reappeared in deep-fried form with the skin crackling and glistening, accompanied by fresh seasonal vegetables and a tasty bean curd dish with a delicious

reflections

sauce. This was as good a simple meal as I have ever enjoyed, anywhere.

In Kunming on a recent visit, I went a bit native. Friends took me to a private restaurant where they proceeded to order braised bear paws and elephant trunk. As I ate my portion, I thought how aghast my environmentalist friends would be. It was well prepared, but rather bland and gelatinous. The only flavour which came through was that of the sauce.

However, the next day I enjoyed a real *tour de force,* a meal two days in the making. It comprised fifty-four dishes, all made from *one* goat. There were twenty-seven cold dishes, including some made from the eyeballs, tail, liver, stomach, and other entrails, and twenty-seven hot dishes featuring braised and stir-fried parts of the same goat. It was an outstanding and impressive accomplishment and, to my astonishment, quite delicious too. The next day, at another private restaurant, I sampled more local fare in the form of toasted goat cheese – goat cheese pan-fried in a wok – a dish certainly of Mongol or Muslim origin or influence. By this time, I felt really deprived when I learned the restaurant was out of the regional speciality, fried grasshoppers, which I have still yet to sample.

I think that the best news concerning the revival of the great cuisine in China is that good and even superb food is being prepared by families in their own kitchens. In a Beijing private home, for example, I had one of the best meals I've ever had in China. It was a classically simple meal and quite delicious. I had the pleasure and privilege of assisting in its preparation. The meal featured *jiaozi,* meat-filled dumplings which were cooked in two styles – fried and boiled. It included minced pork stuffed between slices of aubergine, then dipped in batter and deep-fried, as well as spring rolls stuffed with cabbage and simply fried. The dishes were accompanied by cold cucumber salad, and by fresh tomatoes sliced and garnished with thousand-year-old eggs. All together, a simple but marvellous and perfect experience.

In my ancestral home outside of Guangzhou, I really enjoyed a meal that included freshly killed, steamed chicken, roasted goose, and vegetables taken fresh from the ground. It was a homey touch that warmed both my heart and my stomach.

Indeed, family-style cooking is now available in many cities in the so-called night markets. Enterprising entrepreneurs, armed with family recipes, cook right out in the streets, making hand-pulled noodles, dumplings in soup, fried pastries, spicy cold and hot noodles, braised eels with garlic, or stir-fried frogs – all at very reasonable prices and quite tasty.

In sum, my many culinary experiences in China lead me to believe that Chinese cuisine, along with the other arts and sciences and culture in general, is slowly but demonstrably on the mend. I know it will continue to move from strength to strength after being so many years in the desert of proletarian functionalism. Cuisine is, after all, one of the glories of Chinese civilisation and one of China's important contributions to world culture.

ACKNOWLEDGEMENTS

This book has been a massive project and there are many people I am deeply indebted to for their support and kind assistance. First, I thank my many friends in China: Luo Kaiye, Huang Shitian, Shen Jianqing, Wang Zhigao, Xu Hairong, Hu Mageng, Zou Zongwen, Wen Hongchun, David Xu, Guan Yang, Nobby Choi, Alan Kung, Herbert G. Sossna, Liang Jin, Washington Tam, Zhao Qiren, Li Weiyi, Chen Yaqu, Hu Biyuan, Hu Hairong, Li Yaoyun, Wang Yulin, Mr. and Mrs. Qu Shoukang, and the entire Qu family from Beijing, Du Shunhua, Miss Li Li, Dailin Liu, Dr. Stefan Simons, Feng Cunli, Albert A. P. Leung, Chang Jie. They introduced me to the real China that endures despite adversity.

I offer my sincere appreciation to Gerry Cavanaugh, Gordon Wing, Mimi Luebbermann and Scott Ewing, who together with Martha Casselman helped me to shape the book and to make it flow coherently.

I owe special thanks to Lynn Pan for her advice and help in the pinyin, and to Jenny Lo who helped me with the research in China. They are my soul mates.

This book was made possible by my publisher, Colin Webb, whose ideas and enthusiasm for the book inspired me. I thank him and the rest of the editorial, design and marketing staff at Pavilion Books, especially Gillian Young.

A fond thank you to Erika Maurer for her help on the manuscript. Her knowledge and love of China was of immense help. And to Susie Maurer as well, for arranging my long trips to China, with all my special requests.

I owe many thanks to The Regent in Hong Kong, for its splendid hospitality, with special thanks to Rudolf Greiner and Lynn Grebstad.

I thoroughly enjoyed working with the photographer of the book who is also a good friend, Leong Ka Tai (pinyin: Liang Jiatai) and his assistant Eric Cheng (pinyin: Zheng Le). It was a learning experience as well as a warm, congenial time.

My family was there to help whenever I needed to know something: Guan Shimin, Tan Qiaoyun, Tan Rongbai, Guan Meixiao, Tan Songfa, Zhou Lishan, and, especially, warm thanks to my auntie, Fang Jiongxiao and my dear mother, Fang Jiongying.

I owe a debt of thanks to other close friends in China: Guan Huoling, Sun Rongcan, Lu Jiayun, Su Mingxiang, He Shufen, Gong Shouhua, Guan Ming, Zhou Ling, Guan Nafen, Yang Duoxiang, Sun Zhanguo, Qi Qin, Zhang Xi, Zhang Deshan, Guan Yang, Lin Deqiong, Wang Daqing, Chen Bo, Hu Zhiyun, Huang Haijia, Ge Wenfeng, Huang Sufeng, Huang Sujiong, Huang Kangze, Huang Ying, Huang Yingmei, Huang Shibing, Lan Shiping, Liu Dezhi, Zhang Ying, Liu Baoyu, Yan Meiyi, Xu Yiping, and Ding Shuiling.

My thanks and appreciation to The Peninsula in Hong Kong and my friends there: Eric Waldburger, Edwin Chan, Erich Schaeli, and Sian Griffiths.

And to Pacific World in Hong Kong, always so accommodating to my special demands, particularly Sophia Cheong, Jacques Arnoux and Albert Ho.

I offer special thanks to T.C. Lai in Hong Kong for supplying the epigrams.

And, finally to the people of China. Their warmth and generosity gives me great hope lor their future. They deserve the best.

Index

Across the Bridge Rice Noodles,
173
Almonds, 65, 68, 87
Asparagus, 98
Aubergine, 41, 75, 115
Fish-flavored, with Pork, 75-76
Stuffed, 131

Bamboo Brush, 61
Bamboo Shoots, 29-30
with Noodle Soup and 196-7
Bamboo Steamers, 62
Bean Curd (doufu), 15, 30, 121,
142, 145
Brown Sauce Doufu, 126
with Cabbage, 91
Chinese Water Spinach with
Fermented, 165
fermented, 30-1
Grandma Chen's, 125
Guizhou-style, 136
pressed seasoned, 31
Red-cooked, Family Style, 18
soft, 30
solid, 30
Tofu Salad, 182
Bean Sauce, 51
Sweet, 52
Yellow, 51
Bean Sprout(s), 23, 31
Salad, 94-5
Stir-fried, with Lily Buds, 217-8
see also Soybean Sprouts
Bean Starch Noodles with
Cucumbers, 127

Bean Thread Noodles, 45-6
with Pork, 137-8
Beans see Black Beans; Green
Beans; Long Beans; Red Bean
Paste Soup; Sweet Bean Sauce;
Yellow Beans
Bear Paws, 230
Beef, 67, 99
Crisp Beef in Chili Sauce, 71-2
Sliced Beef with Broccoli, 145
Sliced Beef Liver with Prawn
Dumpling, 190
Soup for the Blood and Skin,
219-220
Bird's Nest, 31-32, 53, 122
Black Beans, 32-33, 34
Broccoli, Chinese, 35, 207
Brown Sauce Doufu, 126
Buns see haozi', Man Tou
Butterfat, 67

Cabbage, 188. 207
Chinese Flowering, 36
Chinese White see Pak Choi
Red-in-Snow, 48
Cabbage, Chinese (Peking
Cabbage), 36, 38
with Bean Curd, 91-92
in "Cream Sauce", 93-94
with Dried Shrimp, 166
Stir-fried, with Mushrooms,
224-5
Cakes, 122, 188, 190, 211
Birthday, 148
"Honey-harmonising-with-oil",
118-9
Mooncakes, 122-124

New Year, 122
Cardamom, 87
Carp, 14, 98, 149
  Red-cooked Grass, with
  Tangerine Peel, 20
  West Lake, in Vinegar Sauce,
  160
Catfish with Noodle Soup, 196
Caul Fat, 33
Celery, Stir-fried, 127, 150
Cheese, Goat, 67, 145
  Dried, 145
  Fresh, 145
  Fried, 145
  Stuffed with Yunnan Ham, 145
  Toasted, 79, 230
Chicken, 104, 118-119, 145
  Across the Bridge Rice Noodles,
  173
  Cooked with Rice, 202
  Mushroom-Chicken Casserole,
  151
  Soup 118, 207
  Spicy, with Fresh Water
  Chestnuts, 162-3
  Steamed, 24-25, 230
  Stewed, with Smoked Ham
  Hock, 220-21
  Yunnan Steamed Pot, 145,
  221-222
Chili(es), 33-34
  Dried Red, 34
  in Emerald Chicken "Meat",
  215
  Fresh, with Stir-fried Corn, 73-4
  Pickled, with Pork, 158
  with Stir-fried Bitter Melon,
  183-4

Stir-fried Chili Pork, 79-80
  with Stir-fried Pork, 157-8
  Stir-fried Whole Mild, 74-5
Chili Bean Sauce, 35, 50
Chili Oil, 34-5
Chili Paste, 100, 149
Chili Powder, 35
Chili Sauce (Dipping Sauce), 50,
  34-5
Crisp Beef in, 71
Chinese Prickly Ash, 209
Chinese Tree Fungus see Cloud
  Ears
Chinese Water Spinach see Spinach
Chinese Wood Ear Fungus, 38
Chives, Chinese, 35-6
Chives, Chinese Yellow, 36, 145
Chopping Board, 62
Chopsticks, 63
Cinnamon, 39
Citrus Peel, 39
Clay or Sandy Pots, 62
Cleavers, 61
Cloud Ears (Chinese Tree Fungus),
  38, 150
  with Stem Lettuce, 155-6
  with Stir-fried Fish Fillets and
  Cucumbers, 181-3
  Stir-fried, with Long Beans and
  Silk Squash, 22-3
Coriander (Chinese Parsley), 39-40
  with Stir-fried Goat, 70-1
Corn, 145, 221-22
  with Rice Porridge, 72-3
  Stir-fried, with Fresh Chilies,
  73-4
Cornflour, 40
Cornmeal, Lamb Steamed with

index

Spice-Flavoured, 82-3
Corn Oil, 46
Cottonseed Oil, 47
Crab, 188
  Mock, 218-9
Cucumbers:
  with Bean Starch Noodles,
  127-8
  Cold, with Garlic, 184
  Salad, 230
  with Stir-fried Fish Fillets, 180
  Stir-fried, with Pork, 150, 158-9
Curry, Beef and Potato, 99
Custard Tarts, 190

Dates, 87, 122
Dian Xin sweet snacks, 190
Dim Sum snacks, 104, 189-191
Donuts, Fried, 229
Doufu see Bean Curd
Duck, 15
  Sichuan-style, 150
  Tea-smoked, 229
  Yunnan Roast, 96-97
Duck Eggs, Salted, 43
Dumplings
  with Chicken Soup, 190
  Green, 188
  Jiaozi (meat-filled), 121, 133-36,
  142, 186, 189, 230
  in Soup (Water Dumplings),
  25-6
  Steamed, with Minced Pork and
  Prawns, 190
  Steamed Pork, 189-9
  Steamed Prawns, with Beef
  Liver, 190

Wontons, 195-6

Eels:
  Braised, with Garlic, 231
  Stir-fried, with Prawns in
  Noodle Soup, 199-200
Egg Noodles see Noodles
Eggs:
  Crepe filled with Meats, 189
  Salt, 188
  Salted Duck, 43
  Sliced Salted, 122
  Stir-fried, with Tomatoes, 81-2
  Stir-fried, with Yellow Chives,
  17
  Thousand-year-old, 230
  Tomato and Egg Summer Salad,
  132-3
  White of, 41
Elephant Trunk, 230
Emerald Chicken "Meat", 215
Equipment, 58-63

"Fantasy Pork", 171-2
Fen Rice Noodles (Sha He
  Noodles), 45
Figs, 65, 68, 87
Fish
  Mandarin, 161-2
  Steamed Fish Southern Style,
  109-110
  Stir-fried Fillets with Cloud Ears
  and Cucumbers, 180
  see also Carp; Catfish; Eels
Fishball Soup, Wenzhou, 189
Fish-flavoured Aubergine with
  Pork, 75-76

235

index

Five-Spice Powder, 39
Flour, Rice, 41-2
Frogs, Stir-fried, 231
Fruit, 122, 123, 145
    Dried, Candied and Pickled,
    187
Fungus Stuffing for Buns, 212
see also Mushrooms

Garlic, 42
    with Cold Cucumbers, 184
    Stir-fried Green Beans and, 130
Garlic Shoots, 42
Ginger root, 42-3
    with Pickled Pig's Feet, 222-23
Ginger Juice, 43
Ginseng with Squab Soup, 223-4
Goat
    Braised Goat Casserole, 77-8
    Steamed with Spice-flavored
    Cornmeal, 82-3
    Stir-fried, with Fresh Coriander,
    70-71
    Toasted Goat Cheese, 79
Goose, 15, 230
Grandma Chen's Bean Curd, 125
Grapes, 68
Green Beans, 149
    Stir-fried, with Chili, 152-3
    Stir-fried, with Garlic, 130
Guizhou-style Bean Curd, 136

Ham, 58
    "Fantasy Pork", 171-2
    Smoked Ham Hock with Stewed
    Chicken, 220-1
Herbs, 208

Hoisin Sauce, 50
Honeysuckle Tea, 212

Ingredients, 29-58
Jellyfish, 121
Sesame, 179-180
Jiaozi (meat-filled
    dumplings), 121, 133-6, 142,
    186, 189, 230
Jujubes, 117

Kohlrabi, 68, 87

Lamb Steamed with Spice-flavored
Cornmeal, 82-3
Leeks, 43-4
Lettuce, 65, 68, 87
Lettuce, Stem, 142, 150
    with Cloud Ears, 155-6
    with Spicy Chicken, 229
Lily Buds, 44
    with Stir-fried Bean Sprouts,
    217-8
"Lions' Heads", 122
Long Beans, Chinese, 37
    Stir-fried, with Silk Squash and
    Cloud Ears, 22-23

Maltose Sugar, 44
Man Tou (steamed bun), 187
Mandarin Fish, 161-2
Mangetout Beans, 54
Meat Balls, Steamed Minced, 145
Melon, 123

index

Watermelon, 145
Winter Melon Salad, 95
Melon, Bitter, 32, 207-8
Minced, with Rice Noodles,
113-14
Stir-fried, with Fresh Mild
Chilies, 183
Milk, Stir-fried, 76-77
Millet, 87
Wine, 189
Minced Chili "Fish", 216-7
Mock Crab, 218-19
Monosodium Glutamate (MSG),
28, 212, 228
Mooncakes, 123
Mung Beans, 46, 94
Bean Thread Noodles, 45-6
see also Bean Sprouts
Mushrooms
Mushroom-Chicken Casserole,
151-52
with Stir-fried Cabbage, 224-5
see also Cloud Ears

Napa Cabbage see Cabbage
Noodle Soup, 190
with Catfish and Bamboo
Shoots, 196-8
Pork and Preserved Vegetable,
203
Stir-fried Eels with Prawns in
199-200
Wonton, 201
Noodles, 44-6
Bean Starch, with Cucumbers,
127-8
Bean Thread, 45-6
Bean Thread, with Pork, 137-8

Cold, 194-5
Fried, with Onions, 105-6
Spicy Sichuan, 192-3
Wheat and Egg, 44-5
Noodles, Rice, 45
Across the Bridge, 173-5
Fen, 45
with Minced Bitter Melon,
113-14
Sweet Sesame, 114-5
with Yellow Chives and Pork,
19

Oils, 46-8
Oyster Sauce, 50
Oysters, Dried, 47

Pak choi (Chinese White
Cabbage), 38
Stir-fried, 111
Pastes:
Chili, 100, 149
Sesame, 51
see also Sauces
Peanut Oil, 47
Peanuts, 48
Pig's Feet (Pig's Trotters), Pickled,
with Ginger, 222-3
Pork:
with Bean Thread Noodles
137-8
"Fantasy", 171-2
with Fish-flavoured Aubergines,
55-6
Meatballs ("Lions' Heads"), 122
Minced, with Stir-fried Celery,

150
with Pickled Chilies, 153-4
and Preserved Vegetable Noodle
Soup, 203
with Rice Noodles and Yellow
Chives, 19
Salt and Pepper Spareribs, 172-3
Stir-fried Chili, 157-8
Stir-fried Cucumbers and, 158-9,
131
with Stir-fried Soybean Sprouts,
23-4
Sweet and Sour, made with
Fruit Juice, 106-7
Tung Po, 177-8
Twice-cooked, 156-7
Prawn:
in Dragon Well Tea, 178-9
Oil-exploded, 164
with Stir-fried Eels in Noodle
Soup, 199-200
White-blanched, 110-11

Red-cooked Grass Carp with
Tangerine Peel, 20
Red-in-Snow Cabbage see
Cabbage
Rice, 48-49
Chicken Cooked with, 202
Deep Fried Glutinous Rice
Cakes, 198-199
Glutinous, 48
Long-grain, 48
"Sizzling Rice", 175-6
Short-grain, 48
Rice Flour, 42
Rice Noodles see Noodles, Rice
with Corn, 72-3

Rice Wine, 49

Safflower Oil, 47
Salad:
Bean Sprout, 94
Cucumber, 230
Tofu, 182-3
Tomato and Egg Summer, 132-3
Winter Melon, 95
Salt, 49
and Pepper Spareribs,
172-3
Sauces, 49-50
Chili (Dipping), 34-5, 50
Chili Bean, 35. 50
"Cream", Cabbage in, 93-4
Hoisin, 50
Oyster, 50
Sweet Bean, 51
Yellow Bean, 51
Sesame:
Jellyfish, 179-80
Oil, 47
Paste, 51
Seeds, 51-2
Shallots, 52
Shark's Fin, 52-3
Shrimp
Cabbage with Dried, 166
Sichuan Peppercorns (flower
peppers), 53
Sichuan Preserved Vegetable, 53-4
Silk Squash (Chinese Okra), 54
with Oyster Sauce, 115-6
Stir-fried, with Long Beans and
Cloud Ears, 22-3
Snow Peas, 54

index

Soup, 125, 155, 169
    for the Blood and Skin, 219-20
    Dumplings in, 205-6
    Yunnan Steamed Pot Chicken
    145, 221-2
Soy Sauce, 54-5
    Dark, 55
    Light, 54
Soybean Oil, 47
Soybean Sprouts, *31*
    Stir-fried with Pork, 23-4
Spareribs:
    Fried Stewed Country, 92-3
    Salt and Pepper, 172-3
Spinach, 55
    Water, with Fermented Bean
    Curd, 165
Spring Rolls, 128-9
Squab:
    Crispy Roast, 112-3
    Soup with Ginseng, 223-4
Star Anise, 55
Steamers, Bamboo, 62
Sugar,
    Maltose, 44
Sunflower Oil, 47
Sweet and Sour Pork made with
    Fruit juice, 106-7
Sweet Bean Sauce, 51
Sweet Sesame Rice Noodles, 114-5

Tangerine Peel, Dried,
    with Red-cooked Grass Carp, 20
Tea,
    Honeysuckle, 212
    Prawn in Dragon Well, 178-9
Three-shredded Dish, 107-8
Tofu Salad, 182-3

Tomato(es),
    and Egg Summer Salad, 132-3
    with Stir-fried Eggs, 81-2
Tung Po Pork, 177-8

Vegetables,
    Pork and Preserved Vegetable
    Noodle Soup, 203
Vinegar, 56
    Black Rice, 56
    Red Rice, 56
    Sauce, with West Lake Carp,
    160-1

Water Chestnuts, 56-7
with Spicy Chicken, 162-3
Watermelon, 145
    Seeds, 122
West Lake Carp in Vinegar Sauce,
    160-1

Wheat Gluten, 57
Wheat Starch, 57
Wine,
    Millet, 189
    Rice, 49
Winter Melon Salad, 95
Wok, 58-9
    accessories, 60-1
Wonton Noodle Soup, 201-2
Wontons (dumplings), 57-8
Chengdu, 195-6

Yunnan Roast Duck, 96-7